Improving Reading Comprehension through Metacognitive Reading Strategies Instruction

Improving Reading Comprehension through Metacognitive Reading Strategies Instruction

Edited by
Kouider Mokhtari

ROWMAN & LITTLEFIELD
Lanham • Boulder • New York • London

Published by Rowman & Littlefield
A wholly owned subsidiary of The Rowman & Littlefield Publishing Group, Inc.
4501 Forbes Boulevard, Suite 200, Lanham, Maryland 20706
www.rowman.com

Unit A, Whitacre Mews, 26-34 Stannary Street, London SE11 4AB

Material in chapters 1 and 2, which have been revised and updated, originally appeared in: Mokhtari, K., & Sheorey, R. (Eds.). (2008). *Reading strategies of first and second language learners: See how they read.* Norwood, MA: Christopher-Gordon Publishers

British Library Cataloguing in Publication Information Available

Library of Congress Cataloging-in-Publication Data
Names: Mokhtari, Kouider, editor.
Title: Improving reading comprehension through metacognitive reading strategies instruction / edited by Kouider Mokhtari.
Description: Lanham, Maryland : Rowman & Littlefield, [2016]
Identifiers: LCCN 2016027082 (print) | LCCN 2016047530 (ebook) | ISBN 9781475831214 (Cloth : alk. paper) | ISBN 9781475831290 (Paper : alk. paper) | ISBN 9781475831306 (Electronic)
Subjects: LCSH: Reading comprehension.
Classification: LCC LB1050.45 .I48 2016 (print) | LCC LB1050.45 (ebook) | DDC 372.47–dc23
LC record available at https://lccn.loc.gov/2016027082

∞™ The paper used in this publication meets the minimum requirements of American National Standard for Information Sciences—Permanence of Paper for Printed Library Materials, ANSI/NISO Z39.48-1992.

Printed in the United States of America

In loving memory of Professor Ravi Sheorey:
A reliable friend, trustworthy mentor, distinguished scholar, and outstanding human being.
Remembered with smiles.

Contents

Foreword

Dispelling the Myths about Metacognitive Reading Strategies Instruction

Kouider Mokhtari is masterful in presenting us with a much needed volume that zooms in on the key concepts, developments, and practices of metacognitive reading strategies instruction. Such instruction aims to help readers acquire a set of text processing techniques to actively monitor their own thinking while reading. Examples include techniques for checking learning goals, monitoring comprehension, making connections with prior knowledge, and strategies for deciding on which techniques to use for different texts and contexts. With the increasing demand of close, analytical reading of complex texts in today's classrooms, one would think that metacognitive reading strategies, which have been proven to be most effective to improve reading comprehension, would occupy a central place in reading pedagogy. Yet they do not, and in fact, the opposite is true. Metacognitive reading strategies instruction is still "not commonly observed in most primary and secondary classrooms" (Baker, 2013, p. 421). This is not surprising, given the fact that systematic reading instruction is often delivered through manufactured programs at the elementary and middle schools, and it is rarely offered in high schools (see Cummings, 2008; Scott, 2009). Two major barriers contributed to this neglect.

One is teachers' lack of knowledge and training in reading instruction in general and in metacognitive reading strategies instruction in particular (Baker, 2013; Pressley, 2002). A review conducted by the National Literacy Panel (2000) was unable to discern how preservice and in-service teachers are taught to teach reading due to the sparse information available on the content of reading instruction in teacher education and teacher professional development and the lack of consistency and clarity in reported techniques, methods, theories, and materials covered in the programs. Without being explicitly taught metacognitive reading strategies themselves or learning how to use them in their own process of learning to teach, or with ongoing support in their in-service teaching, it is difficult for teachers to actively use these strategies explicitly and consistently in their classrooms.

The other barrier concerns misconceptions about metacognitive reading strategies instruction. One misconception is related to the age group appropriate for such strategies. The field has overwhelmingly focused on the development and training of adolescent learners to help them gain metacognitive reading strategies so that they can better "read to learn." The underlining assumption of emphasizing metacognitive reading strategies instruction for this age group is that children in the lower grades who are learning to read are not capable of, or do not need to, gain such strategies. Similarly for high school and college students, it is assumed that they have already learned or possessed those skills and their metacognitive skills in other areas or aspects of life would automatically transfer to reading. However, recent research findings on the positive effects of metacognitive strategies instruction for elementary students as well as for college students in North America and abroad suggest that metacognitive reading strategies instruction should start early in school and should continue in postsecondary education. It should be continuous and should not start only in middle school or stop as students reach high school or college.

Another related misconception is that strategy (metacognitive reading strategies included) is seen as a quick-fix instructional activity that can be offered any time as needed. This "remedial" conception of the function of strategy instruction often fails to recognize that the process of strategy learning, especially that of turning a strategy (conscious and intentional use of techniques and approaches) into a skill (routinized, automatic use of strategies with different genres of texts in different contexts) takes time and requires repetition and practice with different texts in different contexts, including the online environment. Therefore, the remedial approach of teaching metacognitive reading strategies in the current school practices is shortsighted and often fails to help learners gain the automaticity of using these strategies or turn them into skills that they can use at their disposal.

Finally, there is an assumption that metacognitive reading strategies are just for reading and they are separate from writing instruction. Given that metacognitive reading strategies application requires multiple levels of text analysis and rigorous transactional relationship with author and text (i.e., active use of background knowledge and making inferences from author's ideas in text) (Kintsch, 2013, also chapters 4 and 5 of this volume), metacognitive reading strategies should not be seen as only beneficial for reading, but also for understanding writing or thinking about thinking of writing. Therefore, making metacognitive reading strategies instruction as an approach of integrated reading and writing practices or "hybrid literate acts" (chapter 6 of this volume) will produce optimal results in improving students' literacy achievement.

Kouider Mokhtari's thoughtfully constructed volume addresses these barriers and dispels the myths surrounding metacognitive reading strategies instruction by featuring research-informed practices that are easily assessable to teachers and practitioners at all levels of instruction—from early elementary to college. Collectively, the chapters advocate continuous development of metacognitive strategies over time to achieve comprehension fluency, and promote starting it early (as early as in Kindergarten or preschool) and ongoing scaffolding as students move through the K–16 school system. The leading experts in the field provide both research developments and proven models of practices (both in face-to-face and in online environments) that teachers need to know in order to successfully implement metacognitive reading strategies in their classrooms. The book covers a wide range of interrelated topics including a comprehensive introduction of the key constructs and contributors of metacognitive reading strategies, clarification of the common confusion between the use of strategies and skills in the current curriculum and standards, assessments, text comprehension and word identification strategies, as well as online reciprocal teaching strategies for learners (including English language learners) ranging from elementary to postsecondary learners.

The breadth and depth of coverage in this book makes it an extraordinary professional development resource for teachers and educators of all levels to integrate effective metacognitive reading strategies instruction into their daily classroom practice. So read on, and help your students become better thinkers and better drivers of their own literacy learning and beyond. I am confident that you, too, will become better thinkers of your thinking about literacy teaching and learning.

Guofang Li, Professor
Vancouver, Canada
Canada Research Chair (Tier 1) in Transnational/Global Perspectives of Language and Literacy Education of Children and Youth
Department of Language and Literacy Education

REFERENCES

Baker, L. (2013). Metacognitive strategies. In H. Hattie & E. M. Anderman (Eds.), *International guide to student achievement* (pp. 419–21). New York: Routledge.

Cummings, B. (2008). Reading instruction for all: A study of the status of *reading instruction in Ohio high schools*. (Electronic Thesis or Dissertation). Retrieved from https://etd.ohiolink.edu/

Kintsch, W. (2013). Revisiting the construction-integration model of text comprehension and its implications for instruction. In D. E. Alvermann, N. J. Unrau, & R. B. Ruddell (Eds.), *Theoretical models and processes of reading, 6th edition* (pp. 807–39). Newark, DE: International Reading Association.

Pressley, G. M. (2002). Metacognition and self-regulated comprehension. In A. E. Farstrup & S. J. Samuels (Eds.), *What research has to say about reading instruction* (pp. 291–309). Newark, DE: International Reading Association.

The National Literacy Panel. (2000). Chapter 5: Teacher education and reading instruction. In *Teaching children to read: An evidence-based assessment of the scientific literature on reading and its implications for reading instruction* (pp. 5:1–19). Available: https://www.nichd.nih.gov/publications/pubs/nrp/documents/report.pdf

Scott, S. E. (2009). *Knowledge for teaching reading comprehension: Mapping the terrain.* Unpublished doctoral dissertation, University of Michigan. Retrieved from https://deepblue.lib.umich.edu/bitstream/handle/2027.42/62201/sarascot_1.pdf

Preface

This book is about metacognition (i.e., the extent to which readers think about their own thinking while reading) and its role in improving reading comprehension among students from primary grades through college. In its most basic interpretation, metacognition refers to the extent to which one is aware of, monitors, reflects on, and regulates thinking in the context of literate acts including reading, writing, listening, and speaking.

The contributors of this book, a select group of outstanding scholars and practitioners, view reading comprehension as fundamentally about metacognition, which is a general capacity to monitor and control one's thinking while reading writing, listening, or speaking. Through their chapter contributions, they advocate for the inclusion of metacognition in our understanding of the decisions readers make in support of skilled reading. They agree that metacognitive monitoring and regulation play an essential role in text understanding, and offer an array of research-supported insights and recommendations in support of direct assessment and instruction of metacognitive strategies as powerful ways of strengthening metacognitive development, and in turn, reading comprehension performance.

The content of the book is intended for a variety of audiences including literacy researchers, teacher educators, classroom teachers, reading specialists, curriculum coordinators, and professional development leaders. The twelve chapters of the book are ideal for use in undergraduate and/or graduate courses focused on metacognition and reading comprehension, teacher study groups, or job-embedded professional development sessions. Chapter content, which is grounded in research and practice, is presented in an easy to read and friendly style and tone that speaks directly to readers. To this end, by design, each chapter begins with a brief opening section framing the key issue in the chapter, provides theoretical, policy, or research support for the issue in question, and concludes with an extended section addressing practical applications or implications for practice. A brief overview of chapter contents follows.

In chapter 1, "The Development of Metacognitive Knowledge and Control of Comprehension: Contributors and Consequences," Linda Baker discusses the role of metacognition in comprehension instruction. Particular focus is placed on developmental differences in metacognition and their implications for metacognitively oriented reading instruction.

In chapter 2, "Skills and Strategies: Their Differences, Their Relationships, And Why They Matter," Peter Afflerbach, P. David Pearson, and Scott Paris propose definitions of reading "skills" and reading "strategies" that clarify their differences and their relationship, and provides illustrative examples that help guide the development of reading curriculum and instruction.

In chapter 3, "Assessing Metacognition in Reading," Marcel V. J. Veenman provides an overview of online and offline assessment methods for metacognition in reading with their pros and cons, along with implications for assessing and students' metacognitive reading strategies.

In chapter 4, "The Construction-Integration (CI) Model of Text Comprehension: A Lens for Teaching the Common Core Reading Standards," D. Ray Reutzel highlights the importance of grounding comprehension instruction firmly within a framework or model of text processing, especially in an era of CCSS in reading where the text takes center. A thorough understanding of text processing will help guide teachers in selecting appropriate reading strategies to teach, when to integrate them into their teaching, and how to effectively teach them in ways that support students' text understanding.

In chapter 5, "Improving Metacomprehension with the Situation-Model Approach," Jennifer Wiley, Keith W. Thiede, and Thomas D. Griffin explore some methodological and conceptual issues, inspired by current theories of text comprehension, which suggest that the nature of the texts and tests used for metacomprehension studies may be a critical factor to consider.

In chapter 6, "The Reading-Writing-Thinking Connection: How Literacy and Metacognition Are Mutually Interdependent," Annamary L. Consalvo and Diane L. Schallert make the case for how intimately interrelated reading, writing, and metacognitive processes are, and describe how the "hybrid literate acts" such as those that take place online, through synchronous chatting or asynchronous postings, blur the lines between reading, writing, and thinking.

In chapter 7, "Improving Adolescents' Reading Comprehension and Engagement Through Strategy-based Interventions," Susan Chambers Cantrell, Janice F. Almasi, and Margaret Rintamaa share lessons learned from two statewide evaluations of supplemental strategy-based interventions for lower-achieving adolescent readers, and outline principles for implementing strategy-based interventions for students in middle and high schools.

In chapter 8, "Preparing College Students to Learn More from Academic Texts through Metacognitive Awareness," Richard L. Isakson and Marné B. Isakson define metacognitive awareness in the context of college reading, discusses the need for its teaching, and describes a model for learning well from academic texts, and a college reading course that uses this model.

In chapter 9, "Improving Reading Comprehension through Metacognitive Reading Strategies Instruction for Students in Upper Grades," Stephan E. Sargent discusses the close relationship between metacognition and reading proficiency, and offers a set of strategies aimed at raising middle grade students' awareness and use of reading strategies while reading.

In chapter 10, "Improving Reading Comprehension through Metacognitive Reading Strategies Instruction for Students in Primary and Elementary Grades," Melinda Smith describes a set of reading strategies aimed at improving students' reading comprehension performance by encouraging metacognitive awareness and self-regulation among primary and elementary grade students.

In chapter 11, "Exploring the Potential of Internet Reciprocal Teaching to Improve Online Reading," Jill Castek describes an adaption of Reciprocal Teaching, a well-known instructional intervention for increasing reading comprehension, to address the skills and strategies required when reading online text.

In chapter 12, "Development of Word Identification in a Second Language," Keiko Koda clarifies reader-text interactions in word form analysis and word meaning retrieval, describes cross-linguistic variations in word form analysis, and discusses their implications for the development of word identification skills in a second language.

I hope you will find this book relevant and valuable in support of your efforts to strengthen your students' metacognitive knowledge and skills, and in turn, improve their reading comprehension performance.

Kouider Mokhtari

Chapter 1

The Development of Metacognitive Knowledge and Control of Comprehension

Contributors and Consequences

Linda Baker

ABSTRACT

The primary objective of this chapter is to review the literature on metacognitive development in relation to reading. The emphasis is on recent investigations of precursors to metacognitive knowledge and control, including executive functions and theory of mind, and on evidence that metacognition and comprehension are strongly intertwined with basic biological, cognitive, linguistic, and motivational processes. Research indicates that the development of metacognition is both cause and consequence of better reading comprehension. Intervention research shows that direct instruction in metacognitive strategies is a powerful way to enhance metacognitive development, and in turn, reading comprehension. Our understanding of developmental mechanisms is improving with more sophisticated research designs and technologies. Nevertheless, there remains a gap between research and practice. A more concerted effort is warranted to give teachers the knowledge and skills they need to foster the transition from other-regulation to self-regulation.

FRAMING THE ISSUE

It has been nearly forty years since researchers became interested in metacognitive knowledge and control as it relates to reading comprehension. The seminal studies by Kreutzer, Flavell, and Leonard (1979) on children's metacognitive knowledge about memory and by Markman (1977) on children's comprehension monitoring while listening set the stage for a long line of research that continues today. Scholarly interest in metacognition remains strong, with hundreds of articles published over the past decade alone, as well as numerous books devoted to the topic. Despite the depth and breadth of the research literature, many questions remain about the causes and consequences of metacognitive development. The purpose of this chapter is to review developmental differences in students' reading-related metacognitive skills, to examine contributors to metacognitive development, and to consider the consequences of metacognitive development on comprehension. Particular attention is given to work completed within the past decade (see Baker, 2008, for a similar treatment of earlier work).

Metacognition as defined in this chapter encompasses both knowledge about cognition and regulation of cognition. Knowledge includes knowledge about the skills, strategies, and resources that are needed to perform a task effectively. Control refers to the use of self-regulatory strategies to ensure successful task completion, including planning, evaluating, monitoring, checking, and revising. Metacognitive control in reading is often conceptualized as comprehension monitoring, which involves deciding whether or not we understand (evaluation) and taking appropriate steps to correct comprehension problems that are detected (regulation).

Most of the methods currently being used to study metacognitive knowledge and control had their origins in the early years of inquiry (Baker & Brown, 1984; Garner, 1987). The methods fall into two broad areas: (1) those where information is collected by means of decontextualized interviews and questionnaires, and (2) those where behavioral information is collected while readers are actively engaged with text. The first approach yields evidence of both knowledge and control, based on self-reports of what readers know about reading and what they think they typically do when they read. The second approach yields evidence of metacognitive control based on how readers respond in more contextualized situations requiring comprehension. Responses include self-reports of what readers are thinking and doing as they read texts, as well as real-time processing measures such as reading times on target sentences and patterns of eye movements through a text. In this chapter I consider the two approaches separately; for expository convenience it should be understood that when I refer to metacognitive knowledge, the evidence comes from interviews and questionnaires, and when I refer to metacognitive control, the evidence comes from tasks that call for participants to evaluate and regulate their comprehension.

I begin this chapter by presenting evidence of developmental change in both metacognitive knowledge and control, from preschool through late adolescence. The chapter then addresses contributors to metacognitive growth, including biological, cognitive, and motivational factors. The next portion of the chapter addresses consequences of metacognitive knowledge and control, first covering correlational research showing that metacognition and comprehension are linked and then intervention research showing that by increasing metacognitive skills, comprehension can also be increased. The final section of the chapter addresses whether and how instructional practices have changed over the years in response to research findings on metacognitive development and its relation to reading comprehension.

MAKING THE CASE FOR DEVELOPMENTAL CHANGE

Most of the research on developmental changes in metacognition is cross-sectional, comparing children of different ages at the same point in time. This allows us to conclude that older children have stronger metacognitive skills than younger children, but in essence it is correlational evidence and does not tell us what may have led to these differences. Longitudinal research provides more insight because it can reveal true growth over time within individual children, as well as the extent to which individual differences in children's metacognition remain stable. Unfortunately, relatively few studies of metacognition have a long-term developmental focus. In most research, participants span relatively short age ranges (e.g., six to eight years, twelve to fifteen years). Grade in school is typically regarded as a proxy for experience or knowledge, and little attention is given to other possible developmental mechanisms (Fox, 2009). Developmental research is complicated by the fact that materials given to one age group may be too hard or too easy for another age group. When age-appropriate materials are used to circumvent this problem, one cannot rule out that age effects were really due to differences in materials. Another complication is that much research has been conducted outside of the United States, and children begin formal schooling at different ages in different countries. Direct instruction is a major mechanism of developmental change in metacognition, as are the accompanying increases in knowledge and experience involving reading. Therefore, when possible, I report grade levels and I indicate nationality of participants when they are not from the United States.

The Development of Metacognitive Knowledge

The Elementary School Years

Many studies have documented increases during the elementary school years in children's metacognitive knowledge of reading and their awareness of metacognitive control strategies. Interview studies have been particularly valuable in showing *qualitative* differences in thinking because of their open-ended question format. Three studies provide converging evidence of a gradual shift in understanding of reading as a decoding process to reading as a meaning-getting process. Myers and Paris (1978) first documented this shift when they questioned children in second and sixth grades about person, task, and strategy variables involved in reading. Eme, Puustinen, and Coutelet (2006) interviewed French children in third and fifth grades and found that the fifth graders were more likely than third graders to cite understanding as characteristic of a good reader, whereas the younger students described a good reader as one who reads quickly without a mistake. In a longitudinal analysis, Annevirta and Vauras (2001) found a similar developmental shift when Finnish children were followed from preschool (kindergarten) through third grade. The interview tapped metacognitive knowledge about memory and learning as well as comprehension. Understanding of memory processes was apparent even in preschool, and understanding of learning was apparent by first grade. Metacognitive understanding of comprehension was latest to develop. An example of a question probing comprehension is: *How would you read a story to be able to understand it and tell it to the class afterwards*? Responses to this question that were coded as *non-developing* were: "reading without any mistakes," "reading it slowly aloud," and "telling it quickly." Responses coded as *developing* were: "I would read it many times and try to say it to myself" and "reading a story and imagining it happening to me." It was only students in third grade and higher who, in response to this question, spoke about evaluating and monitoring their understanding.

Quantitative increases in metacognitive awareness have also been documented through interview studies. In a study using the same assessment tool as that used by Annevirta and Vaurus (2001), Annevirta, Laakonen, Kinnunen, and Vauras (2007) again showed increases in metacognitive knowledge in a longitudinal study of Finnish children followed from preschool to grade 3. They tested for a cumulative effect but did not find one; that is, children with initially high metacognitive knowledge did not develop more in their metacognitive knowledge than children with low metacognitive knowledge, and the converse also was not true, However, children showed more growth from first to second grade than they did from preschool to first grade, perhaps reflecting the increased opportunities to learn about themselves as learners once formal schooling began.

Working with older elementary school children, Paris and Jacobs (1984) also assigned scores based on the quality of responses to open-ended questions tapping knowledge about evaluation (*What would help you become a better reader*), planning (*If you could only read some sentences in the story because you were in a hurry, which ones would you read*?), and regulation (*What do you do if you come to a word you don't understand*?). Although fifth graders had somewhat higher scores overall than third graders, the distribution of scores had considerable overlap. Comparable numbers in both grades had low or moderate levels of awareness; only at the highest level of awareness were there more fifth graders. What this latter finding illustrates is that knowing a child's age will not provide a full picture of his or her level of metacognitive development. Individual differences must also be taken into account. Differences in reading skill are almost always associated with differences in metacognitive knowledge, as will be discussed later in the chapter.

Quantitative increases in metacognitive awareness as children progress through school have also been documented through multiple-choice questionnaires and rating scales. Multiple-choice questionnaires typically include response options that reflect what children might say in open-ended interviews. Paris and Jacobs (1984) used their interview data to develop the Index of Reading Awareness, an informal tool that has been used subsequently by researchers and classroom teachers. A multiple-choice instrument was recently used by Lecce, Zocchi, Pagnin, Palladino, and Taumoepeau (2010). An example of a question that taps the understanding of reading as a meaning-getting process is: *In your opinion, when you read, the most important thing is: (a) To read loudly and clearly; (b) To read exactly and without hesitation every word; (c) To understand the content of the text;* or *(d) To read as quickly as possible.* In a cross-sectional study, with Italian second and fourth graders, the older children showed a more mature knowledge of reading goals and simple strategies than the younger children. In a short-term longitudinal study, fourth graders' metacognitive knowledge scores did not increase over eleven months, but scores remained stable (i.e., they were significantly correlated).

Perhaps the most widely used approach for gathering self-report data about metacognition is to use a rating scale. Rating scales have been developed for use with elementary school students and are widely used with secondary students and college students as well. Students are presented with a set of statements and are asked to indicate how often each statement is true of themselves. For example, the statement "*I know when I understand something*" might have response options ranging from "*never*" through "*sometimes*" to "*always*." Although a few scales have undergone extensive psychometric testing and are available for use by other researchers, most investigators develop their own measures. This makes it difficult to compare results across studies.

Sperling, Howard, Miller, and Murphy (2002) developed and validated a questionnaire called the Jr. Metacognitive Awareness Inventory (MAI; based on an instrument developed for adults by Schraw and Dennison, 1987) to tap metacognitive knowledge as well as metacognitive regulation. This questionnaire has a general academic focus as opposed to being specific to reading. One version of the Jr. MAI is intended for grades 3–5; it includes twelve questions and a three-choice response scale. Another version is intended for students in grades 6–9; it includes the same twelve items plus an additional six items tailored more to middle schoolers and has a five-choice rating scale. In the validation study, the expected developmental progression in metacognition was not found for the elementary school version; in fact, third graders scored as well as fourth and fifth graders.

The Secondary School Years

Developmental increases in metacognitive knowledge of reading have been found frequently among samples of adolescents as well as children. In a longitudinal study, Roeschl-Heils, Schneider, and van Kraayenoord (2003) found that children who score high on assessments of metacognitive knowledge in elementary school (grade 3 or 4) continued to do so in middle school (grade 7 or 8). Moreover, eighth graders had higher levels of metacognitive knowledge than seventh graders, illustrating continued growth during adolescence. Kolić-Kehovec, Rončević Zubković, and Pahljina-Reinić (2014) assessed a sample of Croatian children longitudinally in fourth, sixth, and eighth grades on metacognitive knowledge of reading strategies and found that strategic knowledge increased steadily across the three time points. Cross-sectional studies yield similar patterns. For example, in a Dutch study, metacognitive knowledge increased with age across grades 6, 8, and 10 (Schoonen, Hulstijn, & Bossers, 1998).

In contrast, this consistent developmental progression during adolescence was not found by Sperling et al. (2002) in their validation study of the Jr. MAI. Eighth and ninth graders had higher scores than seventh graders, but sixth graders had scores comparable to the older students. Moreover, in an analysis that examined how children from grades 3 through 9 performed on the twelve common items, children in some of the elementary grades had higher scores than children in secondary grades.

One of the few metacognitive rating scales that focuses exclusively on reading is the Metacognitive Awareness of Reading Strategies Inventory (MARSI). It was developed by Mokhtari and Sheorey (2002) and validated with children in grades 6 through 12. It taps three different types of reading strategies, referred to as global (*I think about what I know to help me understand what I read*), support (*I summarize what I read to reflect on important information in the text*), and problem-solving (*I adjust my reading speed according to what I'm reading*). Each item is rated on a five-point scale with respect to how often the reader does the described activity. The scale was constructed with the expectation that the items would be appropriate for all secondary students, and scale reliability was high for each separate grade. Mean scores at each grade level were not reported in this study, so it does not help to resolve conflicting evidence about developmental progression in adolescent readers.

Synthesizing across these studies, it appears that metacognitive awareness of reading is low at the outset of formal schooling but develops quickly over the next several years. By third grade, many children score as high as children several years older than themselves. The emerging understanding that the goal of reading is to get meaning is probably the most significant accomplishment, and it may drive much of the growth that is seen up to grade three or four, the time when most children have mastered the code-based skills of reading. The questions that are used to assess metacognitive knowledge and regulation are very similar from late elementary school onwards, with inconsistent evidence of developmental progression. This suggests that self-report inventories are less useful for tracking developmental change in fluent readers than they are for shedding light on individual differences.

The Development of Metacognitive Control

We focus in this section on control as reflected in behavioral studies. A few preliminary comments are in order about two widely used measures of metacognitive control: error detection and think-alouds. Rather than using tasks that depend on readers' spontaneous reports indicating they are evaluating and regulating their comprehension, researchers in the late 1970s adopted the error-detection approach originally used in studies of comprehension monitoring while listening (Markman, 1977). In this approach, errors or problems are introduced into texts, and various indices are used to determine whether readers notice the problems and attempt to resolve them. Verbal reports, reading times, and patterns of eye movements are frequent indicators of problem detection. Neuroimaging methods are increasingly being used as well, but rarely with children (Baker, Zeliger-Kandasamy, & DeWyngaert, 2014). Caution is needed in interpreting results of these studies for several reasons. The nature of the errors that are introduced is a critical factor. For example, when information presented in different parts of the text is internally inconsistent, detection is more difficult than when information is inconsistent with respect to knowledge of the world. In addition, whether or not a problem will be reported depends on the readers' goals for reading, the criteria they adopt for evaluating their understanding, their threshold for deciding when a problem is serious enough to report, and whether they used "fix-up" strategies that resolved the intended comprehension difficulty (Baker & Cerro, 2000).

Another approach used in early research and continuing today is to ask readers to reflect on their reading processes, either immediately after reading a passage or during the process itself. Concurrent reports, also known as think-alouds, have revealed that skilled readers use complex processes to construct an interpretation of a passage. For example, they adjust their approaches to reading depending on task demands, and they monitor and regulate their understanding (Fox, 2009; Pressley & Afflerbach, 1995). Caution is also needed when think-aloud approaches are used, but careful attention to established guidelines can make verbal reports a good source of information. Of particular concern is that limitations in young children's ability to reflect on and articulate their mental processes may mask incipient comprehension-monitoring skills.

The Preschool Years

Many have argued that metacognition is a late-developing skill (e.g., Pintrich & Zusho, 2002), but there is now considerable evidence that preschool children possess rudimentary metacognitive skills (Annevirta et al., 2007; Baker, 2005; Whitebread et al., 2009). In the literacy domain, much of this evidence comes from research showing successful comprehension monitoring of orally presented texts. Variants of error-detection tasks are used most frequently in this research. In an early study, Baker (1984a) found that preschoolers were fairly successful at identifying information in simple stories that conflicted with what they already knew (e.g., that ice cream does not grow in gardens) but much less successful detecting inconsistencies in the text (e.g., a rabbit's fur is described as "snow white" in one part of the story and brown in another). In this cross-sectional study, first graders outperformed the preschoolers, and third graders outperformed the first graders. The older children also had most difficulty with internal inconsistencies, given the demands they put on memory processes.

Emerging comprehension-monitoring abilities are apparent in even younger children, ranging in age from 30 months to four years (Skarakis-Doyle, 2002; Skarakis-Doyle and Dempsey, 2008). In these studies, nonverbal measures of problem detection are particularly valuable. The children listened to familiar stories that had been modified to include different types of errors, as when an action was changed from singing to swimming in a context where swimming did not make sense. Children were videotaped as they listened to the stories read aloud, and tapes were coded for nonverbal as well as verbal evidence of problem detection. Nonverbal evidence appeared earlier in development than verbal, and older children were faster to show evidence of problem detection than younger children.

The Elementary School Years

Children in the elementary school grades have been the focus of much of the research on metacognitive control from 1980 through the present. Consistently, developmental differences have been shown in children's comprehension monitoring, both cross-sectionally and longitudinally (see Baker, 1994; 2005). However, developmental differences are often qualified by individual differences. In an early study examining children's use of different standards for evaluating their comprehension (Baker, 1984b), sixth graders who were good readers performed better on an error-detection task than fourth graders. However, poorer readers in sixth grade performed no better than poorer readers in fourth grade. Academic language skill more generally is also an important source of variation in metacognitive skills, as shown in a short-term longitudinal study by Connor and colleagues (2015). Eye movements were tracked as fifth grade students read sentence pairs where a word in the second sentence was either semantically plausible or implausible in relation to the first sentence. This processing measure was valuable in providing evidence of the two components of comprehension monitoring, evaluation, and regulation. Students had longer gaze durations on the target word when it was semantically implausible than when it was plausible; this was taken as evidence that students monitored their understanding and found a problem. Students also spent more time rereading the context sentence, taken as evidence of an effort to repair understanding. The different response patterns were stronger for better readers and those with better language skills. From the beginning of the school year to the end, only those students who had strong academic language skills improved in their comprehension monitoring.

The Secondary School Years

A considerable amount of research has also been conducted with students in middle schools and high schools. These studies often address conditions under which metacognitive control might falter, and they have shown that developmental differences are greater when tasks are more complex. In a study of fourth and sixth graders asked to think aloud as they read informational text, the older students used more metacognitive strategies when reading easy versus difficult text, whereas the younger readers did not modify their behaviors as a function of text difficulty (Cote, Goldman, & Saul, 1998). In another think-aloud study involving fifth, seventh, and ninth graders, older students reported a more diverse range of reading strategies (Moore & Scevak, 1997). Using an error-detection task, Hacker (1997) found increasing levels of problem detection among students in grades 7, 9, and 11, with the greatest differences again appearing for errors involving inconsistencies within the text. Poorer readers at all grade levels reported fewer errors than more skilled readers.

Age-related differences in metacognitive regulation were reported by Franks et al. (2013), who compared the reading behaviors of students in fifth, eighth, and tenth grades as well as in college. Students were asked to either evaluate or generate logical conclusions in narrative texts, and reading behaviors were tracked by examining lookbacks to relevant segments of the text. Students in the three younger age groups looked back more frequently when they had to evaluate the conclusions rather than generate them. However, the college students looked back equally often for both tasks. Lookbacks are an adaptive strategy for reinstating task-relevant information in memory, and the authors concluded that "Students appear to have become proficient at this metacognitive behavior by the time they are in college, and to apply it more generally as a useful comprehension strategy, rather than differentially with different task demands" (p. 162).

Real-time evidence of comprehension monitoring is now available from neuroimaging studies using functional magnetic imaging (fMRI) or event-related potentials (ERPs) (see Baker et al., 2014, for a review). Biological support for the distinction between the two components of comprehension monitoring comes from fMRI work showing that different regions of the brain are involved in the detection (evaluation) and integration (regulation) components of comprehension monitoring (Ferstl, Rinck, & von Cramon, 2005). Different neural responses are revealed when readers encounter different types of comprehension difficulties, as when readers encounter passages that contain referential ambiguities as opposed to semantic anomalies (Nieuwland, Petersson, & Van Berkum, 2007). Individual differences in reading skill and in working memory capacity are associated with differences in brain activation as readers process challenging text (Fieback, Vos, & Friederici, 2004; Prat, Mason, & Just, 2011). A recent intriguing finding is that the use of reading strategies that include metacognitive components elicits different neural activation patterns than the use of strategies involving less cognitive effort (Moss, Schunn, Schneider, & McNamara, 2013).

Developmental Relations between Metacognitive Knowledge and Control

A long-standing question in the literature is whether children need to have a sufficient level of internalized metacognitive knowledge before they can use it effectively to guide their own learning (Brown, 1980). Results of recent studies converge to offer an affirmative answer. Annevirta and Vaurus (2006) selected three groups of children who had participated in their longitudinal study discussed previously (Annevirta & Vaurus, 2001). The groups differed in their preschool levels of metacognitive knowledge (high, intermediate, and low). Only those children who had high metacognitive knowledge in preschool demonstrated any comprehension monitoring, and for most of them, it was not until second grade. Children who started out with low metacognitive knowledge showed very little growth in metacognitive control, whereas those with high metacognitive knowledge showed considerable growth. Schmitt and Sha (2009), working with a cross-sectional sample of Chinese students in the third, fifth, and seventh grades, assessed metacognitive knowledge with a questionnaire and an interview, and they assessed metacognitive control with an error-detection task and a cloze task. Results showed steady age-related increases on both aspects of metacognition, but the knowledge component increased at a faster pace than the control component.

It also appears that metacognitive knowledge is necessary but not sufficient for metacognitive control. In the Annevirta & Vaurus (2006) study, no children with low metacognitive knowledge had good metacognitive control, but some children with higher levels of knowledge did not demonstrate control. In the Eme et al. (2006) study discussed earlier, both third- and fifth-grade students, when asked to think aloud during an authentic reading task, focused on comprehension difficulties at the level of individual words rather than at higher levels of meaning construction, and they did not use strategies to help address their misunderstandings. Thus, despite the fact that the older children exhibited the metacognitive knowledge that reading was a meaning-getting process, their actual behaviors reflected the same word level focus as the younger children. In other words, possessing metacognitive knowledge is no guarantee that it will be used productively while reading. A similar conclusion is supported by Hacker's (1997) study with adolescents; although some students had the knowledge necessary to monitor their understanding at the appropriate levels, they nevertheless did not use that knowledge. In this latter case, the interpretation might be that the students had the skill but lacked the will to activate appropriate monitoring strategies, given the effort required to do so.

CONTRIBUTORS TO METACOGNITIVE DEVELOPMENT

We have just seen that the development of metacognitive knowledge contributes to the development of metacognitive control. Here we consider selected factors that contribute to metacognitive development. These include neurobiological maturation and the development of reading fluency, executive function, theory of mind, and comprehension. Self-system factors such as motivation and perceived competence in reading are also addressed. All of the research is correlational, which means that we cannot really conclude a causal role of any of these factors. In many cases, the correlations may simply indicate that metacognitive skills develop concurrently with other cognitive and linguistic skills. However, longitudinal research designs allow for stronger inferences to be made about possible developmental precursors.

Neurobiological Underpinnings of Metacognitive Development

Neuroscience research indicates that developmental changes in metacognition are related to maturation of the prefrontal cortex, the portion of the brain involved in executive function. Evidence is currently indirect, to the extent that executive function includes processes typically regarded as metacognitive in nature, such as planning, monitoring, and error correction and detection (Fernandez-Duque, Baird, & Posner, 2000). Maturation of the prefrontal lobes begins early in childhood and is not complete until late adolescence or early adulthood. Developmental increases in executive function occur at the same time there is rapid prefrontal maturation, first during early childhood and then during late adolescence. This long developmental time course helps explain why metacognitive control of reading continues to improve into the college years. As neuroimaging technology becomes more accessible for use with children, we may soon know more about how developmental changes in brain structure and function are related to development of metacognitive control.

Automatic versus Deliberate Processing: A Developmental Challenge

Skilled readers demonstrate a balance between automatic and deliberate processing of text. Brown (1980) captured this distinction well in a seminal paper. Skilled readers "proceed merrily on automatic pilot, until a triggering event alerts them to a comprehension failure. While the process is flowing smoothly, their construction of meaning is very rapid, but when a comprehension failure is detected, they must slow down and allot extra processing capacity to the problem area. They must employ debugging devices and strategies, which take time and effort" (p. 455). An important question for educators is how to help children transition from the slow and effortful processing characteristic of beginning readers *whenever* they read to effortful processing only when necessary. As Clay (1998) asserted, "We need to have children successfully monitoring and controlling their literacy acts, but with minimal conscious attention" (p. 68). With repeated experience, children learn to decode and to monitor their comprehension sufficiently well that they do not have to allocate attention to the processes; it is only when an obstacle is noted that attention is directed to the problem area (Samuels, Ediger, Willcut, & Palumbo, 2005). When conscious attention is required, monitoring competes for valuable working memory resources that are involved in comprehension per se.

Scholars disagree as to whether comprehension monitoring is necessarily a conscious process. Neuroimaging and eye-movement methods, which do not require readers to make overt responses, provide evidence of automaticity (Baker et al., 2014; Connor et al., 2015). Conscious metacognitive control can help readers compensate for weaknesses in decoding and working memory. For example, they can compensate by pausing, looking back, rereading, and sounding out words (Walczyk, Marsiglia, Johns, & Bryan, 2004).

The Role of Working Memory and Other Executive Functions

Executive functions are higher order cognitive abilities involved in goal-directed behavior. Metacognition is sometimes regarded as an executive function and sometimes it is seen as a separate construct. However, the skills involved in metacognitive control, such as error detection, correction, and planning, are regarded by neuroscientists as executive functions largely under the control of the prefrontal cortex (Fernandez-Duque et al., 2000). Working memory is the executive function most often implicated in the development of comprehension monitoring. Other executive functions have also been implicated, including inhibition and cognitive flexibility (Cartwright, 2015).

For many years, a primary explanation of the weak metacognitive control exhibited by younger and poorer readers was that they had limited cognitive resources (i.e., working memory) but only recently has this explanation been tested empirically. Many researchers interested in metacognition now include direct measures of working memory in their studies. Working memory tasks require participants to hold information that is presented to them in short-term memory while simultaneously manipulating that information or processing new information. For example, in a numerical task, people listen as a string of digits is presented to them and then they must recall the digits backward. The length of the digit string that they can recall correctly is an indication of working memory capacity. A task frequently used by reading researchers requires people to read or listen to sentences in sets of increasing size, and they must verify the truth value of each sentence at the same time they hold in memory a set of words for subsequent recall.

An important question that has been raised recently is whether executive functions are necessary precursors of metacognitive skills. Research on this question is limited, but it was addressed by Bryce, Whitebread, and Szűcs (2015) in a study with five- and seven-year-old children. They found that working memory and metacognitive skills (as demonstrated in a planning task that did not involve reading) were more strongly correlated in the younger children than in the older children. The authors suggested that weaknesses in metacognitive monitoring and control in young children may be due to their less developed executive functioning. On this view, the rapid improvements in metacognitive skills seen during the early years of formal schooling may be caused, at least in part, by the increase in executive control that occurs with maturation of the prefrontal cortex in preschool children.

As suggested previously, working memory constraints make it difficult for children who are just learning how to read to monitor their understanding. But even once the code-based skills have been mastered and children are fluent at word reading, individual differences in working memory are still associated with differences in metacognitive control. A number of studies by Oakhill and her colleagues in England have documented this outcome. For example, Oakhill, Hartt, and Samols (2005) found that fifth graders who performed poorly on a test of numerical working memory also performed more poorly on several error-detection tasks, especially when inconsistent sentences in the text were more widely spaced and so put a greater burden on working memory. (See also Cain, Oakhill, & Bryant, 2004; Oakhill & Cain, 2012.) Associations of working memory with metacognitive control have also been found in tasks other than error detection (Chrysochoou, Bablekou, & Tsigilis, 2011).

Working memory plays a role in comprehension monitoring while listening as well as in reading, and it might be even more important given the lack of permanence of orally presented text. In her study of Korean kindergarteners and first graders, Kim (2015) documented that children who had better working memory capacity had better performance on an error-detection task. Strasser and del Rio (2014) had similar findings with Chilean preschoolers.

Researchers are also beginning to address whether other executive functions contribute to metacognitive control. One important executive function that plays a role in self-regulated behavior is inhibitory control, the ability to resist distraction and sustain attention. The Stroop task familiar to many adults is an inhibitory control task, and a developmentally appropriate variant is to ask children to say *boy* when confronted with a picture of a girl and vice versa. Kim and Phillips (2015) found that inhibitory control was significantly correlated with error detection in kindergarten and first-grade children, as did Strasser and del Rio (2014). Longitudinal evidence was provided by Roebers, Cimeli, Röthlisberger and Neuenschwander (2012) in a sample of Swiss children who were assessed at the end of first grade and again at the end of second grade. Inhibitory control was assessed, as well as cognitive flexibility, the ability to mentally switch between two concepts. The metacognitive task required children to spell a set of words varying in difficulty, to indicate their confidence in the correctness of the spellings, and to revise their spellings if they thought it necessary. Relations between metacognition and executive functions were strong, both concurrently and longitudinally. Moreover, executive function skills in first grade had a direct effect on metacognitive control in second grade, providing additional support for the notion that executive functions might be developmental precursors.

The Role of Theory of Mind

Theory of mind is another cognitive factor thought to contribute to metacognitive development. In fact, some consider it to be a type of executive function, along with metacognition itself (Cartwright & Guajardo, 2015). Theory of mind reflects the understanding that people have mental states that are not directly accessible to other people. Children begin to develop a theory of mind during the preschool years, and it gradually becomes richer and more complex moving into adulthood (Kuhn, 2000). Is it the case that children need to develop a theory of mind before they are able to reflect on their own cognitive processes or regulate their own mental activity in relation to a specific task?

This possibility was examined in relation to reading by Lecce et al. (2010) in their study of Italian children. One indicator of theory of mind is the ability to use mental state terms such as *think* and *feel*. Participants were asked to write an ending for stories involving episodes of daily life that called for the use of such terms. In a cross-sectional study, fourth graders showed a better understanding of mental states than second graders, as well as more mature metacognitive knowledge. In a longitudinal study, the authors asked whether knowledge of mental states preceded metacognitive knowledge about reading. They found that mental state knowledge assessed early in fourth grade did predict metacognitive knowledge 11 months later, but only when the mental state terms dealt with cognition, not emotion. The authors thus obtained evidence for the proposed developmental sequence.

Theory of mind is particularly important in relation to narrative comprehension because the mental states of characters are usually critical to the story line. Thus, it might also play a role in comprehension monitoring of narrative materials. Relations between theory of mind and metacognitive control were examined in the research with kindergartners and first graders discussed previously (Kim, 2014; Kim & Phillips, 2015; Strasser & del Rio, 2014). In all three studies, theory of mind, assessed with the commonly used false belief task, was moderately to strongly related to comprehension monitoring.

The Role of Reading Comprehension Ability

Most of the research on relations between metacognition and comprehension postulates a directional relation such that increases in metacognition lead to increases in comprehension. The possibility exists, however, that the relation works in the opposite direction, such that weaknesses in comprehension contribute to weaknesses in metacognitive control. Oakhill et al. (2005) favored the latter interpretation of their results, suggesting that better comprehension monitoring may be a consequence of better reading comprehension skills, as did Connor et al. (2015). This makes sense if one considers that successful comprehension entails the construction of a coherent mental model of the text. If readers have difficulty constructing such a model, they will have difficulty evaluating whether or not the content makes sense.

What aspects of comprehension might play a role in such a connection? van der Schoot, Reijntjes, and van Lieshout (2012) examined whether the poor comprehension monitoring skills of poor comprehenders resulted from difficulty in creating a strong mental model of a text or from difficulty in updating the model as new information comes in. Participants were Dutch fifth and sixth graders identified as either good or poor comprehenders who were matched on age and decoding skills. They read passages in which an inconsistent or consistent statement about a character's action was adjacent to or widely separated from a description of the character. Good comprehenders spent more time reading the target statement when it was inconsistent with prior context, regardless of whether the descriptive statement was near or far. In contrast, the poor comprehenders only spent more time on the inconsistent statement when it was adjacent to the description. This is evidence that the problem comes from creating the mental model, not from updating it, because when it was possible to update the model in a local context, poor comprehenders apparently did so. When eye movements were tracked in a second study, neither good nor poor readers made many regressions to the sentence describing the character, but good comprehenders were more likely to reread the sentence that was far back in the text. When working memory assessed by a reading span task was controlled, these differences were reduced in magnitude but not eliminated, demonstrating again the important independent contribution of working memory to comprehension monitoring.

In reality, the relation between metacognition and comprehension is most likely a reciprocal one, such that increases in one domain facilitate development in the other domain, which in turn facilitates further development in the original domain. To address this possibility, Annevirta, Laakkonen, Kinnunen, and Vauras (2007) examined the cumulative developmental interaction of metacognitive knowledge and comprehension in their longitudinal study described previously–Annevirta & Vaurus, 2006. In addition to assessing metacognitive knowledge in preschool, grade 1, and grade 2, they also assessed reading comprehension in grades 1, 2, and 3. Children's level of metacognitive knowledge was strongly associated with their level of reading comprehension across all school years, consistent with a large body of research. The unique contribution of this study is tentative support for a developmental cycle: the more children grew in metacognitive knowledge over time, the more they grew in reading comprehension over time.

The Role of Motivation

Self-system variables such as motivation, interest, perceived competence, and attributional beliefs may also play a role in metacognitive development. Researchers working within the self-regulated learning tradition view the use of motivational strategies as one of three components of self-regulated learning, with cognitive and metacognitive strategies as the other two (Dignath & Buttner, 2008). Correlations between motivation for reading and metacognitive knowledge about reading have been reported consistently in the literature, and longitudinal studies show that the relations are stable over time (Kolić-Kehovec, Rončević Zubković, & Pahljina-Reinić, 2014; van Kraayenoord, Beinicke, Schlagmüller, & Schneider, 2012; Roeschl-Heils et al., 2003). The Roebers et al. (2012) study discussed previously showed strong relations between metacognitive control and self-concept about reading in their sample of Swiss first and second graders studied longitudinally. Moreover, the authors suggested that having a positive conception of oneself as a reader is a precursor to the development of metacognitive control, and they offered as support the evidence that grade 1 self-concept predicted grade 2 metacognitive control.

Correlations between motivation and metacognition most likely do not reflect a causal relation but rather that a student with high reading motivation will be more willing to put forth the effort to use metacognitive strategies. Situational interest is also an important consideration. For example, when fourth grade poor comprehenders engaged in a game-like comprehension-monitoring task that was more interesting than the traditional school-like task, their error detection was as good as that of their peers who were better comprehenders (De Sousa & Oakhill, 1996).

CONSEQUENCES OF METACOGNITION

We now know that metacognitive knowledge and control of reading increase with age and that a variety of other factors may be precursors to metacognitive development. The important practical question is what this means for educators interested in promoting reading comprehension. Countless correlational studies have been conducted over the years that demonstrate simple connections between metacognition and comprehension, but current researchers conceptualize metacognition as just one of many contributors to comprehension. In other words, comprehension depends on the successful coordination of multiple cognitive and linguistic factors, including vocabulary knowledge, executive functions, oral language competencies, theory of mind, and code-based skills such as word identification. In addition, self-system factors such as motivation, interest, and perceived competence play a role. Using multiple regression and path analysis, researchers today are examining the extent to which metacognition predicts reading comprehension in conjunction with other predictors, and they are asking whether certain variables affect comprehension indirectly via their effect on metacognition. In essence, many of these studies examine both contributors to metacognition and consequences of metacognition. The intervention research of today also reflects this multicomponent view of comprehension, and there is consensus that fostering students' metacognitive knowledge and control is necessary but not sufficient for improving reading comprehension. Experimental interventions therefore entail instruction in metacognitive strategies, as well as cognitive and sometimes motivational strategies. In this section, I highlight some recent findings in the correlational and intervention research.

Metacognition as a Contributor to Comprehension: Evidence from Correlational Studies

Metacognitive knowledge. Correlational evidence of interconnections among metacognitive knowledge, reading comprehension, and other variables comes from a number of studies, many of which have already been mentioned. For example, van Kraayenoord et al. (2012) investigated the relations among metacognitive knowledge, self-concept, interest, word identification, and reading comprehension in third and fourth graders in Australia. Reading comprehension was most strongly predicted by word identification, as would be expected, but metacognitive knowledge and reading self-concept were also significant predictors. In a path model, word recognition and metacognitive knowledge both predicted reading comprehension directly. Motivation had a direct effect on reading comprehension as well as an indirect effect via metacognitive knowledge and word identification. Similar interrelations among self-reports of metacognitive knowledge and control, motivation (interest in reading and self-concept), and comprehension have been found among third- and fourth-grade students and seventh- and eighth-grade students (Roeschl-Heils et al., 2003). Kolić-Vehovec et al.'s (2014) longitudinal study of Croatian children in fourth, sixth, and eighth grades included assessments not only of metacognitive knowledge of reading strategies and attitudes toward reading, but also reading comprehension. Strategic knowledge was associated with reading comprehension at all three time points. In a test of a path model, girls' attitudes toward recreational reading predicted metacognitive knowledge, which in turn predicted reading comprehension. Although a considerable body of research corroborates connections between metacognitive knowledge and reading comprehension, it is important to acknowledge that many studies have found weak connections (Sperling et al., 2002). The discrepancies may well reflect differences in how metacognitive knowledge is assessed, which are often substantial.

Metacognitive Control. Studies that include behavioral measures of metacognitive control in relation to comprehension have a long history with older children, adolescents, and adults, but a new line of research focuses on preschoolers. A growing interest in the comprehension skills of preschoolers has led to research on metacognitive control in relation to listening comprehension. Three recent studies have already been cited for showing connections between executive functions, theory of mind, and comprehension monitoring (Kim, 2015; Kim & Phillips, 2014; Strasser & del Rio, 2014). These studies were based on the perspective that comprehension depends on a number of higher-level skills, including comprehension monitoring, which in turn depend on other more basic skills. Only the results related to comprehension monitoring are summarized here.

Strasser and del Rio (2014) examined how depth and breadth of vocabulary knowledge, inference making, executive functions (inhibition and working memory), theory of mind, and comprehension monitoring (error detection) contributed to two measures of story comprehension among Chilean kindergartners. They found that comprehension monitoring was an independent predictor of comprehension when measured by a task requiring children to generate a story from a wordless picture book, a challenging activity that requires integration and manipulation of information. In contrast, when the comprehension task involved simple recall of story information, comprehension-monitoring skills did not play a role. Kim and Phillips (2014) demonstrated that inhibitory control, vocabulary knowledge, theory of mind, and comprehension-monitoring skills predicted kindergartners' as well as first graders' listening comprehension of stories. Kim (2015) obtained similar results in a study with Korean kindergartners and first graders, but it also showed that the effect of working memory on comprehension was mediated by comprehension monitoring. Because children in Korea learn to read in kindergarten, it was possible to include measures of reading as well as listening in her study. Results of path modeling showed that reading comprehension was fully mediated by listening comprehension and word reading. What this means is that children's performance on an error-detection task presented orally did not directly predict reading comprehension, although the two measures were correlated.

Longitudinal research by Oakhill and colleagues illustrates connections between comprehension monitoring and reading comprehension in the later elementary school years. Cain, Oakhill, and Bryant (2004) examined the joint contributions of comprehension monitoring, working memory, and inference making to reading comprehension in a longitudinal study of children in grades 3 through 6. Comprehension monitoring was assessed with error-detection tasks using age-appropriate materials containing embedded inconsistencies. Working memory and comprehension monitoring were significant predictors of comprehension. Comprehension monitoring accounted for unique variance once working memory and other background variables (word reading skill, verbal ability) were controlled. These relations held across all three measurement points. In a subsequent study Oakhill & Cain (2012) tested a longitudinal path model to examine how multiple variables contributed to the prediction of reading comprehension over time. Results are again reported selectively. Comprehension monitoring in grade 3 predicted comprehension monitoring in grade 4, which in turn predicted reading comprehension in grade 6. Reciprocal connections were also revealed in that grade 3 comprehension predicted grade 4 comprehension monitoring. This latter finding provides further evidence that comprehension is a contributor to metacognitive control, as discussed earlier.

Metacognition as a Contributor to Comprehension: Evidence from Intervention Studies

The early evidence of developmental and ability-related differences in metacognitive skills led quite quickly to efforts to increase these skills through direct instruction (Baker & Zimlin, 1989) and to the design of metacognitively oriented interventions to promote reading comprehension (Jacobs & Paris, 1984; Palincsar & Brown, 1984). The intervention programs often entailed the teaching of multiple cognitive and metacognitive strategies, such as predicting upcoming text, clarifying unknown words and concepts, summarizing what was read, and generating substantive questions about the text. Key features of effective interventions were identified, including explicit explanation of how, when, and why to use cognitive and metacognitive strategies, teacher modeling, guided practice, and peer collaboration. An important instructional goal was to foster a gradual transition from *other-regulation* to *self-regulation*.

On the basis of the training studies carried out in the 1980s and 1990s, two influential national committees concluded that metacognition is important to reading comprehension and can and should be taught (The National Reading Panel (NRP), 2000; Snow, Burns, & Griffin, writing for the National Research Council, 1998). The number of intervention studies with a metacognitive component has continued to grow in the twenty-first century. Recent meta-analyses confirm and extend the NRP meta-analysis (Cromley & Azevedo, 2007; Dignath & Buttner, 2008; Dignath, Buttner, & Langfelt, 2008). Length constraints do not permit detailed discussion of the recent intervention research, but see Baker et al. (2015) for a review. I focus here on conclusions from the meta-analyses and a few recent studies that bear on those conclusions.

In their meta-analyses, Dignath and colleagues took a broad perspective, examining strategies interventions in different content domains (math, reading-writing, and others), at different grade levels (primary [i.e., grades 1–6] and secondary), and with different instructional components (cognitive strategies, metacognitive strategies, metacognitive reflection, and motivation). Effect sizes were based on the outcomes of strategy knowledge/use and achievement. The Dignath et al. (2008) meta-analysis focused on the primary level, whereas Dignath and Buttner (2008) included all grade levels. Of particular relevance for this chapter are the conclusions related to developmental differences.

Comparison of outcomes in grades 1 through 6 showed that students at all levels had better reading achievement after training than students in comparison groups. Moreover, the magnitude of the benefits was comparable across grade levels. This latter finding conflicts with earlier meta-analyses (e.g., NRP, 2000) that found greater benefits from metacognitively oriented instruction for older elementary students, but it may be that the more recent intervention studies are methodologically stronger. Dignath et al. (2008) also found that children in the early primary grades showed greater increases in their strategy knowledge and use than students in the upper primary grades. This nonintuitive finding may have arisen because older children, including those in comparison classrooms, already had a repertoire of strategies that they used effectively. This interpretation is consistent with the evidence presented earlier of better metacognitive control among older elementary school children.

The Dignath and Buttner (2008) meta-analysis that included studies of primary and secondary students showed that strategy instruction had a much stronger effect on the reading achievement of students in secondary school than in primary school, although all students benefited more than their peers in comparison classrooms. The effects of strategy instruction on the development of metacognitive knowledge and control were stronger for secondary students. This finding may reflect in part that older students have already acquired some metacognitive knowledge from their more extensive schooling history and so are better able to build on prior experiences. The meta-analysis also revealed that secondary students benefited more than primary students when the instructional programs included metacognitive reflection. Metacognitive reflection fosters conditional knowledge about metacognition, the understanding of conditions under which particular strategies are most useful and the benefits of using them. The differences in treatment effectiveness associated with schooling level may reflect developmental improvements in factors that contribute to metacognition, such as those identified earlier in the chapter. Maturation of the prefrontal cortex, which peaks during adolescence, may underlie many of these increases as well as the increases in metacognitive functioning per se.

A common component of strategies instruction is peer collaboration, where children work together to practice the trained strategies. Although many researchers have found that interventions involving peer collaboration are effective, Dignath and Buttner (2008) did not find a large effect size when comparing studies that did or did not include peer collaboration. It appears that the way collaborative learning opportunities are structured is an important factor and one that can contribute to age-related differences in treatment effectiveness. To illustrate, Van Keer and Verhaeghe (2005) compared performance of second and fifth graders in Belgium who participated in teacher-led whole-class strategies instruction, reciprocal same-age peer tutoring, or reciprocal cross-age peer tutoring. The second graders gained in reading comprehension from teacher-led and cross-age tutoring activities, but not from same-age tutoring, whereas fifth graders in all three conditions showed greater gains relative to peers in a comparison group. In other words, peer collaboration was not more effective than whole-class groupings. From a developmental perspective, the findings confirm that children as early as second grade can benefit from multiple-strategies instruction, but they also show that the strategies need to be practiced with more knowledgeable others (i.e., teachers or older students) as opposed to same-age peers. In another study comparing different collaborative group structures, Spörer, Brunstein, and Kieschke (2009) also did not find an advantage of peer collaboration (reciprocal teaching in pairs or in small groups) over whole group strategies instruction, but they did find that only the students working in small groups maintained their gains at a long-term follow-up. Participants in this study were German students in grades three through six. Students at all grade levels benefited from all three types of intervention, improving in their strategy use and in their reading comprehension. The different developmental results across the two studies may be due to the greater mastery of basic word reading skills of third graders relative to second graders, and/or their greater experience working with peers.

Meta-analysis has shown stronger effects when a motivational component is included relative to programs focused on metacognitive and cognitive strategies alone (Dignath & Buttner, 2008). In one such study, Berkeley, Mastropieri, and Scruggs (2011) implemented a strategy instruction program for struggling readers in grades 6 through 9. One of their treatment groups received additional instruction in using self-talk to increase persistence and flexible strategy use, and to make connections between the use of strategies and academic outcomes. This latter group showed greater gains over the long term in metacognitive strategy awareness and reading comprehension than students who received metacognitive training alone, with no apparent differences in treatment effectiveness across grade levels.

The role of executive functioning in school achievement has received a great deal of attention in recent years, but few researchers have attempted to increase students' executive functions as a way to increase metacognitive control and comprehension (Cartwright, 2015). As discussed previously, working memory limitations make it difficult for students to hold information from the text in memory while processing subsequent text, interfering with construction of a mental representation and effective monitoring of comprehension. To address these issues, Carretti et al. (2013) developed a multiple-strategies intervention that also included instruction in working memory skills and text integration. Classroom teachers in Italy administered the instruction to fourth and fifth graders. Children receiving intervention showed greater gains in metacognitive knowledge and control than a standard-instruction comparison group, and they showed improvement in working memory and reading comprehension, with gains maintained over an eight-month period. Working memory capacity is often considered to be an individual difference that is not amenable to instruction, so it is important that these results be replicated.

One age group that was not addressed in any of the meta-analyses is preschool children, a gap in coverage attributable to the lack of relevant research. Given the evidence of rudimentary comprehension-monitoring skills among preschoolers, it is reasonable to expect that children might be receptive to metacognitively oriented instruction well before they become fluent at word reading (Baker, 2005; Baker et al., 2015; Williams & Atkins, 2009). After all, the processes of monitoring for comprehension are similar in listening and reading, and children can be sensitized early on to the need to check their understanding. In research and practice, attention is now being directed to enhancing the oral comprehension skills of preschoolers in the hope that this will transfer to improved reading comprehension in subsequent years (DeBruin-Parecki, van Kleek, & Gear, 2015).

A large-scale study in France by Bianco et al. (2010) illustrates the potential of early metacognitive intervention. The researchers compared two different approaches to comprehension instruction, one of which involved explicit instruction in component processes of comprehension, including comprehension monitoring and inference generation, and the other involved shared storybook reading. Children received a series of lessons on inconsistency detection, designed to make them aware that comprehension difficulties can occur and that one must think how to resolve them. Early lessons called for children to identify anomalies in pictures (e.g., two butterflies in a goldfish bowl) and explain what was wrong with the picture. More complex lessons called for children to identify inconsistencies between text content and an accompanying picture. Once the component skills were learned, they were used in lessons designed to help children build a coherent mental representation of texts.

The shared storybook intervention involved repeated readings of storybooks and discussion of the stories, but no explicit instruction in comprehension. The intervention was begun when children were in prekindergarten and it continued through kindergarten. Results revealed that the explicit comprehension instruction led to improved comprehension, but the storybook reading intervention did not. What was particularly encouraging is that the children who received explicit comprehension instruction continued to increase steadily in their comprehension during first grade, when no intervention was provided. Also of importance is that children benefited more from the training if they participated for two years rather than just one. This result is consistent with another of the conclusions of the Dignath and Buttner (2008) meta-analysis: effect sizes were stronger in studies with longer durations.

IMPLICATIONS AND IMPACT: HAVE CLASSROOM PRACTICES CHANGED?

Based on an extensive research base, we now know a great deal about how to foster metacognitive development in instructional settings and how to help ensure that the instruction enhances reading comprehension. However, a significant conclusion of the Dignath and Buttner (2008) meta-analysis of strategy training research is that effects are much stronger when the interventions are delivered by researchers rather than classroom teachers. What this suggests is that effective implementation of strategies instruction is not easy, and that considerable knowledge and practice is required. Researchers customarily assess whether individual teachers implemented their program as intended. When they find weaknesses in implementation fidelity, they also find that students in those teachers' classes did not benefit as much from the instruction they received.

During the 1980s and 1990s, when metacognition first acquired such popular appeal, many articles were written for teachers on the importance of metacognition and how to foster it (Baker & Cerro, 2000). However, classroom observations, teacher interviews, and analyses of literacy textbooks and curriculum materials revealed scant attention to metacognition in the reading curriculum (Baker, 1994). Thanks in part to the report of the National Reading Panel (2000) and similar initiatives in other countries, teacher education programs are now more likely to address metacognition, and metacognition is more likely to be included in curriculum guidelines, standards, and basal series. Despite these positive trends, classroom literacy instruction designed to promote metacognitive knowledge and control may still not be the norm. Observational studies continue to show relatively little attention to metacognitive strategies in classroom instruction (Dignath-van Ewijk, Dickhauser, & Büttner, 2013). Teacher surveys reveal similar outcomes. For example, in a survey of 278 Irish primary (elementary) teachers, Concannon-Gibney and Murphy (2010) learned that the teachers did not know much about metacognition. Few teachers engaged in the explicit teaching of comprehension, and this was true for both experienced and novice teachers. Teachers in the early grades had a strong emphasis on decoding and bottom-up reading instruction, whereas teachers in the upper grades focused on having their students read for pleasure. The authors' conclusion echoes that of many others: "The importance of cognitive flexibility, metacognition and explicit comprehension strategy instruction in reading needs to be promoted among all educators" (p. 122).

Despite the fact that there still does not seem to be much emphasis on metacognition in routine classroom practice, anecdotal evidence indicates successful outcomes for schools that make concerted efforts to foster metacognition. For example, Thiede, Redford, Wiley, and Griffin (2012) examined differences in metacognitive control as a function of how long students had been attending a charter school that has a curriculum emphasizing use of metacognitive strategies. The seventh- and eighth-grade students who had been attending the school for more than four years were better at judging their comprehension of text than newcomers, and they were better able to regulate their study efforts. Additional anecdotal evidence comes from intervention studies where students in "standard practice" comparison classrooms gained in metacognitive knowledge and strategy use from pretest to posttest (e.g., Caretti et al., 2013; McKeown, Beck, & Blake, 2009). It turned out that teachers in these upper elementary classrooms were using curricula that included metacognitive instruction, and apparently students were benefiting from it. Schoolwide adoption of a metacognitively oriented curriculum can benefit even the youngest and weakest readers, as shown at Benchmark School for struggling readers. Beginning in the primary grades, children are taught to use a variety of comprehension and comprehension-monitoring strategies, and their use of these strategies improves their comprehension (Pressley & Gaskins, 2006).

Teachers who would like to take the initiative in their own professional development will continue to find a large number of books and articles written explicitly for practitioners. Teaching tips and instructional resources are available to help teachers at all levels foster metacognitive knowledge and control (Israel et al., 2005). Teachers who are interested in evaluating the metacognitive knowledge and skills of their students can ask them to complete questionnaires that were designed, at least in part, with teachers in mind (Bauserman, 2005; Mokhtari & Reichard, 2002). Questionnaires designed for teachers themselves to rate their students' levels of metacognitive control are also available (Whitebread et al., 2009). Use of these instruments has the added advantage of enhancing teachers' and students' awareness of the importance of metacognition and self-regulated learning.

CONCLUSION

The primary objective of this chapter was to review the literature on metacognitive development in relation to reading. Age-related changes were documented in metacognitive knowledge and control in research involving many different age groupings and methods. Recent investigations yielded evidence of precursors to metacognitive knowledge and control, including executive functions and theory of mind. Research has shown that metacognition and comprehension are strongly intertwined with basic biological, cognitive, linguistic, and motivational processes. The development of metacognition can be considered both cause and consequence of better reading comprehension. Intervention research shows that direct instruction in metacognitive strategies is a powerful way to enhance metacognitive development, and in turn, reading comprehension. Adolescents tend to benefit more from these instructional interventions, but they are effective from the earliest years of schooling. Our understanding of developmental mechanisms is increasing with more sophisticated research designs and technologies. Nevertheless, there remains a gap between research and practice. A more concerted effort is warranted to give teachers the knowledge and skills they need to foster the transition from other-regulation to self-regulation.

REFERENCES

Annevirta, T., & Vauras, M. (2001). Development of metacognitive knowledge in primary grades. *European Journal of Educational Psychology, 16*, 257–82.

Annevirta, T., & Vauras, M. (2006). Developmental changes of metacognitive skill in elementary school children. *The Journal of Experimental Education*, *74*, 197–225.

Annevirta, T., Laakkonen, E., Kinnunen, R., & Vauras, M. (2007). Developmental dynamics of metacognitive knowledge and text comprehension skill in the first primary school years. *Metacognition and Learning, 2*, 21–39.

Baker, L. (1984a). Spontaneous versus instructed use of multiple standards for evaluating comprehension: Effects of age, reading proficiency and type of standard. *Journal of Experimental Child Psychology, 38*, 289–311.

Baker, L. (1984b). Children's effective use of multiple standards for evaluating their comprehension. *Journal of Educational Psychology, 76*, 588–97.

Baker, L. (1994). Fostering metacognitive development. In H. Reese (Ed.), *Advances in Child Development and Behavior* (Vol. 25, pp. 201–39). San Diego: Academic Press.

Baker, L. (2005). Developmental differences in metacognition: Implications for metacognitively-oriented reading instruction. In S. E. Israel, C. C. Block, K. L. Bauserman, & K. Kinnucan-Welsch (Eds.), *Metacognition in literacy learning: Theory, assessment, instruction, and professional development* (pp. 61–79). Mahwah, NJ: Erlbaum.

Baker, L. (2008). Metacognitive development in reading: Contributors and consequences. In K. Mokhtari & R. Sheorey (Eds.), *Reading strategies of first and second language learners: See how they read* (pp. 25–42). Norwood, MA: Christopher Gordon.

Baker, L., & Brown, A. L. (1984). Metacognitive skills and reading. In P. D. Pearson, M. Kamil, R. Barr, & P. Mosenthal (Eds.), *Handbook of research in reading* (Vol. 1, pp. 353–95). New York: Longman.

Baker, L., & Cerro, L. (2000). Assessing metacognition in children and adults. In G. Schraw & J. Impara (Eds.), *Issues in the measurement of metacognition* (pp. 99–145). Lincoln, NE: Buros Institute of Mental Measurements, University of Nebraska.

Baker, L., DeWyngaert, L. U., & Zeliger-Kandasamy, A. (2015). Metacognition in comprehension instruction: New directions. In S. R. Parris & K. Headley (Eds.), *Comprehension instruction: Research-based best practices* (3rd ed., pp. 72–87). New York: Guilford.

Baker, L., Zeliger-Kandasamy, A., & DeWyngaert, L. U. (2014). Neuroimaging evidence of comprehension monitoring. *Psychological Topics, 23,* 167–87.

Baker, L., & Zimlin, L. (1989). Instructional effects on children's use of two levels of standards for evaluating their comprehension. *Journal of Educational Psychology, 81*, 340–46.

Bauserman, K. L. (2005). Metacognitive Processes Inventory: An informal instrument to assess a student's developmental level of metacognition. In S. E. Israel, C. C. Block, K. L. Bauserman, & K Kinnucan-Welsch (Eds.), *Metacognition in literacy learning: Theory, assessment, instruction, and professional development* (pp. 165–80). Mahwah, NJ: Erlbaum.

Berkeley, S., Mastropieri, M. A., & Scruggs, T. E. (2011). Reading comprehension strategy instruction and attribution retraining for secondary students with learning and other mild disabilities. *Journal of Learning Disabilities, 44*, 18–32.

Bianco, M., Bressoux, P., Doyen, A., Lambert, E., Lima, L., Pellenq, C., & Zorman, M. (2010). Early training in oral comprehension and phonological skills: Results of a three-year longitudinal study. *Scientific Studies of Reading*, *14*, 211–46.

Bryce, D., Whitebread, D., & Szűcs, D. (2015). The relationships among executive functions, metacognitive skills and educational achievement in 5 and 7 year-old children. *Metacognition and Learning, 10,* 181–98.

Cain, K., Oakhill, J., & Bryant, P. (2004). Children's reading comprehension ability: Concurrent prediction by working memory, verbal ability, and component skills. *Journal of Educational Psychology, 96*, 31–42.

Carretti, B., Caldarola, N., Tencati, C., & Cornoldi, C. (2013). Improving reading comprehension in reading and listening settings: The effect of two training programmes focusing on metacognition and working memory. *British Journal of Educational Psychology, 83,* 1–17.

Cartwright, K. B. (2015). Executive function and reading comprehension: The critical role of cognitive flexibility. In S. R. Parris & K. Headley (Eds.), *Comprehension instruction: Research-based best practices* (3rd ed., pp. 56–71). New York: Guilford.

Cartwright, K. B., & Guajardo, N. R. (2015). The role of hot and cool executive functions in prereader comprehension. In A. DeBruin-Parecki, A. van Kleek, & S. Gear (Eds.), *Developing early comprehension: Laying the foundation for reading success* (pp. 151–77). Baltimore, MD: Brookes.

Chrysochoou, E., Bablekou, Z., & Tsigilis, N. (2011). Working memory contributions to reading comprehension components in middle childhood children. *The American Journal of Psychology, 124*, 275–89.

Clay, M. M. (1998). *By different paths to common outcomes*. York, Maine: Stenhouse.

Concannon-Gibney, T., & Murphy, B. (2010). Reading practice in Irish primary classrooms: Too simple a view of reading? *Literacy, 44*, 122–30.

Connor, C. M., Radach, R., Vorstius, C., Day, S. L., McLean, L., & Morrison, F. J. (2015). Individual differences in fifth graders' literacy and academic language predict comprehension monitoring development: An eye-movement study. *Scientific Studies of Reading, 19,* 114–34.

Cromley, J. G., & Azevedo, R. (2007). Testing and refining the direct and inferential mediation model of reading comprehension. *Journal of Educational Psychology, 99*, 311–25.

DeBruin-Parecki, A. van Kleek, A., & Gear, S. (Eds.) (2015), *Developing early comprehension: Laying the foundation for reading success* (pp. 19–34). Baltimore, MD: Brookes.

Dignath, C., & Buttner, G. (2008). Components of fostering self-regulated learning among students: A meta-analysis on intervention studies at primary and secondary school level. *Metacognition and Learning, 3,* 231–64.

Dignath, C., Büttner, G., & Langfeldt, H. P. (2008). How can primary school students learn self-regulated learning strategies most effectively? A meta-analysis on self-regulation training programmes. *Educational Research Review, 3*, 101–29.

Dignath-van Ewijk, C., Dickhauser, O., & Büttner, G. (2013). Assessing how teachers enhance self-regulated learning: A multiperspective approach. *Journal of Cognitive Education and Psychology, 12,* 338–58.

Eme, E., Puustinen, M., & Coutelet, B. (2006). Individual and developmental differences in reading monitoring: When and how do children evaluate their comprehension? *European Journal of Psychology of Education, 21,* 91–115.

Fernandez-Duque, D., Baird, J. A., & Posner, M. I. (2000). Executive attention and metacognitive regulation. *Consciousness and Cognition, 9,* 288–307.

Ferstl, E. C., Rinck, M., & von Cramon, D. Y. (2005). Emotional and temporal aspects of situation model processing during text comprehension: An event-related fMRI study. *Journal of Cognitive Neuroscience, 17*, 724–39.

Fiebach, C. J., Vos, S. H., & Friederici, A. D. (2004). Neural correlates of syntactic ambiguity in sentence comprehension for low and high span readers. *Journal of Cognitive Neuroscience, 16*, 1562–75.

Fox, E. (2009). The role of reader characteristics in processing and learning from informational text. *Review of Educational Research, 79*, 197–261.

Franks, B., Therriault, D., Buhr, M., Chiang, E., Gonzalez, C., Kwon, H., . . . Wang, X. (2013). Looking back: Reasoning and metacognition with narrative texts. *Metacognition and Learning, 8*, 145–71.

Garner, R. (1987). *Metacognition and reading comprehension.* Norwood, NJ: Ablex.

Hacker, D. J. (1997). Comprehension monitoring of written discourse across early-to-middle adolescence. *Reading and Writing, 9*, 207–40.

Israel, S. E., Block, C. C., & Bauserman, K. L. (Eds.) (2005). *Metacognition in literacy learning: Theory, assessment, instruction, and professional development.* Mahwah, NJ: Erlbaum.

Kim, Y. (2015). Language and cognitive predictors of text comprehension: Evidence from multivariate analysis. *Child Development, 86*, 128–44.

Kim, Y., & Phillips, B. (2014). Cognitive correlates of listening comprehension. *Reading Research Quarterly, 49*, 269–81.

Kolić-Vehovec, S., Zubković, B., & Pahljina-Reinić, R. (2014). Development of metacognitive knowledge of reading strategies and attitudes toward reading in early adolescence: The effect on reading comprehension. *Psychological Topics, 23*, 77–98.

Kreutzer, M. A., Leonard, C., Flavell, J. H., & Hagen, J. W. (1975). An interview study of children's knowledge about memory. *Monographs of the Society for Research in Child Development*, 1–60.

Kuhn, D. (2000). Metacognitive development. *Current directions in psychological science, 9*, 178–81.

Lecce, S., Zocchi, S., Pagnin, A., Palladino, P., & Taumoepeau, M. (2010). Reading minds: The relation between children's mental state knowledge and their metaknowledge about reading. *Child Development, 81*, 1876–93.

Markman, E. (1977). Realizing that you don't understand: A preliminary investigation. *Child Development, 48,* 986–92.

McKeown, M. G., Beck, I. L., & Blake, R. G. K. (2009). Rethinking reading comprehension instruction: A comparison of instruction for strategies and content approaches. *Reading Research Quarterly, 44*, 218–55.

Moore, P. J., & Scevak, J. J. (1997). Learning from texts and visual aids: A developmental perspective. *Journal of Research in Reading, 20*, 205–23.

Myers, M., & Paris, S. (1978). Children's metacognitive knowledge about reading. *Journal of Educational Psychology, 70,* 680–90.

Mokhtari, K., & Reichard, C. A. (2002). Assessing students' metacognitive awareness of reading strategies. *Journal of Educational Psychology, 94,* 249–59.

Moss, J., Schunn, C. D., Schneider, W., McNamara, D., & VanLehn, K. (2011). The neural correlates of strategic reading comprehension: Cognitive control and discourse comprehension. *Neuroimage, 58*, 675–86.

National Reading Panel (2000). *Teaching children to read: An evidence-based assessment of the scientific research literature on reading and its implications for reading instruction.* Bethesda, MD: National Institute of Child Health and Human Development

Nieuwland, M. S., Petersson, K. M., & Van Berkum, J. J. A. (2007). On sense and reference: Examining the functional neuroanatomy of referential processing. *NeuroImage, 37*, 993–1004.

Oakhill, J. V., & Cain, K. (2012). The precursors of reading ability in young readers: Evidence from a four-year longitudinal study. *Scientific Studies of Reading, 16*, 91–121.

Oakhill, J., Hartt, J., & Samols, D. (2005). Levels of comprehension monitoring and working memory in good and poor comprehenders. *Reading and Writing, 18*, 657–86.

Palincsar, A., & Brown, A. (1984). Reciprocal teaching of comprehension-fostering and comprehension-monitoring activities. *Cognition and Instruction*, 2, 117–75.

Pintrich, P. R., & Zusho, A. (2002). The development of academic self-regulation: The role of cognitive and motivational factors. In A. Wigfield & J. S. Eccles (Eds.), *Development of achievement motivation* (pp. 249–84). San Diego: Academic Press.

Prat, C. S., Mason, R. A., & Just, M. A. (2011). Individual differences in the neural basis of casual inferencing. *Brain and Language, 116*, 1–13.

Pressley, M., & Afflerbach, P. (1995). *Verbal protocols of reading: The nature of constructively responsive reading*. Hillsdale, NJ: Lawrence Erlbaum Associates Inc.

Pressley, M., & Gaskins, I. (2006). Metacognitively competent reading is constructively responsive reading comprehension: How can such reading be developed in students? *Metacognition and Learning, 1,* 99–113.

Roebers, C. M., Cimeli, P., Röthlisberger, M., & Neuenschwander, R. (2012). Executive functioning, metacognition, and self-perceived competence in elementary school children: An explorative study on their interrelations and their role for school achievement. *Metacognition and Learning, 7*, 151–73.

Roeschl-Heils, A., Schneider, W., & van Kraayenoord, C. E. (2003). Reading, metacognition and motivation: A follow-up study of German students 7 and 8. *European Journal of Psychology of Education, 18*, 75–86.

Schoonen, R., Hulstijin, J., & Bossers, B. (1998). Metacognitive and language-specific knowledge in native and foreign language reading comprehension: An empirical study among Dutch students in grades 6, 8 and 10. *Language Learning, 48,* 71–106.

Schmitt, M., & Sha, S. (2009). The developmental nature of meta-cognition and the relationship between knowledge and control over time. *Journal of Research in Reading, 32*, 254–71.

Skarakis-Doyle, E. (2002). Young children's detection of violations in familiar stories and emerging comprehension monitoring. *Discourse Processes, 33*, 175–97.

Skarakis-Doyle, E. & Dempsey, L. (2008). The detection and monitoring of comprehension errors by preschool children with and without language impairment. *Journal of Speech, Language, and Hearing Research,* 51, 1227–43.

Snow, C. E., Burns, M. S., & Griffin, P. (Eds.). (1998). Preventing reading difficulties in young children. National Academies Press.

Sperling, R. A., Howard, B. C., Miller, L. A., & Murphy, C. (2002). Measures of children's knowledge and regulation of cognition. *Contemporary Educational Psychology, 27,* 51–79.

Spörer, N., Brunstein, J. C., & Kieschke, U. (2009). Improving students' reading comprehension skills: Effects of strategy instruction and reciprocal teaching. *Learning and Instruction, 19*, 272–86.

Strasser, K., & del Rio, F. (2014). The role of comprehension monitoring, theory of mind, and vocabulary depth in predicting story comprehension and recall of kindergarten children. *Reading Research Quarterly, 49*, 169–87.

Van Keer, H., & Verhaeghe, J. P. (2005). Effects of explicit reading strategies instruction and peer tutoring on second and fifth graders' reading comprehension and self-efficacy perceptions. *Journal of Experimental Education, 73*, 291–329.

Van der Schoot, M., Reijntjes, A., & Lieshout, E. (2012). How do children deal with inconsistencies in text? An eye fixation and self-paced reading study in good and poor reading comprehenders. *Reading and Writing, 25*, 1665–90.

van Kraayenoord, C. E., & Schneider, W. E. (1999). Reading achievement, metacognition, reading self-concept and interest: A study of German students in grades 3 and 4. *European Journal of Psychology of Education, 14*, 305–24.

van Kraayenoord, C. E., Beinicke, A., Schlagmuller, M., & Schneider, W. (2012). Word identification, metacognitive knowledge, motivation, and reading comprehension: An Australian study of grade 3 and 4 pupils. *Australian Journal of Language and Literacy, 35*, 51–68.

Walczyk, J. J., Marsiglia, C. S., Johns, A. K., & Bryan, K. S. (2004). Children's compensations for poorly automated reading skills. *Discourse Processes, 37*, 47–66.

Whitebread, D., Coltman, P., Pasternak, D. P., Sangster, C., Grau, V., Bingham, S., Almeqdad, Q., & Demetriou, D. (2009). The development of two observational tools for assessing metacognition and self-regulated learning in young children. *Metacognition and Learning, 4*, 63–85.

Williams, J. P., & Atkins, J. G. (2009). The role of metacognition in teaching reading comprehension to primary students. In D. J. Hacker, J. Dunlosky, & A. C. Graesser (Eds.), *Handbook of metacognition in education* (pp. 26–45). New York: Routledge.

Chapter 2

Skills and Strategies

Their Differences, Their Relationships, and Why They Matter

Peter Afflerbach, P. David Pearson, and Scott Paris

ABSTRACT

In the literature on reading, two words, *skill* and *strategy*, are widely used, yet inconsistently defined. This is unfortunate, as skills and strategies are central to all students' reading success. Helping ELL (English Language Learning/Learners) students develop to their potential presents a series of challenges that demand our full effort and attention, and consistent conceptualization of skill and strategy can help us in these efforts. In this chapter, we propose that detailed definitions of these words and agreement in the use of these words are of utmost importance as we conceptualize and describe reading. Just as important is the consistent use of skill and strategy when we develop reading curriculum.

FRAMING THE ISSUE: CURRENT USES OF *SKILL* AND *STRATEGY* IN PROFESSIONAL DISCOURSE

In this section, we describe what we believe to be a state of confusion in the use of *skill* and *strategy*. The genesis of this chapter was prompted, in part, by the fact that the terms *skill* and *strategy* represent practically and theoretically important concepts, but appear to have different meanings for different people. Because skills and strategies are the focus of reading instruction and because they are used by successful readers, we must strive to use these terms in predictable and regular ways.

Our experience is shaped by the observation of (and participation in) our profession's discourse, and this suggests that it is important to distinguish skill from strategy, while acknowledging their developmental relationships. To set about investigating our hypothesis that skill and strategy are used inconsistently, we sampled from the professional discourse, including our colleagues' ideas, state education department documents, school district documents, commercial instructional materials, and federal government publications. Our first query was to colleagues (professors, teachers, graduate, and undergraduate students), as we asked them to define or characterize skill and strategy. The responses we received varied, and included the following:

"Strategies are the hallmark of skillful reading."
"We learn skills and apply strategies."
"Skills make up strategies."
"Strategies lead to skills."
"Skill is the destination, strategy is the journey."
"We learn strategies to do a skill."
"Skills are automatic, strategies are effortful and mediated."
"We use strategies as tools."
"Strategies that work require a skill set."
"We have to pay attention in learning skills, but eventually we use them automatically."
"You don't think about skills, and you do think about strategies."

Our interpretation of this sample suggests that people are ready and willing to define or characterize skills and strategies. We note also that there is considerable variation in how professionals define the two terms, and how the two terms are situated in relation to one another. Following our questions to colleagues, we turned to the use of skill and strategy in state department of education and school district official documents. Consider how skill and strategy are used by the State of Washington in describing grade-level expectations for reading:

> In first grade, students apply concepts of print, phonological and phonemic awareness, oral language *skills*, and phonics. They continue to expand their reading vocabulary and demonstrate comprehension by participating in a variety of responses. Students choose and read a variety of books for pleasure.
>
> In second grade, students become fluent as readers and apply comprehension and vocabulary *strategies* to a wide variety of literary and informational text. They demonstrate comprehension by participating in discussions, writing responses, and using evidence from text to support their thinking. Reading for pleasure continues to be an enjoyable habit.
>
> In third grade, students select and combine *skills* to read fluently with meaning and purpose. They apply comprehension and vocabulary *strategies* to a wider variety of literary of literary genres and informational text. Students demonstrate comprehension by participating in discussions, writing responses, and

> using evidence from text to support their thinking. They read for pleasure and choose books based on personal preference, topic, or author. (State of Washington, 2015; italics added)

In the above example, skills are first mentioned in relation to oral language in kindergarten and then again in first grade. It is not until second grade that strategies are expected, in this case as they relate to comprehension and vocabulary. In third grade, students are described as again using vocabulary and comprehension strategies. Note also that third graders are expected to "combine skills to read fluently with meaning and purpose." Skills are portrayed as important early in the career of developing readers, with skills followed by strategies. There is a clear affiliation of skills with mechanics of reading (such as phonics). In contrast, strategies appear affiliated with meaning-making aspects of reading. There is no account of how skills and strategies might be related to one another, mutually exclusive of one another, or developmental in nature.

We next consulted the information on teaching ELL students included on the New York State Education Department website. There, we found the following information on "progressions," or a means to help ELL students continue their reading development (italics added):

> Bilingual Common Core Progressions
>
> Taken together, the New Language Arts Progressions and the Home Language Arts Progressions present tools for teachers to develop grade-level instruction for students with varying levels of language proficiency and literacy. When used together, New Language Arts Progressions and the Home Language Arts Progressions provide a roadmap to develop bilingual Common Core *skills* for all students—*skills* that are necessary for our increasingly global society.

The related discussion of classroom discussion focuses on how teachers can use their knowledge of students, reading, and language development to develop appropriate instruction:

> Using the Progressions to Design Instruction
>
> The New and Home Language Arts Progressions are designed to help all teachers plan instruction and develop appropriate expectations for students at different levels of language and literacy levels. The development of academic language rests on content area texts. Teachers can target grade appropriate text and develop *strategies* to provide multiple points of entry for their students. The following are some examples of how teachers can use the progressions to plan and assess language.

> Differentiate linguistic scaffolds that students will require: Entering students for example, will be able to develop their listening, reading, speaking and writing *skills* by focusing on key words in text, while Emerging students will focus on key phrases and short sentences in the new language. Transitioning students will need less explicit teaching of language and can replicate models, while Expanding students can be supported with tools such as glossaries while Commanding students can be expected to work more independently.
>
> Determine the specific scaffolds that target the content area demands: Recognizing the precise way in which content should be broken down for students learning a new language or developing their home language is key for selecting scaffolds. . . . The Progressions can support teachers in understanding how to create content area scaffolds such as graphic organizers, sentence starters and rubrics that target the content area standard and match the students' language ability in the new or home language.
>
> (*Teacher's Guide to Implement the Bilingual Common Core Progressions* 2015; italics added)

We have several observations related to the above website excerpts. First, we appreciate the attention given to how teachers might help ELL students continue their language development. Second, we note that teachers are expected to use instructional strategies to foster with this development. Third, and in contrast, student language development is characterized as growth in "listening, reading, speaking and writing *skills*"—there is no mention of reading strategies. Fourth, as scaffolding is introduced as a potentially powerful teaching method, there is no mention of how teachers might scaffold language skills, or strategies. Thus, a consideration of a state board of education's grade-level expectations for grades 1–3 and a state's general approach to language development for ELL learners suggests varied conceptualizations of reading strategies and skills.

Up to this point we could not detect a solid theme for the skill and strategy information that we gathered from various sources. We next consulted an authoritative reading research source, the National Reading Panel Report (2000), and found the following account:

> The rationale for the explicit teaching of comprehension skills is that comprehension can be improved by teaching students to use specific cognitive strategies or to reason strategically when they encounter barriers to understanding what they are reading.

The above account continued our experience of finding skill and strategy featured in consequential discourse of our profession, but here reading skills and reading strategies appear to be used interchangeably.

MAKING THE CASE: THE CONSEQUENCES OF INCONSISTENT USE OF SKILL AND STRATEGY

Before going further, we want to pose the question, "Is it really necessary to dwell on how different people use the term *skill* or *strategy* in different situations?" We believe that it is, and that the distinction between skills and strategies is extremely important, for both theoretical and practical reasons. The research evidence is clear: skills and strategies are different (Paris, Lipson & Wixson, 1983; Pressley & Afflerbach, 1995). Additionally, how teachers think about skill and strategy is of utmost importance because we cannot possibly teach well those things that we don't carefully define and fully understand. Definitions are important because they are the foundation for how we think about the constructs related to reading success. They provide a common language for practitioners and theorists, and they provide the touchstone for discussions of whether ideas (as expressed by an individual or a group) have a connection to the reality that research findings represent. The body of research demonstrates that skill and strategy are different, and this has important implications for our conceptualization of them and for how we might introduce them and help students learn them. Theory-driven instruction and teachers who are reflective practitioners are agents of positive change in schools. Both rely on precise definitions and clarity of conceptualization to realize their promise.

Despite the current inconsistency in the use of reading skill and reading strategy, there is a rich history of research and instruction associated with the two terms. A century of research has contributed to our understanding of the nature of developing and accomplished reading (Davis, 1944; Huey, 1908; Snow, 2002; Thorndike, 1917). Successful readers possess abilities and knowledge that allow them to construct meaning from text. These readers work within the constraints of human memory systems (Atkinson & Shiffrin, 1968), manage their goal-oriented approaches to reading (Brown, 1975; Flavell & Wellman, 1977), and identify and remember important information in text and monitor and evaluate their reading (Pressley & Afflerbach, 1995). They do so in increasingly diverse types of texts, from the printed page to the electronic page (Afflerbach & Cho, 200). Implicated, if not described in considerable detail, reading skill and reading strategy are requisite for successful reading.

The findings from a century of reading research regularly find their way into reading instruction (Pearson & Fielding, 1991; Pressley, 2000; Smith, 1965). This reading instruction is marked by its own set of terms. These terms, including "skill and drill," "whole language," and "balanced approach," also appear to defy consistent definition (Goodman, 1975; Pearson, 2004). Because reading instruction marks a major intersection of theory and practice, clarity in the use of terms would appear to be of critical importance, as this helps connect what is taught in reading with what is known about reading.

DEFINITIONS AND CHARACTERIZATIONS OF *SKILL* AND *STRATEGY*: A MODEST PROPOSAL

In this section, we consider the commonalities and distinctiveness of "skills" and "strategies." *Reading skills* are *automatic actions* that result in decoding and comprehending of texts with speed, efficiency, and fluency, usually without the reader's awareness of the components or controls involved. Reading skills operate without the reader's deliberate control or conscious awareness. They are used out of habit, practiced, and mastered to the point where they function automatically. As such, they usually are deployed much faster than strategies because they do not require the reader's conscious decision-making. This has important, positive consequences for each reader, as all reading work is conducted within the boundaries of our limited working memory systems. That is, the more reading work we can do automatically and without the allocation of memory resources, the more of these resources we have to take on complex reading demands and remembering and applying what we learn from reading.

Reading strategies are *deliberate, goal-directed attempts to control and modify* the reader's efforts to decode text, understand words, and construct meanings of text. The reader's deliberate control of work, the goal-directedness of the work, and the reader's awareness of work define a strategy. Control and working toward a goal characterize the strategic reader who selects a specific path to a reading goal (i.e., the means to a desired end). For example, the reader who deliberately pauses after each paragraph to evaluate understanding while reading with the goal of summarizing the text is using strategies. Awareness helps the reader select an intended path, the means to the goal, and the processes used to achieve the goal. The reader can examine the strategy, monitor its effectiveness, and revise the goal or means to the goal (or both), if necessary. If the evaluation of reading at the end of each paragraph signals a lack of understanding, the reader may reread, slow the rate of reading, or consult an authoritative source to determine word meaning. Indeed, the hallmark of strategic readers is the flexibility and adaptability of their actions as they read. Thus, whether a reader's actions are under automatic or deliberate control is a key difference between skill and strategy.

It is important to note that reading strategies, however mindful and effortful, are not always successful. Thus, the determination of a reader as strategic and a definition of reading strategies do not necessarily imply only positive and useful actions. A reader may choose an inappropriate goal, such as reading at a fast pace because a text is deemed familiar, and then fail to comprehend the text in its entirety. Or, a reader may make several predictions about the contents of a text and the author's purpose, without sufficient prior knowledge to inform the predictions. In these cases, strategies are selected and employed, but they are faulty. The actions are strategic, connecting specific means to specific goals, but they are inappropriate and ineffective for reading. It is important that readers have strategic stances toward reading text, but being strategic does not guarantee success. It is the appropriateness of the goal, the means, and the path to connect them that must be negotiated in every situation in order to be strategic and successful. This is fundamentally different from a skill that is well practiced and executed in the same manner across situations.

Consider a further example that will clarify the distinction between skill and strategy, as well as demonstrate their relationship. Suppose a student determines he has only a vague understanding of a paragraph as he reaches the end of it. He wants to do something that will increase his comprehension so he slows down and asks, "Does that make sense?" regularly as he reads at the completion of each sentence and paragraph. This is a reading strategy—a deliberate, conscious, metacognitive act. The strategy is prompted by the student's knowing that the act of constructing meaning is not going well, and the strategy is characterized by a slower rate of reading and a deliberate act of self-questioning that serves his goal of monitoring and building better comprehension. If this strategy is successful, the student may continue to use it throughout the school year. With months of practice, the strategy requires less effort and attention, and the student uses it with increasing speed and efficiency. When the strategy becomes effortless and automatic (i.e., the question "Does that make sense?" is asked automatically, almost subconsciously, at the end of reading sentences and paragraphs), the reading strategy has become a reading skill. In this developmental example, skill and strategy differ in their intentionality and their automatic/nonautomatic status. Yet, they are clearly related as practiced and successful strategies evolve into skills.

For all readers, the progression from effortful and deliberate strategies to automatic use of skills while reading occurs at many levels—decoding, fluency, comprehension, and critical reading. Novice readers need to associate visual patterns of letters with their phonemic pronunciations and a hoped-for consequence of our instruction is that their decoding progresses from deliberate to fluent actions. Indeed, we expect developing readers to learn, practice, and master such work to the point of automaticity. Students, especially where reading instruction focuses on constructing meaning, learn to find or construct main ideas, to skim text, and to reread first as deliberate actions and, with practice, later accomplish the same actions with less effort and awareness. In this view of learning, deliberate reading strategies can transition into fluent reading skills. We note that reading skills and reading strategies may serve the same goals and may result in the same behaviors. For example, readers may decode words, read a text fluently, or find a main idea using either skills or strategies (or both). The distinction may not be important to the student or teacher at a single point in time, but across time movement from deliberate and effortful reading to more fluent and automatic reading is a good thing, representing expected student reading development.

Practice alone may not be sufficient for some students to make progress from deliberate, resource-consuming strategy to facile skill use. Instruction about how and why to use strategies can be quite effective; for example, providing students with information about how to summarize and predict text while showing the rationale for using these strategies (National Reading Panel, 2000). As we focus on metacognition in skill use, scaffolded and guided practice that helps developing readers move toward accomplished reading may also be required. Some readers may need to be persuaded that effective reading is one result of strategy use, and teachers may need to encourage student to use and practice the strategies. In this view, fluent reading skills are more "advanced" actions than reading strategies because they are faster, more efficient, and require less thinking and social guidance. However, it is important to promote both skilled and strategic reading because students need to know how to read strategically. Paris and his colleagues (Paris, Lipson, & Wixson, 1983; Paris, Wasik, & Turner, 1991) described reading strategies as "skills under consideration" to denote that the same actions could be either a skill or strategy, depending on the readers' awareness, control, intention, and the specific reading situation.

There are two specific situations in which it is useful to be a strategic reader. The first occasion to use appropriate strategies is during initial learning. Effective strategy instruction involves teachers modeling specific strategies. These comprehension strategies include predicting, inferencing, summarizing, deriving vocabulary, determining claims and evidence in argumentative texts, and understanding subtexts and reading critically. These strategies can be embedded in dialogic reading with teachers. The strategies represent a range of relative difficulty (as always, relative to the situation in which readers use the strategies) and some may seem basic and elementary. Yet, these strategies, described, modeled, and supported by teachers and classmates, help students direct their attention, choose actions, and successfully carry them out. It is here that we encounter a seeming paradox: while we hope for increasing automatic skill use for our students, we introduce and teach strategies in a manner that is comprehensive, sometimes slow and always about the detail of successful strategy use. We hope that these strategies are learned well and that they evolve into skills. A crucial part of reading development is the shifting control for using strategies, first in response to teachers and peers and later as self-initiated strategies. Fluent reading begins with strategies that integrate intentions, actions, and goals, and fluency increases with repeated practice. From here, developing readers can undertake increasingly complex tasks in relation to the increasingly difficult texts they read.

Careful reading and trouble-shooting, prompted by a reader's metacognition, is a second occasion when strategic reading is required. Practice may help readers develop fluent decoding, word recognition, and understanding, but when reading does not go smoothly, strategic intervention may be required. For example, if a text includes unfamiliar content, many difficult words and convoluted syntax, or if a reading-related task is too challenging (e.g., summarize and then synthesize these essays on the Civil War into a single coherent review), readers' usual skills may not work, and deriving word meaning and comprehension may suffer. Strategic readers who are metacognitively aware of the specific difficulties can generate alternative actions. For example, as difficulties are encountered, readers may slow their reading rate, reread, focus on words perceived to be important, or ask for help with new words. Strategic readers are problem solvers as they detect problems, determine when their goals are not accomplished, and generate alternative means to reach the goals. Thus, trouble-shooting, or cognitive monitoring and repair, are essential aspects of strategic metacognitive routines, including reading. In this sense, strategies can compensate when usual skills fail.

PEDAGOGICAL AND ASSESSMENT IMPLICATIONS

Several years ago, the lead author presented a lesson on explicit teaching of reading comprehension strategies. During the lesson, elementary education students read an exceedingly challenging text and thought aloud about the reading strategies they used to try to construct meaning. Upon completing the reading task, students cataloged their comprehension strategies, described them, and then segued into a discussion of how modeling and explaining reading strategies through scaffolded instruction was a key factor in elementary students' reading development. As we were filing out of the classroom, one of the undergraduate students attending the class approached me and asked, "If reading comprehension strategy instruction is so important, and so powerful, how did readers become expert before strategy instruction?" The question invited examination of the assumptions that underlie reading comprehension strategy instruction, and presaged the remainder of this chapter: how and why reading strategy instruction matters, and why the distinction between strategy and skill is critical.

With explicit teaching, teachers can explain, model, and use reading strategies. Teachers must break down reading into the different operations that make it successful. This helps students become aware of the operations, understand how they work together, and practice combining them in the skilled performance that is reading. This cognitive disassembly or "defossilizing" a skilled action into smaller teachable and learnable parts (Vygotsky,

1978) is often challenging for teachers. It is not always easy to identify the components of accomplished reading and determining the possible sources of difficulty that readers may encounter, but it is possible as demonstrated by reciprocal teaching (Palincsar & Brown, 1984). For example, breaking apart complex cognitive activity requires thorough and precise task analysis. A task analysis helps us focus on what exactly we are asking students to do. When we request students to make predictions about text contents or author motives, we can analyze the task and determine that students must have prior knowledge for the text content and why authors write, respectively, to make such prediction. They must have a strategic means for combining their applicable prior knowledge with information in text to generate an accurate and useful predication. In addition, the reader must have a means of monitoring the accuracy and usefulness of the prediction as reading begins and progresses.

Professional development activities can help teachers learn how to conduct such task analyses by which they will best understand the procedural knowledge underlying a skilled action. By analogy, it is like the perceptive coach who observes and diagnoses subtle components of a complex performance and then offers advice about what the athlete needs to improve, how to do so, and how to coordinate the new actions. This involves demonstrating strategies and accompanying these strategies with detailed explanation of how to implement the strategy, along with rationale for why one would choose to be so strategic.

Classroom interventions that help students become strategic readers include this metacognitive layer of discussion (e.g., Palincsar & Brown, 1984; Paris, Cross, & Lipson, 1984; Pressley, Almasi, Schuder, Bergman, & Kurita, 1994). It is clear that students who learn about reading strategies can use the knowledge to become fluent and skilled and to monitor and make efficient their own reading. This thoughtful and deliberate use of the strategies may also provide a motivational advantage for students. Reading skills are motivated by goals of fluency, effortlessness, and accuracy; they give rise to the student reader's pride in ability, not effort. In contrast, reading strategies are motivated by control, good decision-making, and adaptability; they reinforce a student's belief in self-efficacy based on both ability and effort (Guthrie & Klauda, 2016; Schunk & Bursuck, 2016). Strategic readers feel confident that they can monitor and improve their own reading so they have both knowledge and motivation to succeed. This is especially important when we work with student readers who, by dint of their past school reading experiences, especially need encouragement and the experience of success.

Based on our conceptualization of skill and strategy, we believe that there are several further implications for instruction. Teachers need to provide explicit instruction to develop both skills and strategies. As students are learning these, frequent practice in applying them while reading accessible texts (i.e., texts that are at the student's current level of competency) can help students practice basic strategies and then shape them into fluent and perhaps automatic skills. However, our challenged readers, including ELL students, may need more than the modeling and explanation that mark successful strategy instruction. These students need to know how and why reading strategies are valuable, two crucial features of learning that may escape students who are asked to practice strategies without the benefit of cognitive explanations. Thus, even "basic" skills can benefit from being taught initially as strategies, but the goal is fluent, proficient, and increasingly automatic use of skills.

We want students to easily recount, summarize, and critique texts without always having to use slow deliberate strategies such as searching back in text and rereading. How can that be accomplished? Teachers need to explain how to think to their students. That is, teachers need to model, describe, and scaffold appropriate reading strategies for students. For example, teachers can search for a main idea in a text and use thinking aloud to demonstrate how they reason about each sentence and idea. They can describe the differences between a topic sentence and a main idea, differences between an explicit and implicit main idea, and differences between a man idea and supporting details in their discussion. The detailed discourse of explanation encourage strategy use. The sooner the strategy is understood, used, and practiced, the higher the probability of it changing to skill use.

This may pose challenges as we devise our paths to successful teaching. As we teach, we may not understand our students' misconceptions about reading and may assume that an explanation given is an explanation understood. We may be challenged in diagnosing difficulties and "defossilizing" automatic skills. Our thoughtful task analysis and carefully planned explication of how to do things may not always reach our students. We may not be adept at making our thinking public (thinking aloud about strategies as we use the strategies), or our verbalizations may be difficult for ELL students to understand. And with diverse student needs, we may not have the instructional time to add the layer of strategy instruction and metacognitive explanations that some readers need. These barriers notwithstanding, we know it can be done. On a more positive note, we know that teachers who provide their students with strategies for taking responsibility for classroom roles (why we should be good and cooperative classroom citizens) are usually also very good at explaining strategies for constructing meaning and determining vocabulary measures because they know the value of explicitly teaching different ways to accomplish a goal. Strategic teachers also set a precedent for intentional, self-regulated learning that spills over into reading instruction. Intentional strategies require that students take responsibility for their learning, and they also insure that students attribute success to their efforts and strategies.

We recommend reading instruction that follows a regular cycle of modeling, explaining, and guiding—all features of learning strategies that encourage students and lead them to increasingly independent practice and fluency. If practice does not lead to fluency, then more diagnostic and strategic teaching is warranted. Assessment must help us determine if a strategy has become so practiced that it has "gone underground" in the form of fluent skill, or if it is missing. However, once the strategy has been learned and transformed into a fluent skill, teachers should introduce more challenging strategies and texts. This allows our students to successfully apply the mix of skills and strategies with increasingly difficult texts and tasks, reflecting school curriculum that does the same. It also helps students develop flexibility in their reading, moving from skill to strategy and strategy to skill as the text and reading situation demand. Teachers also should consider re-teaching so that important strategies such as making inferences, finding main ideas, and summarizing are taught several times each year and, perhaps, across different school years. The scope and complexity of these strategies are enormous, and there is ample variety of text difficulty and genre variety to practice so that the skills become automatic. The general rule is to teach students many strategies, teach them early, re-teach them often, and connect assessment with re-teaching.

We should point out that the skill or strategy designation applies to a repertoire of actions or processes more than it does to readers. Developing readers certainly become more "skilled," as they learn and practice, just as athletes, accountants, and cabinetmakers become more skilled. However, the progression from effortful and deliberate strategy use to fluent skill use is contingent on factors other than a reader's increasing proficiency. There is always a text or a task lurking just beyond the horizon, waiting to humble any reader, even the most talented one. In other words, readers should not be surprised (and should be prepared) when they encounter what we call "Waterloo" texts (after the downfall of Napoleon)—texts that push us to our skillful and strategic limits. These texts force the reader, however experienced, to revert to a highly strategic (i.e., deliberate, intentional, and step-by-step) journey through its pages. Consider the following text, taken from a study that examined think-aloud protocol data of expert readers' strategies (Afflerbach, 1990). As you read, try to keep track of the strategies you use to try to construct meaning:

> It is legitimate to further characterize the broadpoint appearance as a major archeological horizon marker for the eastern seaboard. In the terms of Willey and Phillips, a horizon is "a primarily spatial continuity represented by cultural traits and assemblages whose nature and mode of occurrence permit the assumption of a broad and rapid spread." That a quick expansion of the broadpoint-using peoples took place is indicated by the narrow range of available radiocarbon dates, along with a correspondingly wide areal distribution of

> components. Once established, the broadpoint horizon developed as a "whole cultural pattern or tradition" in its own right by persisting and evolving over an expansive region for 500 to 1000 years.

Most readers find this text challenging, and report that they use an impressive array of strategies to try to begin to construct meaning for the text. If you noted that the text led you to slow your rate of reading, reread portions of the text, focus on particular words (e.g., broadpoint), parse sentences into smaller (hopefully more comprehensible) parts, but that you failed to comprehend the text anyway, then you have had a "Waterloo text experience." This experience can serve many purposes, including a reminder of what an extraordinary task it is to comprehend unfamiliar text, how resourceful we are at choosing and employing strategies when our metacognitive awareness signals to us the need to do so, and how skill and strategy use may be related to the particular characteristics of the reading demand. Thus, readers never outgrow the need to consult their strategy repertoire. Proficient readers monitor their work, deploying the appropriate mix of skill and strategy as guided by the exigencies of the particular reading task.

One key to effective strategy instruction is assessment so that teachers can introduce strategies that are on the leading edge of each student's reading proficiency. Teachers need to assess processes in both skilled and strategic modes. Measures of fluent reading (such as words correct per minute) and question-answering are typically used to assess reading skills, but teachers may be unsure what to do if a student scores poorly when these skills are measured. We find it difficult to make inferences about students' growth and needs from such assessment. In this situation, an appropriate procedure is to assess the strategies. If a student cannot recount the contents of an expository text, the teacher should ask the student to try to identify the topic of the text. If a student cannot retell a narrative text, the student should be asked to identify the order of key events or use a graphic organizer to query if the student understands narrative elements and their relations. If students cannot answer multiple-choice questions quickly, the teacher should ask them to think aloud as they read the stem and response options and ask them to show how they search for confirming or disconfirming evidence in the text. Experienced teachers know how to diagnose dis-fluency and the lack of proficiency by checking the strategies that students should be using. The main reason for assessing strategies is to find clues about what is being done or is being done incorrectly so that teachers can identify and re-teach needed strategies. Strategy assessments are formative; when done well, they provide diagnostic information that helps shape our understanding of students and plan instruction. In contrast, skill assessments are summative. We should avoid trying to use skill assessments for diagnostic teaching or failing to assess strategy use so students are given repeated cycles of the same instruction and inappropriate, unhelpful assessments. We should not be surprised that students find this frustrating and unhelpful, or that the mismatch of assessment to skill or strategy results in wasted effort. Many teachers are not trained to assess students' reading in a strategic mode, even though this is a critical ability. There are limited commercial resources for assessing strategies. That is why most strategy assessments are informal and embedded in instruction, and why asking students to explain their thinking during or after reading provides such important insights for both teachers and students.

CONCLUDING REMARKS

In this chapter, we argued for the importance of clearly conceptualizing and defining skill and strategy, and noting their differences and relationships. We identified a need to distinguish between reading skills and strategies, provided definitions and examples of the distinctions between reading skill and strategy, and discussed implications for instruction and assessment. We conclude by revisiting our major points and providing additional commentary. In our opinion, it is important that the terms *skill* and *strategy* be used to distinguish automatic processes from deliberately controlled processes, respectively. At the heart of accomplished reading is a balance of both—automatic application and use of reading skills, and intentional, effortful employment of reading strategies—accompanied and coordinated by the ability to shift seamlessly between the two when the situation calls for it. The difficulty of the reading task, influenced by text, task, reader, and contextual variables, will determine this shifting balance. When students possess content domain knowledge, read accessible texts, and work toward attainable goals, we will observe students applying their usual skills. In contrast, when knowledge for the text content is sketchy, texts are challenging, and reading tasks are complex, the reader's skill/strategy mix will tilt toward the more strategic reading that is required. The distinction between reading skill and strategy is important for understanding how readers continue to learn, how they repair difficulties while reading, and how they read fluently or puzzle and problem solve. While automatic and fluid application of reading skills is a goal of instruction, we must remember that a particular reading skill is often preceded by a period in which the developing reader must be strategic. Developing readers must learn comprehension and vocabulary strategies before they can be expected to apply them accurately, quickly, and with increasing automaticity. Developing readers must learn to be metacognitive, and it is at the stage of conscious application of strategies that readers come to understand how reading works and how to identify and fix problems. Strategies represent a window on the intricate workings of the reader's mind. Metacognition also works to inform the reader of the optimal mix of skills and strategies, providing regular updates on the suitability and success of ongoing reading work.

Skillful readers are motivated because skill affords high levels of performance with little effort whereas strategic readers are motivated to demonstrate control over reading processes with both ability and effort. Skill and strategy complement one another and when they do so they can provide student readers with motivation and self-efficacy from both sources. In other words, students can complete a reading task efficiently and thoroughly, thinking, appropriately, "I am good at this *and* I can work through the tough spots." Effective use of skills and strategies also encourages students' appreciation of the value of reading. In the final analysis, when we examine the broader goals of reading and examine reading holistically, we want readers to be both skilled and strategic. To characterize students as "skilled" readers is to recognize that they can orchestrate a wide array of processes to make reading "work," optimally or even automatically. To characterize students as "strategic" readers is to recognize that they are flexible and adaptable to particular circumstances—and when the situation calls for it, they can select just the right strategy to overcome any temporary roadblock they might encounter.

When teachers are teaching strategically, they help students to analyze reading tasks, to consider various approaches to performing the tasks, and to choose the most appropriate actions and strategies to reach the goal. Teaching skills involves practice and feedback to improve speed and efficiency (which taken together amount to what we call fluency). One challenge for teachers of reading is fully investigating the strategy-skill connection and determining how an effortful strategy can become an automatic skill. A related challenge is designing instruction that makes clear the steps of strategies while providing practice so that strategies, when appropriate, may transform themselves into skills.

We are convinced that the current lack of consistency in use of the terms *skill* and *strategy* reflects an underlying confusion about how the two are conceptualized. Such inconsistency can render our instruction less effective, even confusing to both our students and us. Consistent conceptualization and use of the terms skill and strategy will have several benefits. First, a clearer conceptualization provides a common language with which to discuss and reflect on the considerable information that is available from the research, practice, and theory related to skill and strategy. Second, clear conceptualization contributes to instructional clarity, where our teaching materials and procedures are referenced to a consistent set of understandings of reading and reading development. Third, we can achieve a certain curricular economy if we regard skills and strategies as two sides of any given process or task; this perspective of commonality could limit the proliferation of "standards" to teach and measure that often results when we add more independent elements to any curriculum. Fourth, this clarity situates our understanding of skill and strategy in an historical context, one marked by the dynamic of new knowledge generated by research, and one that is subject to ongoing discussion and revision.

REFERENCES

Afflerbach, P. (1990). The influence of prior knowledge of expert readers' main idea construction strategies. *Reading Research Quarterly, 25*, 31–46.

Afflerbach, P., & Cho, B. (2009). Identifying constructive reading comprehension processes. In S. Israel & G. Duffy (Eds.), *Handbook of Research on Reading Comprehension* (pp. 69–90). Mahwah, NJ: Erlbaum.

Atkinson, R. C., & Shiffrin, R. M. (1968). Human memory: A proposed system and its control processes. In K. W. Spence & J. T. Spence (Eds.), *The psychology of learning and motivation: Advance in research and theory* (Vol. 2, pp. 89–195). New York: Academic Press.

Brown, A. L. (1975). The development of memory: Knowing, knowing about knowing, and knowing how to know. In H. W. Reese (Ed.), *Advances in child development and behavior* (Vol. 10, pp. 103–52). San Diego, CA: Academic Press.

Davis, F. B. (1944). Fundamental factors of comprehension of reading. *Psychometrika, 9*, 185–97.

Flavell, J. H., & Wellman, H. M. (1977). Metamemory. In R. V. Kail & J. W. Hagen (Eds.), *Perspectives on the development of memory and cognition* (pp. 3–33). Hillsdale, NJ: Erlbaum.

Goodman, K. (1975). Acquiring literacy is natural: Who skilled Cock Robin? In F. Gollasch (Ed.), *Language & literacy: The selected writings of Kenneth S. Goodman* (Vol. 2, pp. 243–49). London: Routledge & Kegan Paul.

Guthrie, J., & Klauda, S. (2016). Engagement and motivational processes in reading. In P. Afflerbach (Ed.), *Handbook of individual differences in reading: Reader, text, and context* (pp. 41–53). New York: Routledge.

Huey, E. (1908). *The psychology and pedagogy of reading*. Cambridge, MA: MIT Press.

National Reading Panel (NRP) (2000). *Teaching children to read: An evidence-based assessment of the scientific research literature on reading and its implications for reading instruction: Reports of the subgroups.* Bethesda, MD: NICHD.

Palincsar, A. S., & Brown, A. (1984). Reciprocal teaching of comprehension-fostering and comprehension-monitoring activities. *Cognition and Instruction, 1,* 117–75.

Paris, S. G., Cross, D. R., & Lipson, M. Y. (1984). Informed strategies for learning: A program to improve children's reading awareness and comprehension. *Journal of Educational Psychology, 76*, 1239–52.

Paris, S. G., Lipson, M. Y., & Wixson, K. (1983). Becoming a strategic reader. *Contemporary Educational Psychology, 8*, 293–316.

Paris, S. G., Wasik, B. A., & Turner, J. C. (1991). The development of strategic readers. In R. Barr, M. Kamil, P. Mosenthal, & P. D. Pearson (Eds.), *Handbook of reading research*, 2nd ed. (pp. 609–40). New York: Longman.

Pearson, P. D. (2004). The reading wars: The politics of reading research and policy-1988 through 2003. *Educational Policy, 18,* 216–52.

Pearson P. D., & Fielding, L. (1991). Comprehension Instruction. In R. Barr, M. L. Kamil, P. Mosenthal, & P. D. Pearson (Eds.), *Handbook of reading research* (Vol. 2, pp. 815–60). New York: Longman.

Pressley, M. (2000). What should comprehension instruction be the instruction of? In M. L. Kamil, P. B. Mosenthal, P. D. Pearson, & R. Barr (Eds.), *Handbook of reading research* (Vol. III, pp. 545–61). Mahwah, NJ: Erlbaum.

Pressley, M., & Afflerbach, P. (1995). *Verbal reports of reading: The nature of constructively responsive reading.* Mahwah, NJ: Erlbaum.

Pressley, M., Almasi, J., Schuder, T., Bergman, J., & Kurita, J. A. (1994). Transactional instruction of comprehension strategies: The Montgomery County Maryland SAIL program. *Reading and Writing Quarterly: Overcoming Learning Difficulties, 10,* 5–19.

Schunk, D., & Bursuck, W. (2016). Self-efficacy, agency, and volition: Student beliefs and reading motivation. In P. Afflerbach (Ed.), *Handbook of individual differences in reading: Reader, text, and context* (pp. 54–66). New York: Routledge.

Smith, N. B. (1965). *American reading instruction.* Newark, DE: International Reading Association.

Snow, C. (2002). *Reading for understanding: Toward an R&D program in reading comprehension.* Washington, DC: Rand.

State of Washington, Grade-Level Expectations for Reading. Retrieved from: http://www.k12.wa.us/CurriculumInstruct/default.aspx, July 1, 2015.

Teacher's Guide to Implement the Bilingual Common Core Progressions; https://www.engageny.org/resource/new-york-state-bilingual-common-core-initiative Retrieved July 1, 2015.

Thorndike, E. (1917). Reading as reasoning: A study of mistakes in paragraph reading. *Journal of Educational Research, 8,* 323–32.

Vygotsky, L. (1978). *Mind in society: The development of higher psychological processes.* Cambridge, MA: Harvard University Press.

Chapter 3

Assessing Metacognition in Reading Processes

Offline versus Online Measures

Marcel V. J. Veenman

ABSTRACT

Metacognitive skills, such as planning, monitoring, and evaluation, are required for the regulation of and control over learning behavior. Individual students vary substantially in the application of metacognitive skills, while metacognitive skillfulness is a profound predictor of reading comprehension. Consequently, adequate assessment methods are needed for the identification of metacognitive deficient students. This chapter reviews the available assessment methods for metacognition in reading by scrutinizing their validity. Offline methods pertain to self-reports of students obtained prior or retrospective to reading (e.g., on a questionnaire), whereas online methods refer to behavioral measures obtained during reading (e.g., through thinking aloud). Empirical evidence from validity studies clearly endorses the use of online assessments of metacognitive skills in reading, while challenging the validity for offline methods. Practical implications are discussed.

Metacognition refers to the declarative knowledge of, and the regulatory control over one's cognitive system (Veenman, Van Hout-Wolters, & Afflerbach, 2006). Baker and Brown (1984) already noticed that metacognition is relevant to reading comprehension. Reading not only pertains to studying texts and textbooks, as reading activities are omnipresent in various school tasks. Many students, however, fail to adequately regulate and control their reading processes (Veenman, 2013a). A review study of Wang, Haertel, and Walberg (1990) revealed that metacognition is a more important predictor of learning outcomes than other cognitive and motivational student characteristics. In the same vein, Veenman (2008) estimated in an overview of studies with students (nine to twenty-six years) performing different tasks in various school domains that metacognitive skillfulness accounted for 40 percent of learning outcomes, which was significantly more than the contribution of intelligence (32 percent). Individual differences in metacognition are also manifest in reading research (Baker, 2005; Pressley & Afflerbach, 1995; Van der Stel & Veenman, 2014; Veenman & Beishuizen, 2004). In order to disclose these individual differences, adequate methods are needed for the assessment of metacognitive knowledge and skills (Veenman, 2016a).

METACOGNITIVE KNOWLEDGE

A first component of metacognition is *metacognitive knowledge*, which pertains to declarative knowledge of the interplay between person, task, and strategy variables (Flavell, 1979). A student may, for instance, recognize that s/he (person) finds reading difficult (task), and that s/he will therefore have to practice with reading exercises at home (strategy). On the other hand, another student may overestimate her/his reading competency and, therefore, skip reading assignments. This second student may likely fail on a reading test.

The example of the second student shows that metacognitive knowledge does *not* necessarily has to be correct, although this knowledge may affect the student's reading behavior. A student may have all sorts of beliefs about herself/himself, the reading task, and the effort needed for reading activities that do not necessarily correspond with reality. Even when the metacognitive knowledge of a student is correct, this does not guarantee that the student will also adequately regulate the reading behavior (Veenman et al., 2006). The student from the first example may have the intention of to doing reading exercises, but may fail to do so for all sorts of reasons. The student may be insufficiently motivated to invest the time and effort, or s/he may be distracted by other appealing pursuits. Moreover, the student may lack the skills required for reading, so that each attempt at practice is frustrated. Thus, correct metacognitive knowledge is an essential, but not sufficient condition for adequate regulation of reading behavior (Veenman, 2016b).

A specific component of metacognitive knowledge is conditional knowledge about when a particular metacognitive strategy or skill should be applied and to what purpose (Brown, 1978; Schraw & Moshman, 1995). Poor students often do not know *what* skill to choose, *when* and *why*. Even adequate conditional knowledge, however, does not guarantee the actual execution of a skill as a student may still miss the procedural knowledge for *how* the skill should be enacted. In fact, conditional knowledge provides an entry to the first stage of skill acquisition, where a metacognitive strategy has to be consciously applied step-by-step and gradually transformed into a skill through proceduralization and repeated practice (Anderson & Schunn, 2000; Veenman, 2016a).

METACOGNITIVE SKILLS

The second component of metacognition, *metacognitive skills*, pertains to the procedural knowledge or skills for the actual regulation of and control over learning behavior. In the last decade, metacognitive skillfulness is also referred to as self-regulation, although both terms originated from different theoretical perspectives (Dinsmore, Alexander, & Loughlin, 2008). Task orientation, goal setting, planning, monitoring, evaluation, recapitulation, and self-reflection are examples of metacognitive skills. These skills directly affect reading behavior and, consequently, they determine outcomes of reading comprehension (Brown & DeLoache, 1978; Pressley & Afflerbach, 1995; Veenman, 2016a).

In order to be effective, students have to employ an orderly sequence of metacognitive skills in the course of reading. Metacognitively proficient students will first prepare for reading by orienting on the task. Students will read the task assignment to identify the nature of the reading task and to determine what the task demands are. The title will be read to find the central theme of the text. Students may skim through the text to get an impression of its structure, its complexity, and the time needed for reading. Meanwhile, prior knowledge can be retrieved from memory, on the one hand enabling a better understanding of the text while reading and, on the other hand, preparing memory for storage of new knowledge. On the basis of this task analysis, an appropriate reading goal needs to be set that matches the assignment. A reading goal should specify what kind of information in the text is relevant to the student, which is the point of departure for planning one's reading activities, preferably before starting to read. Reading plans pertain to focusing on relevant parts of the text, the allocation of reading time, and selecting methods for processing the content. Metacognitively poor readers, on the other hand, only read the assignment superficially. They tend to skip the title of the text and immediately start reading linearly, from begin to end (Van der Stel & Veenman, 2010; Veenman & Beishuizen, 2004).

During the execution phase, metacognitively proficient students usually adhere to the preconceived plan, unless there are legitimate reasons for revision of the plan. Moreover, they keep a close watch on their reading behavior to check their understanding of words, phrases, and paragraphs. Watching over one's own functioning from a helicopter view is referred to as monitoring or process control. When noticing confusion or misunderstanding, action is taken to remedy a lack of understanding by consulting a dictionary, by backtracking and rereading the text carefully, or by purposefully navigating through the text in search of information (Pressley & Afflerbach, 1995). Metacognitive proficient students also keep track of whether their understanding of the text brings them closer to their reading goal. If not, they may decide to change their reading plan or to reset their reading goal. Students with poor monitoring skills, on the other hand, either do not notice their miscomprehension or they do not take action to remedy their lack of understanding (Veenman, 2016a).

After reading the text, metacognitively proficient students evaluate their comprehension of the text against their reading goal. By rereading the assignment, they may verify whether task requirements have been met with. If not, they may reread certain parts of the text or review their notes. Moreover, they often make a concise summary of the text to recapitulate main ideas and conclusions. Finally, they may occasionally reflect on the reading process to improve future reading. For metacognitively poor students, on the other hand, the reading task ends abruptly when the last word in the text has been read (Veenman, 2016a). Thus, the evaluation phase is practically skipped too. More detailed descriptions of metacognitive processes in reading can be found in Pressley and Afflerbach (1995) and Veenman (2016a).

DEVELOPMENT OF METACOGNITIVE SKILLS

Metacognitive skills already develop at a basic level during preschool or early primary-school years, but they become more sophisticated and academically oriented when formal educational requires the utilization of metacognition (Veenman, 2016b). From the age of eight, children show a steep increase in frequency and quality of metacognitive skills (Alexander, Carr, & Schwanenflugel, 1995; Van der Stel & Veenman, 2014; Veenman & Spaans, 2005; Veenman, Wilhelm, & Beishuizen, 2004). At all ages, however, profound individual differences in metacognitive skills are found, indicating a differential developmental pace of metacognitive skills among students.

Under the age of fourteen, metacognitive skills appear to be substantially domain or task-specific. The same students may vary in metacognitive skills applied to reading, problem-solving, or discovery-learning tasks (Van der Stel & Veenman, 2014; Veenman & Spaans, 2005). According to Veenman and Spaans (2005, p. 172), “metacognitive skills may initially develop on separate islands of tasks and domains that are very much alike.” Between the age of fourteen and fifteen, however, metacognitive skills generalize across tasks and domains. In a longitudinal study, Van der Stel and Veenman (2014) followed twelve-year olds for three successive years. Each year, the participating students performed a reading task in history and a problem-solving task in mathematics. Principal component analysis on metacognitive-skill measures for both tasks revealed an increasing general factor and a diminishing domain-specific factor over the years. At the age of fifteen years, metacognitive skills were entirely general by nature. Apparently, the separate metacognitive repertoires for reading and problem-solving were merged into one general repertoire. Other studies have corroborated the general nature of metacognitive skills beyond the age of fifteen (see Veenman, 2016b). These findings have implications for the assessment of metacognitive skills for reading. Under the age of fourteen, metacognitive assessments should be embedded in a reading context. For instance, questionnaires should explicitly inquire after metacognitive activities in reading and observations should focus on actual reading activities. Beyond the age of fourteen, however, assessments of metacognition for different tasks and domains share common variance to a large extent. Consequently, metacognitive assessments situated in another domain may also bear relevance to metacognition in reading (Veenman & Verheij, 2003).

ASSESSMENT OF METACOGNITIVE SKILLS

There are various reasons for adequately assessing metacognitive skills. A first reason pertains to assessing students' metacognition in order to label them as metacognitively poor or proficient. Obviously, distinguishing metacognitive capacities could be relevant for selecting persons for a particular job or upon entry of a numerus-clausus study at university. More importantly, such a screening of students is required prior to metacognitive instruction and training. For metacognitively proficient students, instruction and training is not merely superfluous and ineffective, it may even interfere with their spontaneous execution of adequate metacognitive skills (Veenman, 2013a). Hence, only students with a metacognitive deficiency in reading should be selected for instruction and training. Secondly, assessments could provide additional information about which metacognitive deficiencies in reading should be addressed. Some students may specifically suffer from poor orientation at the onset of a reading task, whereas others lack monitoring skills during reading. Identifying specific deficiencies could make instruction and training more effectively tailored to the needs of a particular student (Veenman, 2013a). Finally, metacognitive assessments are required in order to establish effects of remedial instruction and training on metacognitive behavior. Most training studies only report effects on performance outcomes, not on metacognitive behavior (Veenman, 2007). Instructional effects on reading comprehension, however, could equally result from confounding variables, such as extended time-on-task. Ultimately, instructional effectiveness is evaluated by ascertaining the causal chain of instruction leading to an improvement in metacognitive reading behavior and, thus, to enhanced reading comprehension (Veenman, 2013a). In order to serve these purposes, adequate and valid assessment methods for metacognitive skillfulness are indispensable.

Offline versus online methods. In assessment instruments for metacognitive skills, offline methods should be distinguished from online methods (Veenman, 2005). Offline methods concern measurements that are administered entirely separated from actual performance on a reading task. For instance, questionnaires presented to students either prior to or after a reading task is a frequently used offline method (Veenman, 2011). Conversely, online methods are applied during the student's performance on a reading task. In studying reading processes, thinking aloud is often used as online method (Pressley & Afflerbach, 1995; Veenman & Beishuizen, 2004). The crucial distinction between both types of method is that offline methods are based on the subjective self-reports from individual students, whereas actual reading behavior is evaluated by an external agency on preset criteria in online methods.

OFFLINE SELF-REPORTS

Questionnaires. For the assessment of metacognitive skills related to reading or text studying, a wide range of questionnaires exists (see Schellings, 2011). Some questionnaires (e.g., MSLQ, Pintrich, & de Groot, 1990; ILS, & Vermunt, 1992) have separate scales for metacognitive strategy use and self-regulation, next to scales for other learner characteristics. Others (e.g., MAI, Schraw, & Dennison, 1994; MARSI, Mokhtari, & Reichard, 2002) entirely focus on metacognition. Students are addressed with questions about (the frequency of) their metacognitive strategy use and skill application. For instance, an item from the MSLQ is: "I ask myself questions to make sure I know the material I have been studying." Students have to answer this question on a Likert scale ranging from 1 (not at all true of me) to 7 (very true of me). Questionnaires can be administered prior to, retrospective to, or entirely disjunct from a reading task. The advantage of questionnaires is that they are effortlessly administered to large groups and that data are easily processed.

Interviews. An interview instrument that was especially developed to assess reading awareness is the Metacognitive Interview (Paris & Jacobs, 1984). A series of open-ended questions are posed to students about evaluating their own abilities for a reading task, goal setting and planning, and monitoring strategies. Independent judges code the students' answers. A broader instrument for assessing self-regulatory strategies is SRLIS (Zimmerman & Martinez-Pons, 1986). In SRLI, students are asked to describe their use of self-regulatory strategies in six learning situations (classroom situation, studying at home, writing assignment, math assignment, preparing for and taking a test, and completing homework when poorly motivated) and these self-reports are scored on fourteen strategy categories. In general, students are retrospectively interviewed, immediately after task performance. Although interviews yield more fine-grained information than questionnaires, the procedure is far more time consuming. Interviews have to be administered individually and coding of answers is labor-intensive. Obviously, this is the reason why Jacobs and Paris (1987) converted their interview instrument into a questionnaire for assessing metacognitive reading strategies, the Index of Reading Awareness, that is frequently used by reading researchers. Similarly, Kitsantas (2000) transformed SRLIS into a questionnaire for different task settings.

Stimulated recall. Stimulated recall is a special interview procedure, designed to support memory processes during retrospective recollection of previous study behavior. Students watch a video recording of their earlier task performance and they are prompted by questions to reflect on their thoughts and behavior (Peterson, Swing, Braverman, & Buss, 1982). For instance, the prompt of "Try to remember what you were thinking about" is given in relation to a particular video fragment. Responses to the questions are transcribed and coded by judges. Although stimulated recall especially facilitates memory of overt behavior, such as in learning-by-doing tasks (Artzt & Armour-Thomas, 1998), it is also used for assessing more covert metacognitive processes in reading (Finkbeiner, Knierim, Smasal, & Ludwig, 2012; Juliebö, Malicky, & Norman, 1998; Kunz, Drewniak, & Schott, 1992). Like any interview procedure, stimulated recall demands investment of time and effort.

Teacher ratings. Teacher ratings of students' metacognition are sometimes used adjacent to other assessment instruments, mostly for reasons of validating new instruments. For instance, Zimmerman and Martinez-Pons (1988) validated the SRLIS against teacher ratings. Teachers were asked to indicate on a five-point scale (never-always) whether individual students applied twelve self-regulatory strategies in class. Overall SRLIS scores correlated 0.70 with teacher ratings. In the same vein, Sperling, Howard, Miller, and Murphy (2002) validated the jr MAI questionnaire, an adaption of the MAI for younger students, against teacher ratings. Teachers received a brief description of prototypical metacognitive behavior and they were asked to give one overall score on a six-point scale for each student. Correlations between the jr MAI and teacher ratings ranged from 0.09 to 0.21. A drawback of teacher ratings is that teachers may lack sufficient knowledge of metacognition to make adequate judgments of students' metacognitive skills (Veenman, Haan, & Dignath, 2009). Moreover, teacher ratings may be biased by their appraisals of competency and personal preferences for particular students.

ONLINE ASSESSMENTS

Thinking aloud is often used as online method for assessing metacognitive reading processes (Presley & Afflerbach, 1995; Schellings, Aarnoutse, &

Van Leeuwe, 2006; Veenman & Beishuizen, 2004). During performance of a reading task, students are requested to merely verbalize their ongoing thoughts and behavior, while refraining from making interpretations (Ericsson & Simon, 1993). Thus, thinking aloud should not be mistaken for introspection. When students are properly instructed, thinking aloud does not interfere with cognitive processes (Ericsson & Simon, 1993) or, more specifically, with metacognitive regulatory processes (Bannert & Mengelkamp, 2008; Veenman, Elshout, & Groen, 1993). It may, however, slightly slow down these processes due to concurrent verbalization efforts. On the other hand, thinking-aloud protocols may be incomplete when students cannot verbalize all ongoing thoughts and fall silent (the tip-of-the-iceberg phenomenon). Thinking aloud may be intrusive to very young or poor readers in particular, because it competes with the resources needed for the execution of basic reading skills. Usually, thinking-aloud protocols are recorded on tape and subsequently transcribed. Two or more "blind" judges independently analyze the protocols according to a detailed codebook (see Pressley & Afflerbach, 1995; Veenman, 2013a). Thus, the thinking-aloud method allows for a fine-grained analysis of metacognitive skills that are either mastered by the student or deficient in the student's repertoire. A disadvantage, however, is the labor-intensive and time-consuming procedure. Therefore, the thinking-aloud method is mainly used in research and for further investigation of individual students with reading deficiencies (Veenman, 2013a), but it is not a practical instrument for screening a large group of students.

Observations. Sometimes the task is not suitable for thinking aloud. For instance, a very easy reading task may only call upon highly automated processes that are not open to verbalization. Conversely, an extremely complex reading task can be very demanding, as a result of which students fall silent. Moreover, a poor verbal proficiency of students may interfere with concurrent reading and thinking aloud. In those cases, thinking aloud can be replaced or complemented by observations through video recordings of the student's reading performance. Video protocols need to be analyzed by multiple judges according a detailed scoring schema of overt behavioral indicators. Observations could pertain to exploratory paging through the text before starting to read linearly, skipping parts of the text, rereading, time allocation to paragraphs, underlining and making notes, navigating through the text (paging back and forth), and facial expressions along with these activities (Lonka, Lindblom-Ylänne, & Maury, 1994; Veenman & Beishuizen, 2004). Unless combined with thinking aloud, behavioral observations do not give direct access to mental processes underlying behavior. For instance, skipping text parts may result as a deliberate choice from time management and relevance appraisals (good metacognition), but equally from sloppy reading and not keeping track of your reading position (poor metacognition). Consequently, judges need to infer the metacognitive nature of behavior by scrutinizing patterns of activities (e.g., stopping with reading, the facial expression of a frown, followed by rereading or paging back). Direct observation, that is, scoring behavior without video recordings, is not recommended for that reason. Obviously, the analysis of video protocols is very time consuming.

Registration of eye movements. Instruments for the registration of eye movement and eye fixations have been used for assessing reading processes in general (Carrithers & Bever, 1984), or metacognitive reading processes in particular (Hyönä, Lorch, & Kaakinen, 2002; Kinnunen & Vauras, 1995). During reading, the head of a student is fixed in a device that registers the motor activities of the eye, the eye-fixation points in the text, and time tags along the line. Kinnunen and Vauras (1995) assessed monitoring through changes in reading time and look backs, while Hyönä et al. (2002) distinguished forward linear reading from reading with look backs. The indices of reading behavior in these studies are rather straightforward, albeit limited in their scope. Much like observations, eye-movement registration only gets access to overt behavior, not to the metacognitive considerations of the student. Therefore, patterns of activities in eye-movement registration need to be carefully selected and tested in order to capture more complex metacognitive reading processes. Previously, fixing the student's head in the device, calibrating the eye movements, and reading with the registration device was an intrusive procedure. Current devices for eye-movement registration are user-friendly and more convenient to the student.

Logfile registration. Recently, researchers have pursued the online registration of metacognitive activities in computer logfiles (Greene & Azevedo, 2010; Veenman, 2013b; Winne, 2014). Students perform a task on the computer and all their activities are logged into a background file. Obviously, the task should lend itself to a computerized version, or otherwise ecological validity is compromised. For reading on the computer, students can read and scroll through a traditional linear text (Dinsmore, Loughlin, Parkinson, & Alexander, 2015; Kunz et al., 1992), or they can read and navigate with links through a hypertext (Hadwin, Nesbit, Jamieson-Noel, Code, & Winne, 2007). Ackerman and Goldsmith (2011) found no differences in reading from computer screen versus paper, as long as study time is externally fixed. When study time is self-paced, however, then reading from screen is detrimental relative to reading from paper due to impoverished metacognition. Consequently, metacognition assessed during self-paced studying from screen may not be entirely representative of metacognitive skills applied to reading from paper.

Logfile data can be semi-automatically analyzed by calculating the frequencies for a selection of activities that are indicative of metacognitive skillfulness (Hadwin et al., 2007; Kunz et al., 1992; Veenman, 2013b). Moreover, trace data in logfile registrations can be inspected for meaningful patterns in time and sequence of activities (Hadwin, et al., 2007; Veenman, 2013b; Winne, 2014). For instance, in the hypermedia environment of *gStudy* (Hadwin et al., 2007), readers are provided with tools for making notes, highlighting text, and making links across concepts during reading. Trace data of study events in the logfiles are used, not only for obtaining frequencies of reading activities and patterns of transitions from one reading activity to the other, but also for detection of dynamic changes in frequencies and patterns over reading time (Winne, 2014). Transition analysis and time-series analysis of logged data are more advanced techniques in the assessment of metacognitive skillfulness (Veenman, 2013b).

Much like behavioral observations and eye-movement registration, logfile registration only captures the concrete, overt behavior of reading activities. It does not give access to the student's metacognitive considerations. Therefore, a set of metacognitive activities or transitions between activities relevant to reading should be selected beforehand on rational grounds and available empirical evidence, and this potential set should be validated with thinking-aloud data (Veenman, 2013b; Veenman, Bavelaar, De Wolf, & Van Haaren, 2014). Validation is required prior to logfile registration, as the coding of student activities during reading is semi-automated. Validation may rule out potential activities or patterns that fail to unequivocally represent metacognitive skillfulness. For instance, in the validation study of Veenman et al. (2014), one of the potential indicators of metacognitive skillfulness was eventually removed from logfile analysis because students performed the activity for diverging reasons, signifying either proficient or poor metacognition. In the end, the adequacy of the automated coding system determines the quality of assessment outcomes. Assessment through logfile registration is minimally intrusive to students. Moreover, it can be administered to large groups at the same time (Dinsmore et al., 2008; Veenman, 2013b).

VALIDITY OF ASSESSMENT METHODS

When evaluating assessment methods, three indices of validity need to be addressed: (1) Internal consistency or reliability of a measure, (2) construct validity, and (3) external or predictive validity (De Groot, 1969). These validity issues are often not adequately attended to in metacognition research (Veenman, 2007, 2011).

Internal consistency. Internal consistency refers to standard reliability measures, such as Cronbach's Alpha, but also to factor analysis for determining the dimensional structure, and to inter-rater reliabilities for establishing consistency in judgments. Reliability indicates to what extent all items on a scale coherently assess the same underlying construct, irrespective of the construct's content. Reliability is especially important in the absence of significant results, as it should be excluded that poor results are due to low internal consistency of the instrument. Factor analysis reveals whether one general factor or multidimensional factors are underlying item scores. Research usually reports reliability indices and factorial structures for questionnaires, but research with other methods often fails to do so (Veenman, 2007). If one aims at assessing metacognitive skillfulness as an aptitude (cf. Veenman, 2016b), rather than some loosely connected components of metacognition, then estimates of reliability and dimensionality are indispensable. Inter-rater reliability represents the extent to which two or more judges converge in their ratings, as expressed by Cohen's Kappa, correlations, or percentage of agreement. It is quite common for research with thinking aloud or observations to disclose inter-rater reliabilities, but indices of convergence are not consistently reported for interviews and stimulated recall.

Construct validity. Most of all, construct validity pertains to content validity, that is, the extent to which key-concepts and key-processes from metacognitive theory are represented and operationalized in the assessment instrument (Veenman, 2011). This is a relevant issue in the design of the instrument. Conversely, once a construct is operationalized through prudent selection of reading activities for the instrument, the content validity of selected activities should be verified. For instance, rereading while thinking aloud is not always the result of monitoring, but rather a side effect of thinking aloud (Veenman & Beishuizen, 2004). Apart from the inspection of content validity, construct validity is also supported by convergent validity (Veenman, 2007). According to convergent validity, different assessment methods for the same construct should point into the same direction, as indicated by high correlations between scores obtained with different methods in a multi-method design (Veenman et al., 2006). Not many studies on metacognitive skillfulness or self-regulation with a multi-method design have been conducted in the past (Dinsmore et al., 2008; Veenman, 2005), although they increasingly become available in the last decade. A review study by Veenman (2005) revealed that offline self-reports of metacognitive self-regulation hardly correspond to actual metacognitive behavior in a task situation, as assessed by online methods. Correlations ranged from –0.07 to 0.31. These findings were corroborated by later multi-method studies for reading (Bannert & Mengelkamp, 2008; Cromley & Azevedo, 2006; Hadwin et al., 2007), and mathematics (Desoete, 2008; Veenman & Van Cleef, 2007). Veenman (2013b) estimated that offline and online measures only have about 2 percent of variance in common ($r = 0.15$ on the average). Apparently, students do not actually do what they earlier said to do, and they do not adequately report what they have done in retrospective (Veenman, 2016b). Moreover, correlations among different offline measurements were low to moderate, whereas correlations among online measures were moderate to high (Cromley & Azevedo, 2006; Veenman, 2005; Veenman et al., 2014). These within-method correlations reveal that offline methods have poor convergent validity, in contrast with online methods.

Poor validity of offline methods may result from problems that are intrinsic to self-reports (Veenman, 2011, 2016b). When responding to offline methods, students need to consult their memory in order to reconstruct their earlier strategic behavior. This reconstruction process may suffer from memory failure and distortion (Ericsson & Simon, 1993; Nisbett & Wilson, 1977). Distortion due to memory failure is likely to increase with the interval between task performance and self-reports. Severe memory problems may occur when offline assessments are administered prior to or entirely disjunct from reading tasks and students have to base their answers on previous reading experiences in the past. In retrospective assessments, reconstructive interpretations may be elicited along with, or instead of correct recollections. Students not only may know more than they tell, they sometimes "tell more than [they] can know" (Nisbett & Wilson, 1977, p. 247). Memory-reconstruction problems can be mitigated by questioning students immediately after reading a text, by making the retrospective questions more task-specific (Schellings, 2011), or by using stimulated recall. Despite these interventions, memory bias in self-reports cannot be fully resolved. Thus, memory-based self-reports may not be representative of the students' actual metacognitive behavior.

A second problem is that questioning may interfere with spontaneous self-reports of students (Schwarz, 1999). Questions may evoke an illusion of familiarity with the strategies that are asked after. Moreover, students may be triggered by questions to label their behavior accordingly. For instance, they may take their loose notes for a summary, when asked after the latter. Incorrect labeling occurs, especially in students with poor declarative metacognitive knowledge (Veenman, 2011). Retrospective questions may even prompt the recall of metacognitive behavior that in fact never occurred. Finally, students may be inclined to give social-desirable answers.

A third problem pertains to the closed answer format of questionnaires. When students have to decide whether they often, regularly, or seldom use a particular reading skill or strategy, they have to compare themselves with others. Students, however, may vary in the reference points chosen: The teacher or the best student, but also the poorest classmate. Even when a student consistently uses the same reference point while answering all questions, disparity in answers occurs *between* students with different reference points. Thus, indices for reliability of the questionnaire may be high, while validity of the instrument is low (Veenman, Prins, & Verheij, 2003).

Online methods do not have these problems. They are based on the actual metacognitive behavior of students during the performance of a reading task, which resolves the first two problems. Moreover, reference problems do not occur in online methods as the metacognitive behavior of all students is rated by external judges or registered by the same device according to a detailed codebook.

External or predictive validity. External validity implies that an assessment instrument should relate to other external variables as expected by the theory. Most reading theories postulate a causal relation between the application of metacognitive skills and reading comprehension (Pressley & Afflerbach, 1995; Veenman, 2016a). Therefore, metacognitive assessments are expected to be adequate predictors of reading comprehension. Veenman (2013b) estimated that, in general, correlations with learning performance range from slightly negative to 0.36 for offline measures and from 0.45 to 0.90 for online measures. Specific studies on reading reported correlations within the same ranges (Bannert & Mengelkamp, 2008; Cromley & Azevedo, 2006; Kunz et al., 1992; Sperling et al., 2002; Van der Stel & Veenman, 2014; Veenman & Beishuizen, 2004; Veenman & Verheij, 2003). Apparently, the external validity for offline assessments is poor, relative to online measures.

CONCLUSION

This overview justifies the conclusion that offline methods suffer from serious validity problems. Although the internal consistency of offline instruments usually is up to par, both construct validity and external validity appear to be poor. Whether generated by questionnaires, interviews, or stimulated recall, all self-reports from offline assessments share this problem. In fact, it is not clear what offline methods essentially measure. Definitely, they do not give access to metacognitive behavior or skills, as evidenced by their lack of correspondence with online measures. Perhaps offline self-reports capture some elements of metacognitive knowledge, but that remains to be investigated further in studies with multi-method designs (Veenman, 2016b; Veenman et al., 2003). Until these validity issues are resolved, researchers and professionals should refrain from using offline methods for the assessment of metacognitive skillfulness in general, and for reading in particular. Nevertheless, offline measures are still omnipresent in metacognition research. In a review of about 200 studies, Dinsmore et al. (2008) estimated that 37 percent of the metacognition assessments (24 percent questionnaires and 13 percent interviews) and 68 percent of the SRL assessments (59 percent questionnaires and 9 percent interviews) relied on offline methods. Some change in assessment practice is obviously needed.

Online methods have shown to uphold high standards of both construct and external validity. Different online methods produce convergent results, while being predictive of learning outcomes in general, and reading comprehension in particular. Thinking aloud, however, is the only online method with direct access to the metacognitive considerations of students (Pressley & Afflerbach, 1995; Veenman, 2013b). Some may argue that the analysis of thinking-aloud protocols is subjective and biased (cf. Ericsson & Simon, 1993), but bias is circumvented by ratings of independent "blind" judges and subjectivity is obviated by inter-rater reliabilities. Thinking aloud is the closest we can get to human thinking processes. The main disadvantage, however, remains the time-consuming and labor-intensive nature of the thinking-aloud procedure. Thinking aloud is not suitable for screening large groups of students on metacognitive deficiencies in reading. With the recent emergence of logfile registration, such as in *gStudy* (Hadwin et al., 2007), an alternative tool for assessing metacognitive skillfulness in reading has become available. More work needs to be done to ascertain that the activities registered in logfiles adequately represent self-regulation and metacognitive skills, for instance, through triangulation of logfile, thinking-aloud, and reading-comprehension data. Moreover, standards should be established for the outcomes of logfile registration, enabling the identification of metacognitively proficient versus deficient readers. Ultimately, logfile registration could become a nonintrusive instrument for screening large groups of students for their metacognitive proficiency in reading. Once deficient students are identified, remedial teachers could resort to the thinking-aloud method for further inspection of metacognitive deficiencies in reading with this selected group of deficient students (Veenman, 2013a).

REFERENCES

Ackerman, R., & Goldsmith, M. (2011). Metacognitive regulation of text learning: On screen versus paper. *Journal of Experimental Psychology: Applied*, *17*, 18–32.

Alexander, J. M., Carr, M., & Schwanenflugel, P. J. (1995). Development of metacognition in gifted children: Directions for future research. *Developmental Review*, *15*, 1–37.

Anderson, J. R., & Schunn, C. D. (2000). Implications of the ACT-R learning theory: No magic bullets. In R. Glaser (Ed.), *Advances in instructional psychology. Volume 5* (pp. 1–33). Mahwah, NJ: Erlbaum.

Artzt, A. F., & Armour-Thomas, E. (1992). Development of a cognitive-metacognitive framework for protocol analysis of mathematical problem solving in small groups. *Cognition and Instruction*, *9*, 137–75.

Baker, L. (2005). Developmental differences in metacognition: Implications for metacognitively oriented reading instruction. In S. E. Israel, C. C. Block, K. L. Bauserman, & K. Kinnucan-Welsch (Eds.), *Metacognition in literacy learning* (pp. 641–79). Mahwah, NJ: Erlbaum.

Baker, L., & Brown, A. L. (1984). Metacognitive skills and reading. In P. D. Pearson (Ed.), *Handbook of reading research* (pp. 353–94). New York: Longman.

Bannert, M., & Mengelkamp, C. (2008). Assessment of metacognitive skills by means of instruction to think aloud and reflect when prompted. Does the verbalization method affect learning? *Metacognition and Learning*, *3*, 39–58.

Brown, A. L. (1978). Knowing when, where, and how to remember: A problem of metacognition. In R. Glaser (Ed.), *Advances in instructional psychology. Volume 1* (pp. 77–165). Hillsdale, NJ: Erlbaum.

Brown, A. L., & DeLoache, J. S. (1978). Skills, plans, and self-regulation. In R. S. Siegel (Ed.), *Children's thinking: What develops?* (pp. 3–35). Hillsdale, NJ: Erlbaum.

Carrithers, C., & Bever, T. G. (1984). Eye-fixation patterns during reading confirm theories of language comprehension. *Cognitive Science*, *8*, 157–72.

Cromley, J. G., & Azevedo, R. (2006). Self-report of reading comprehension strategies: What are we measuring? *Metacognition and Learning*, *1*, 229–47.

De Groot, A. D. (1969). *Methodology, Foundations of inference and research in the behavioral sciences.* The Hague: Mouton.

Desoete, A. (2008). Multi-method assessments of metacognitive skills in elementary school children: how you test is what you get. *Metacognition and Learning*, *3*, 189–206.

Dinsmore, D. L., Alexander, P. A., & Loughlin, S. M. (2008). Focusing the conceptual lens on metacognition, self-regulation, and self-regulated learning. *Educational Psychology Review*, *20*, 391–409.

Dinsmore, D. L., Loughlin, S. M., Parkinson, M. M., & Alexander, P. A. (2015). The effects of persuasive and expository text on metacognitive monitoring and control. *Learning and Individual Differences*, *38*, 54–60.

Ericsson, K. A., & Simon, H. A. (1993). *Protocol Analysis.* Cambridge: MIT Press.

Finkbeiner, C., Knierim, M., Smasal, M., & Ludwig, P. H. (2012). Self-regulated coorperative EFL reading tasks: Students' strategy use and Teachers' support. *Language Awareness*, *21*, 57–83.

Flavell, J. H. (1979). Metacognition and cognitive monitoring: A new area of cognitive-developmental inquiry. *American Psychologist*, *34*, 906–11.

Greene, J. A., & Azevedo, R. (2010). The measurement of learners' self-regulated cognitive and metacognitive processes while using computer-based learning environments. *Educational Psychologist*, *45*, 203–09.

Hadwin, A. F., Nesbit, J. C., Jamieson-Noel, D., Code, J., & Winne, P. H. (2007). Examining trace data to explore self-regulated learning. *Metacognition and Learning*, *2*, 107–24.

Hyönä, J., Lorch, R. F., & Kaakinen, J. K. (2002). Individual differences in reading to summarize expository text: Evidence from eye fixation patterns. *Journal of Educational Psychology*, *94*, 44–55.

Jacobs, J. E., & Paris, S. G. (1987). Children's metacognition about metacognition: Issues in definition, measurement, and instruction. *Educational Psychologist*, *22*, 255–78.

Juliebö, M., Malicky, G. V., & Norman, C. (1998). Metacognition of young readers in an early intervention programme. *Journal of Research in Reading*, *21*, 24–35.

Kinnunen, R., & Vauras, M. (1995). Comprehension monitoring and the level of comprehension in high- and low-achieving primary school children's reading. *Learning and Instruction*, *5*, 143–65.

Kitsantas, A. (2000). The role of self-regulation strategies and self-efficacy perceptions in successful weight loss maintenance. *Psychology and Health*, *15*, 811–20.

Kunz, G. C., Drewniak, U., & Schott, F. (1992). On-line and off-line assessment of self-regulation in learning from instructional text. *Learning and Instruction*, *2*, 287–301.

Lonka, K., Lindblom-Ylänne, S., & Maury, S. (1994). The effect of study strategies on learning from text. *Learning and Instruction*, *4*, 253–71.

Mokhtari, K., & Reichard, C. A. (2002). Assessing students' metacognitive awareness of reading strategies. *Journal of Educational Psychology*, *94*, 249–59.

Nisbett, R. E., & Wilson, T. D. (1977). Telling more than we know: Verbal reports on mental processes. *Psychological Review*, *84*, 231–59.

Paris, S. G., & Jacobs, J. E. (1984). The benefits of informed instruction for children's reading awareness and comprehension skills. *Child Development*, *55*, 2083–93.

Peterson, P. L., Swing, S. R., Braverman, M. T., & Buss, R. (1982). Students' aptitudes and their reports of cognitive processes during direct instruction. *Journal of Educational Psychology*, *74*, 535–47.

Pintrich, P. R., & De Groot, E. V. (1990). Motivational and self-regulated leaning components of classroom academic performance. *Journal of Educational Psychology*, *82*, 33–40.

Pressley, M., & Afflerbach, P. (1995). *Verbal protocols of reading: The nature of constructively responsive reading*. Hillsdale, NJ: Erlbaum.

Schellings, G. (2011). Applying learning strategy questionnaires: Problems and possibilities. *Metacognition and Learning*, *6*, 91–109.

Schellings, G., Aarnoutse, C., & Van Leeuwe, J. (2006). Third-grader's think-aloud protocols: Types of reading activities in reading an expository text. *Learning and Instruction*, *16*, 549–68.

Schraw, G., & Dennison, R. S. (1994). Assessing metacognitive awareness. *Contemporary Educational Psychology*, *19*, 460–75.

Schraw, G., & Moshman, D. (1995). Metacognitive theories. *Educational Psychology Review*, *7*, 351–71.

Schwarz, N. (1999). Self-reports. How questions shape the answers. *American Psychologist*, *54*, 93–105.

Sperling, R. A., Howard, B. C., Miller, L. A., & Murphy, C. (2002). Measures of children's knowledge and regulation of cognition. *Contemporary Educational Psychology*, *27*, 51–79.

Van der Stel, M., & Veenman, M. V. J. (2014). Metacognitive skills and intellectual ability of young adolescents: A longitudinal study from a developmental perspective. *European Journal of Psychology of Education*, *29*, 117–37.

Veenman, M. V. J. (2005). The assessment of metacognitive skills: What can be learned from multi-method designs? In C. Artelt & B. Moschner (Eds.), *Lernstrategien und Metakognition: Implikationen für Forschung und Praxis* (pp. 75–97). Berlin: Waxmann.

Veenman, M. V. J. (2007). The assessment and instruction of self-regulation in computer-based environments: A discussion. *Metacognition and Learning*, *2*, 177–83.

Veenman, M. V. J. (2008). Giftedness: Predicting the speed of expertise acquisition by intellectual ability and metacognitive skillfulness of novices. In M. F. Shaughnessy, M. V. J. Veenman, & C. Kleyn-Kennedy (Eds.), *Meta-cognition: A recent review of research, theory, and perspectives* (pp. 207–20). Hauppage: Nova Science Publishers.

Veenman, M. V. J. (2011). Alternative assessment of strategy use with self-report instruments: A discussion. *Metacognition and Learning*, *6*, 205–11.

Veenman, M. V. J. (2013a). Training metacognitive skills in students with availability and production deficiencies. In H. Bembenutty, T. Cleary, & A. Kitsantas (Eds.), *Applications of Self-Regulated Learning across diverse disciplines: A tribute to Barry J. Zimmerman* (pp. 299–324). Charlotte, NC: Information Age Publishing.

Veenman, M. V. J. (2013b). Assessing metacognitive skills in computerized learning environments. In R. Azevedo & V. Aleven (Eds.), *International Handbook of Metacognition and Learning Technologies* (pp. 157–68). New York/Berlin: Springer.

Veenman, M. V. J. (2016a). Metacognition. In P. Afflerbach (Ed.), *Handbook of Individual Differences in Reading: Reader, Text, and Context* (pp. 26–40). New York: Routledge.

Veenman, M. V. J. (2016b). Learning to self-monitor and self-regulate. In R. Mayer & P. Alexander (Eds.), *Handbook of research on learning and instruction* (2nd rev. ed.). New York: Routledge.

Veenman, M. V. J., Bavelaar, L., De Wolf, L., & Van Haaren, M. G. P. (2014). The on-line assessment of metacognitive skills in a computerized environment. *Learning and Individual Differences*, *29*, 123–30.

Veenman, M. V. J., & Beishuizen, J. J. (2004). Intellectual and metacognitive skills of novices while studying texts under conditions of text difficulty and time constraint. *Learning and Instruction*, *14*, 619–38.

Veenman, M. V. J., Elshout, J. J., & Groen, M. G. M. (1993). Thinking aloud: Does it affect regulatory processes in learning. *Tijdschrift voor Onderwijsresearch*, *18*, 322–30.

Veenman, M. V. J., Haan, N., & Dignath, C. (2009). *An observation scale for assessing teachers' implicit and explicit use of metacognition in classroom settings.* Paper presented at the 13th Biennial Conference for Research on Learning and Instruction, EARLI. Amsterdam.

Veenman, M. V. J., Prins, F. J., & Verheij, J. (2003). Learning styles: Self-reports versus thinking-aloud measures. *British Journal of Educational Psychology*, *73*, 357–72.

Veenman, M. V. J., & Spaans, M. A. (2005). Relation between intellectual and metacognitive skills: Age and task differences. *Learning and Individual Differences*, *15*, 159–76.

Veenman, M. V. J., & Van Cleef, D. (2007). Validity of assessing metacognitive skills for mathematic problem solving. In A. Efklides and M. H. Kosmidis (Eds.), *9th European Conference on Psychological Assessment. Program and Abstracts* (pp. 87–88). Thessaloniki: Aristotle University of Thessaloniki.

Veenman, M. V. J., Van Hout-Wolters, B. H. A. M., & Afflerbach, P. (2006). Metacognition and Learning: Conceptual and methodological considerations. *Metacognition and Learning*, *1*, 3–14.

Veenman, M. V. J., & Verheij, J. (2003). Identifying technical students at risk: Relating general versus specific metacognitive skills to study success. *Learning and Individual Differences*, *13*, 259–72.

Veenman, M. V. J., Wilhelm, P., & Beishuizen, J. J. (2004). The relation between intellectual and metacognitive skills from a developmental perspective. *Learning and Instruction*, *14*, 89–109.

Vermunt, J. D. H. M. (1992). *Leerstijlen en sturing van leerprocessen in het hoger onderwijs.* [Learning styles and regulation of learning processes in higher education.] Lisse: Swets & Zeitlinger.

Wang, M. C., Haertel, G. D., & Walberg, H. J. (1990). What influences learning? A content analysis of review literature. *Journal of Educational Research*, *84*, 30–43.

Winne, P. H. (2014). Issues in researching self-regulated learning as patterns of events. *Metacognition and Learning*, *9*, 229–37.

Zimmerman, B. J., & Martinez-Pons, M. (1990). Student differences in self-regulated learning: Relating grade, sex, and giftedness to self-efficacy and strategy use. *Journal of Educational Psychology*, *82*, 51–59.

FURTHER READINGS

Pressley, M., & Afflerbach, P. (1995). *Verbal protocols of reading: The nature of constructively responsive reading.* Hillsdale, NJ: Erlbaum.

Veenman, M. V. J. (2011, 2016). Learning to self-monitor and self-regulate. In R. Mayer & P. Alexander (Eds.), *Handbook of research on learning and instruction* (2nd rev. ed.). New York: Routledge.

Veenman, M. V. J. (2016). Metacognition. In P. Afflerbach (Ed.), *Handbook of individual differences in reading: Reader, text, and context* (pp. 26–40). New York: Routledge.

Chapter 4

The Construction-Integration (CI) Model of Text Comprehension

A Lens for Teaching the Common Core Reading Standards

D. Ray Reutzel

ABSTRACT

Teaching the CCSS literature and informational text reading standards through the lens of Kintsch's *Construction-Integration Model of Text Comprehension* (Kintsch, 2013) helps teachers "to analyze texts in meaningful ways" recognizing that text comprehension is a complex process employing multiple levels of text processing (Kucan, Hapgood, & Palincsar, 2011, p. 76). Grounding comprehension instruction in a strong theoretical framework like that offered by Kintsch (2013) helps teachers to select CCSS reading standards to support students as they construct and integrate knowledge from the complex texts they read.

> *The Latin root of the word "comprehend" suggests to "wrestle with something."*
>
> *Robert Calfee, 2009*

INTRODUCTION

Reading comprehension is the irrefutable goal of reading instruction and the very heart of the act of reading (Durkin, 1993). Although there may be disparity among definitions, goals, and means for achieving reading comprehension among researchers and practitioners, virtually all educators would agree that reading comprehension is the *sine qua non* of reading instruction. What conceivable purpose could there be in pronouncing words on a page of text, either mechanistically or even expressively and artfully, without comprehending the meaning of those words individually and collectively? And yet, we know intuitively and empirically that comprehending itself involves a delicate balance among several essential elements—reader background knowledge, fluent decoding of an abstract system of printed symbols, and knowledge of language and language functions—that are used by readers to actively construct meaning from and make sense of text (Israel & Duffy, 2009; Keene & Zimmerman, 2013).

Students who say words quickly, even if expressively, are not much better off than the illiterate, since the meaning of and the attendant potential for growth in knowledge embodied in the words, phrases, and text escape their grasp. Young children who are unable to construct meaning and make sense from spoken language itself, let alone from printed texts, struggle early on and throughout their academic careers (Fielding, Kerr, & Rosier, 1998; Israel & Duffy, 2009; National Reading Panel, 2000; National Early Literacy Panel, 2008; Snow, Burns, & Griffin, 1998). Comprehension is a wrestle with text that results in the text giving up its meaning to the reader. To reveal the secrets for successfully comprehending text to students, teachers will need to understand and have knowledge of the theoretical components and processes of human text processing.

This chapter highlights the importance of grounding comprehension instruction firmly within a framework or model of text processing, especially in an era of CCSS in reading where the text takes center stage. Without such a theoretical understanding of human text processing, teachers will not know which, when and how to effectively teach comprehension strategies to support their students' wrestle with text to construct meaning.

FRAMING THE ISSUE: THEORETICALLY GROUNDED READING COMPREHENSION INSTRUCTION

Over the past several decades, various literacy scholars, national panels, and professional groups have defined comprehension in a variety of ways. One of the most complete and highly developed models of reading comprehension is Kintsch's *Construction-Integration* (CI) model of text comprehension (Duke et al., 2011). Kintsch (2013) defines reading comprehension as "automatic meaning construction via constraint satisfaction [perception], without purposeful, conscious effort" (p. 808). What this means is that students who comprehend do so effortlessly by combining their background knowledge of the world and language with the content of the text. Kintsch's (2013) definition of comprehension is qualitatively different than many other definitions of reading comprehension because it places a premium on the initial need for conscious cognitive effort, affective engagement, and active text processing moving over time to a point of comprehension fluency. Kintsch (2013) emphasizes the need initially for readers to use cognitively demanding processes like meaning extraction, construction, and integration. With informed instruction, student attention and engagement move from effortful, conscious, and active processing to becoming automatic, effortless, and fluent. Pressley (2002, p. 395), as has Kintsch, noted the need for developing fluency in comprehension. He inquired, "What does it take to develop such fluent comprehenders? We do not know, but I think it should be a high priority to find out."

The problem of helping students develop into fluent comprehenders is one that has for many years vexed scholar, teacher and student alike. Scholars have sought to understand the processes, components, and mechanisms that are involved in comprehending text. Teachers have sought to understand how to effectively teach students comprehension strategies. Students have sought to understand how others seemingly without effort comprehend a variety of texts.

Fortunately, scholars over the past several decades have labored with some success to reveal the processes, components, and mechanisms involved in comprehending text. Similarly, most teachers now routinely teach students a bevy of comprehension strategies. Students may have learned comprehension strategies but still do not know how or when to apply their strategy knowledge to comprehend increasingly complex texts. Scholars have not effectively bridged the gap between theory and instructional practices when it comes to the teaching of reading comprehension. Consequently, many teachers know about and teach a burgeoning set of comprehension strategies but may not understand what is going on in the minds of their learners to help them develop the ability to be strategic about their application of comprehension strategies to the processing of text. Consequently, many teachers are teaching students how to use comprehension strategies without a sufficient understanding of how text is successfully processed in the human mind. Without this knowledge, comprehension instruction is focused on teaching students strategies or discussing text as the end goal of comprehension instruction instead of framing this instruction within a broader framework, model , or theory of text comprehension.

MAKING THE CASE FOR THEORETICALLY GROUNDED COMPREHENSION INSTRUCTION

Evidence continues to amass that many classroom teachers do not have enough knowledge about text comprehension processes to effectively teach reading comprehension (DeWitz, Jones, & Leahy, 2009; Duke, Pearson, Strachan, & Billman, 2011; Kucan, 2009; Kucan, Hapgood, & Palincsar, 2011; Reutzel, Clark, Jones, & Kumar, 2016).

Most teacher preparation programs, school district professional development workshops, and even federally sponsored teacher practice guides have emphasized the *what* and *how* of teaching reading comprehension rather than focusing on increasing teachers' knowledge and understanding of the process of how readers actually accomplish the astonishing feat of comprehending text. Teachers need help to understand text comprehension processes in order to effectively analyze text and then subsequently provide effective, informed comprehension instruction (Kucan, Hapgood, & Palincsar, 2011; Shanahan, et al., 2010). To emphasize this point, Kucan, Hapgood, and Palincsar (2011, p. 76) concluded the following in a large-scale research study of teachers' reading comprehension instruction:

> We found the majority of teachers (85%) in this study demonstrated very limited ability to analyze the CoLTS [science] texts in meaningful ways. We connect this lack of expertise to a larger construct, namely, that the *teachers were not working from a model of text comprehension that foregrounds the integration of text information and the possible obstacles to that integration* [emphasis added]. Specifically, the majority of teachers did not refer to text coherence or to identifiable factors that might impede a reader in building a coherent representation of text ideas.

In another recent study of primary grade teachers' knowledge about text structures in informational texts, Reutzel, Jones, Clark & Kumar (2016, pp. 92–93) stated the following:

> Teacher education programs will need to increase attention to training inservice and preservice teachers in text analysis skills (Shanahan, 2013). Our experiences as teacher educators suggest that this is an area where considerable new attention needs to be focused in preparing teachers to teach the CCSS effectively and to assist them in developing the insights and skills necessary to determine the appropriate text complexity-reader match for providing effective comprehension instruction using informational texts. (Duke, Halliday & Roberts, 2013)

Unfortunately, it appears that a focus on learning how or which comprehension strategies to teach does not necessarily help teachers develop a framework for understanding the processes students use to comprehend text. Without a framework for understanding text comprehension processes, teachers will unfortunately be at a loss as to how to properly diagnose and intervene with students who struggle to comprehend the texts they read.

Since teachers are often quite accomplished readers themselves, they are not likely to think much about comprehension processes and the demands various texts place upon younger, less proficient readers. Developing conscious awareness and knowledge of text comprehension processes is important because in so doing teachers are able to select appropriate priorities and instructional practices as well as to be able to identify text-based obstacles that may impede their students' text comprehension. In what follows, I describe what comprehension instruction looks like when it is informed using Kintsch's *Construction-Integration Model of Text Comprehension* as a lens or framework to foreground the analysis and teaching of text comprehension to younger and less proficient readers.

The *Construction-Integration Model of Text Comprehension* is composed of two cognitive processes: *construction* and *integration*. The *construction* process involves two levels of text comprehension processing: (1) *microstructure* and (2) *macrostructure*. These two levels of text comprehension processes result in the construction of a *textbase*. A *textbase* is a mental model of the text constructed in the reader's mind representing ideas and connections among ideas in the text assisted by the reader's background knowledge. In essence, a *textbase*, when properly constructed, represents what the text actually says.

The *integration* process involves integrating information drawn from the constructed *textbase* to create a *situation model* of the text. A *situation model* is more than what the text says; it is what the text means. To illustrate how the two CI processes work, *construction* and *integration*, I describe what goes on inside the mind of a less proficient reader beginning with the first process or level of the CI model: *Construction*.

CONSTRUCTION: BASIC COMPREHENSION PROCESSES

Jorge is a first-grade student. He has selected an informational text to read, titled *Sand* (Clyne & Griffiths, 2005). As he begins reading, he must be able to recognize the illustrations and decipher the symbols on each page of the book (e.g., sand, rock, wind, rain, waves, deserts, dunes, beaches, etc.).

Once decoded, the words, phrases, and sentences Jorge reads are placed into his working memory. Jorge must then link the decoded words, phrases, and sentences in working memory to other word meanings, images, and experiences he has stored in his background knowledge or long-term memory. Next, he must link words, phrases, and sentences together in the text to construct a running list of related propositions or ideas in his working memory. When Jorge is successful at this task, he is constructing a *microstructure* of the text (Perfetti & Stafura, 2014).

Jorge reads the first sentence in the book *Sand*: "What is sand?" Jorge fluently decodes each word in this sentence, leaving sufficient cognitive resources available to focus his attention on constructing a *microstructure* of the text. As each word is decoded, it is entered into Jorge's working memory. Then, each decoded word in the sentence is associated with its meaning. . . .

> *What* . . . a word used to ask a question about a person, place, thing or idea (noun) . . .
>
> *Is* . . . a verb indicating a state of being or existence. . . .
>
> *Sand* . . . an object like dirt, but found at the beach or in boxes at the local city park.

As construction of a microstructure of the text proceeds, assisted by Jorge's knowledge of word meanings and language, he constructs a mental model what the text actually says called a microstructure. It is important to know if students can accurately and fluently construct meaning for sentences before one can reasonably expect students to link sentence meanings together into larger meaningful units.

Next Jorge reads, *Sand is many tiny pieces of rock.* As the words in this second sentence are fluently decoded and associated with other word meanings stored in working memory, links are constructed in Jorge's mind between the word meanings in this second sentence (*many, tiny, pieces,* and *rock)* and the concept of *sand* represented in the first sentence (see figure 4.1, Reutzel, Clark, Jones, & Gillam, 2016).

Younger, less proficient readers often need to be helped to establish coherence between and among ideas represented at the local level of text comprehension—words, phrases, sentences, and paragraphs. Authors can help

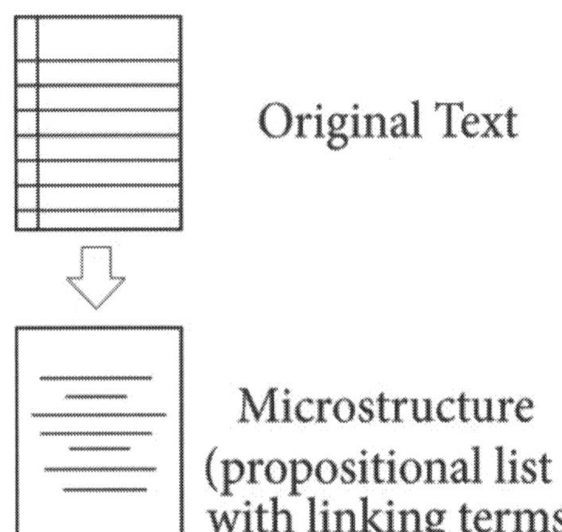

Figure 4.1 CI Model: Constructing the Microstructure of Text

by providing cohesion connectors or *signal words* in the text. Signal words help readers like Jorge explicitly link new ideas to others already stored in working memory into a string of propositions or idea units represented in the text. For example, the word *because* in a sentence signals that ideas in one sentence often link to ideas in a second sentence in a chain of cause and effect. A word like *similarly* in a sentence signals that ideas represented in a new proposition are to be linked with the ideas represented in previous propositions. When authors omit these signal words, readers, like our first-grader, Jorge, must infer or impose relationships among the ideas in a text (Pearson, 1974).

As Jorge reads the next sentence in *Sand*, he reads, *How is sand made?* The text continues:

> *Wind blows on rocks.*
> *Rain falls on rocks.*
> *Waves crash on rocks.*
> *The wind, rain, and waves break the rock into tiny pieces.*
> *The rock becomes sand.*

Continuously using the processes to construct sentence meanings described to this point, the *microstructure* of ideas constructed in Jorge's mind continues to grow with input from the text as he consults his lexicon, background knowledge, and knowledge of language including sentence structure and signal words.

To help Jorge construct a microstructure of the text, his teacher points out to him that each new paragraph in the *Sand* text begins with a question and then each question is answered. Given this insight into the text's organization or text structure, Jorge organizes the information in his microstructure into a coherent mental model of the *Sand* text called a *macrostructure* representing a question-answer text structure.

When authors provide a clearly recognizable organization of the ideas in a text including text features and signal words, construction of a globally coherent model of the text or *macrostructure* is made much easier for younger or less proficient readers. Conversely, when authors fail to do so, readers must infer or impose a structure on the ideas extracted from the text in order to construct a *macrostructure* (Graesser, 2007; Kintsch & Kintsch, 2005; Kintsch, 2013). When readers are able to organize the *microstructure* of a text into a *macrostructure* of a text, they have constructed what Kintsch (2013) calls a *textbase* as shown in figure 4.2 (Reutzel et al., 2016).

Kintsch (2013, p. 811) explains, "Cooperative and attentive readers will more or less form the same *text base—micro* and *macrostructures*—as invited by the author of the text."

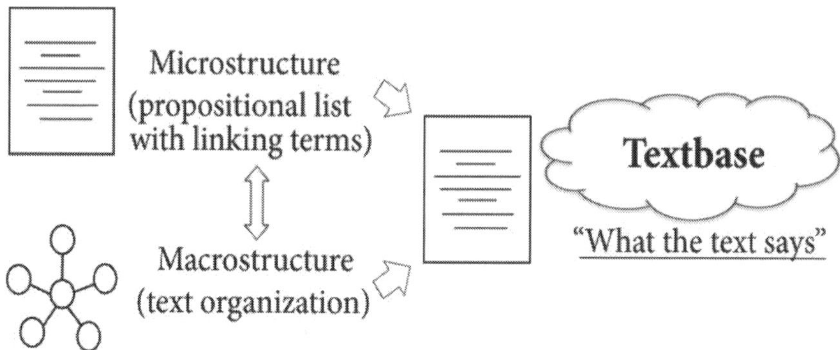

Figure 4.2 CI Model: Constructing Macrostructure of a Text—Combining It with Microstructure to Construct a Textbase

INTEGRATION: WHAT'S THE SITUATION HERE?

Once the construction of an accurate, complete, and well-organized *textbase* is achieved, readers can progress to the next level of comprehension processing described in the CI model of text: *Integration*.

A *situation model* is created when ideas contained in the *textbase* are combined with knowledge stored in a reader's background. A *situation model* is a reader's mental representation of the *situation* in the text. Jorge forms a situation model by linking the contents of the *textbase* he constructed from the *Sand* text to his personal experiences with sand—such as being buried in sand at the beach, building sandcastles, or playing with his grandmother's hour glass (see figure 4.3, Reutzel et al., 2016).

Because each situation model is a composite of information used to construct a textbase and information stored in a reader's network of background knowledge and experiences, it can often contain information that is somewhat different from the original text and from that of other students' interpretations. Because each reader's background knowledge of the text varies, the situation model formed varies similarly although the core information in the situation model should be based on the contents of the text information. Thus, the integration process readers use to form a situation model is greatly dependent on each reader's abilities to do the following:

1. Construct an accurate and coherent textbase from the original text;
2. Access and integrate background knowledge and prior experiences with information in the constructed textbase; and
3. Make inferences to fill in gaps among the ideas provided by the author and those needed to make sense of the text.

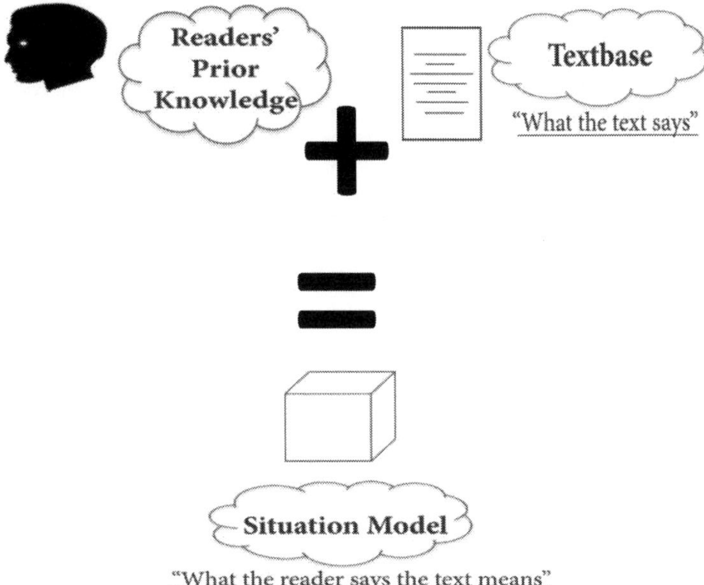

Figure 4.3 CI Model: Integrating the Textbase with the Readers' Prior Knowledge to Form a Situation Model of Text

As a result, it is difficult to predict with absolute certainty the contents of the situation models individual readers may create. However, this is not to suggest that readers are allowed to construct a situation model containing anything they want.

A satisfactory *situation model* must conform to two important constraints (Duke et al., 2011). First, the situation model must align with ideas represented in the text base. Second, it must correspond to the way the reader views the world using the lens of his/her background knowledge and prior experience. So, a situation model does not represent what the text actually says as much as it represents what the reader has decided the text means (see figure 4.3). Duke et al. (2011, p. 54) explain: "If the *text base* [emphasis added] is an account of what the text says, then the *situation model* [emphasis added] can be thought of as an account of what the text means."

The creation of a *situation model* is often what most teachers really want when they think about their students' reading comprehension. Teachers are not very interested in whether or not students can recite the words or sentences in a text verbatim. Rather, they are interested in whether or not students can describe a satisfactory *situation model* that makes sense in relation to the parameters dictated by the text and the connections their students have made to their background knowledge.

According the CI model of text comprehension, the creation of a situation model of the text does not complete the integration process (Kintsch, 2103). To complete the integration process, readers must take conscious steps to integrate the contents of the meaning contained in the situation model into their world knowledge network stored in long-term memory (see figure 4.4, Reutzel et al., 2016).

After Jorge forms a situation model of the *Sand* text, he will need to be helped to take conscious, active steps to *integrate* the contents of his situation model of the *Sand* text into his network of world knowledge. To do this, Jorge may consciously link the concept of sand to his categorical knowledge of soil or dirt types. He may, with help from his teacher, learn to use a question-answer graphic organizer to ask and answer questions about sand in the text. This conscious, effortful linking of known world knowledge about soil or dirt (stored in long-term memory) with new knowledge about sand from the *Sand* text (held in working memory) is necessary for less proficient readers—and even some more accomplished readers—to transfer the contents of their situation model into their background knowledge store.

Kintsch (2013) cautions teachers and readers against *encapsulated knowledge*. Encapsulated knowledge is only retrievable when specific cues from a particular text are employed to access information stored in background knowledge. Encapsulated knowledge has not been consciously integrated into the background knowledge network of a reader. As such, encapsulated knowledge remains linked to a single text or situation model. It remains isolated from the generalized contents of the reader's background knowledge network.

Integrating the information contained in the situation model into information stored in the world knowledge base is quite typical of adult, fluent readers, but it is not an automatic process to be assumed with younger, less proficient readers. According to Kintsch (2013, p. 812), integration of the

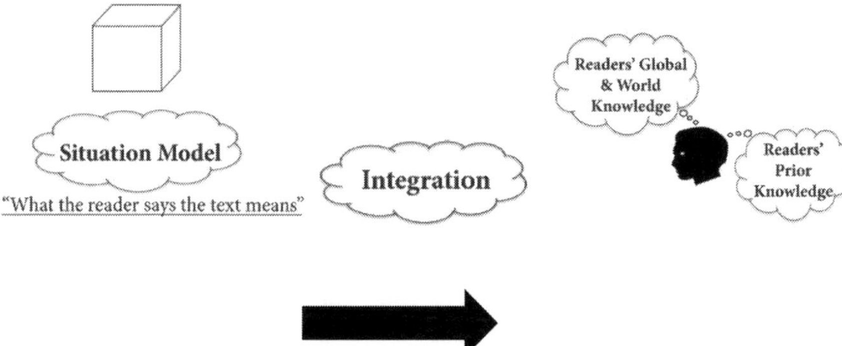

Figure 4.4 CI Model: Integrating Contents of the Situation Model into the Readers' World Knowledge Network

contents of a situation model into one's world knowledge network stored in long-term memory requires "strategic action and effort on the part of the reader/learner." To integrate the contents of a situation model into world knowledge, younger and less proficient readers must actively integrate new knowledge with old, often consciously employing a variety of comprehension strategies including dialogic text discussion, to do so. Encapsulated knowledge represents an incomplete text comprehension process where the virtuous cycle of comprehension described by Duke et al. (2011)—*knowledge begets comprehension begets knowledge*—is disrupted or remains incomplete.

Figure 4.5 represents the complete CI text comprehension model with its two components, construction and integration, labeled showing how text comprehension is composed of multiple levels of comprehension processing (Reutzel et al., 2016).

Teachers who understand the CI model of text comprehension are better equipped to support their students' text comprehension processes through well-planned and sequenced strategy instruction and guided comprehension discussion. Students who are taught to use the text as an evidentiary base for constructing or elaborating their text-based mental models on their own rather than over relying upon teachers frontloading text information prior to reading will have increased capacity to independently comprehend complex texts required in CCSS reading anchor standard 10. Conversely, teachers with limited theoretical understandings of the CI model of text comprehension will

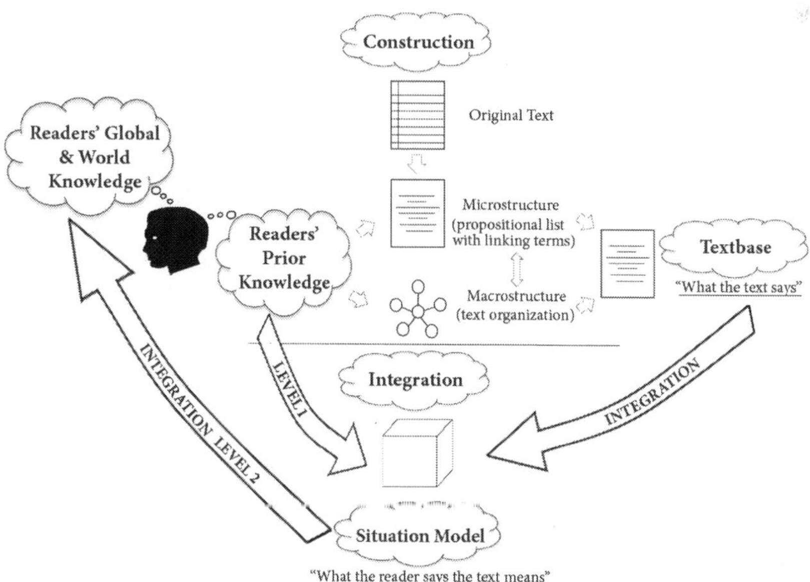

Figure 4.5 Total CI Model: Virtuous Cycle of Comprehension

likely continue to provide comprehension instruction largely foregrounded by Schema Theory replete with all of the well-intentioned, but often excessive, teacher frontloading of text-based information. In so doing, teachers may unintentionally undercut students' opportunities to develop independence in comprehending texts at increasingly complex levels as found in CCSS reading anchor standard 10.

Kucan, Hapgood, and Palincsar. (2011, p. 78) stated, "Recent models of text comprehension and text analysis are important aspects of the specialized knowledge that teachers need in order to think about a text in ways that will allow them to support their students in making sense of it." This is particularly true when teaching to the CCSS reading standards. In the next section of this chapter, I discuss how the CI model can inform and guide teaching of the CCSS reading standards. I begin by describing how theoretical knowledge of the CI model can make a difference in how teachers can effectively teach literature using the CCSS reading standards.

PEDAGOGICAL IMPLICATIONS: USING CI THEORY AS A LENS FOR TEACHING THE CCSS LITERATURE STANDARDS

Step 1. Selecting an Appropriately Complex Text. Our first-grade teacher, Ms. Hicks, has selected a story, "Little Bear Goes to the Moon" from the book *Little Bear* (Minarik, 1957). This book is a Level 1 Beginning Reading book in the *I Can Read Book* series. CCSS ELA/Literacy Standard 10 for Reading Literature in first grade is: *With prompting and support, read prose and poetry of appropriate complexity for grade 1.* Ms. Hicks believes this book could successfully be used in a group shared reading, fits well with the theme of the unit, presents an engaging topic for young children, and uses repetition of words and sentences. She checks the Lexile level of the book and finds it is rated as a 370L. There is not a Text Complexity Grade Band presented in the CCSS ELA/Literature for grades K–1; however, the Lexile rating is below the Grade Band for grades 2–3 of 450L–725L. Ms. Hicks decides this story may be appropriate for use with her first-grade students if given necessary supports, so she digs a bit deeper into the story text.

Ms. Hicks determines potential supports and obstacles the story may present her students as they read:

- Quantitative Supports: many high frequency words, appropriate sentence length, repetition of some sentences and difficult words.
- Qualitative Supports: illustrations match text presented, easy-to-follow plot structure with clear identification of the problem faced by the characters.
- Quantitative Obstacles: difficult words include carrots, potatoes, tomatoes, but only used on the second page of the story and are presented in a rhythmic pattern.

- Qualitative Obstacles: none noted.
- Reader-Task Considerations: text fits well with the identified task and presents an engaging story.

Based on her examination of the text, Ms. Hicks decides this story text is appropriately complex and challenging, given support, for her students at this point in the year.

Step 2: Planning Comprehension Instruction to Construct a Microstructure of Literature. Ms. Hicks turns her attention now to selection of CCSS ELA/Literacy standards and comprehension strategies for her lesson. She selects Reading Anchor Standards for Literature #1–3, Cluster #1: *Key Ideas and Details* to identify grade-specific standards to help her students construct a microstructure of the text. Given the strong plot structure of the story, she selects reading anchor standard #3: *Describe characters, settings, and major events in a story, using key details.* Next, she considers comprehension strategies that will enable her students to identify the key ideas and details of the plot—characters, settings, and major events. Ms. Hick references the *IES K–3 Reading Comprehension Practice Guide* to select an evidence-based reading comprehension strategy for use in this lesson (Shanahan et al., 2010). She decides to teach her students how to ask and answer questions about three components of story structure—characters, settings, and major events. She decides also to use a story structure graphic organizer to support her students' use of this comprehension strategy. Ms. Hicks knows this strategy, coupled with the use of graphic organizers, can be used with other stories and will prepare her students for future lessons focused on the construction of story macrostructure. In this lesson, Ms. Hicks will teach students how to ask and answer questions to identify the characters, settings, and major events in a story using explicit instruction, teacher think-alouds, a "W" word graphic organizer, and whole-class discussion.

A LESSON TO SUPPORT CONSTRUCTION OF STORY MICROSTRUCTURE

CCSS Anchor Standard Cluster #1

Key Ideas and Details: Reading Literature Anchor Standard #3 (Kindergarten): *With prompting and support, identify characters, settings, and major events in a story.*

Materials: An enlarged copy of *Little Bear* (Minarik, 1957) or a regular-size copy and a document camera, markers, large chart paper divided into three columns prepared as shown below.

Lesson Objective/Explanation: (Teacher wording is in italics.) *We will learn how to ask and answer questions to help us better understand important parts of stories. We will be asking and answering the three questions shown on this chart: Who, Where, and What? As I read this story aloud to you, be thinking about these three questions: Who is the story about? Where is the story taking place? and What is happening in the story?*

Teacher Modeling

1. Teacher and students, using shared reading, read the story "Little Bear Goes to the Moon" from the book *Little Bear.*
2. *Did you listen carefully and think about Who, Where, and What? Let's read the story again and raise your hands when we hear an answer to the questions of Who, Where, or What. As I read, I am going to ask myself Who, Where, and What about the story.* Teacher reads page 1 of the story and (as students raise their hands) presents a think-aloud about the Who presented on this page. Teacher explains that *the Who of a story is also called the characters* and explains the importance of characters for a story. Teacher also emphasizes that *when reading a story, asking and answering the question, "Who are the characters in the story?" will help us to better understand the story.* Teacher writes or draws the characters presented on page 1 of the story on the chart.

3. Teacher reads page 2 of the story and discusses the Where of the story and the first What of the story (in this case, the first What is the problem of the story). Teacher provides the label of "setting" for the Where and the label of "events" for the What. Teacher continues to write or draw the answers on the chart and discuss the importance of asking and answering these questions.
4. Teacher continues to read aloud and explain and discuss the Who, Where, and What of the story, articulating how use of the strategy of asking and answering questions about these three components increases understanding of the story. As students begin to understand the concept of asking and

Who?	*Where?*	*What?*

answering questions about the Who, Where, and What, teacher moves to guided practice.

Guided Practice (with gradual release of responsibility): Teacher draws students into collaborative use of the strategy of asking and answering questions about these three important story components. For example,

Teacher-Guided Practice: *As I read this next page, continue to listen carefully to this story and raise your hand when you hear an answer to a Who, Where, or What question.* Teacher continues reading. When a student raises his/her hand, teacher and student(s) discuss the Who, Where, or What and teacher or student adds the answers to the chart.

Gradual Release of Responsibility Guided Practice: *Continue to listen carefully to this story, asking yourself and answering Who, Where, or What questions. I'll stop at the end of each page and you can tell your reading partner your question and answer. We'll share our questions and answers with each other and add the answers to our chart.*

Independent Practice: Depending on the responsiveness of the students, independent practice of the strategy might be applied during this shared reading or reserved for a subsequent independent reading. Over time, independent practice of the strategy can progress to students completing a Who, Where, What Question/Answer graphic organizer with a partner or individually. For example:

- Independent Practice during this shared reading: *Continue to listen and read carefully, asking yourself and answering Who, Where, or What questions. When you hear an answer to a question, raise your hand and we'll draw or write the answer on our chart.*
- Independent Practice during Subsequent Shared Readings: *When you ask and answer a Who, Where, or What question, draw or write the answer on your Partner Question/Answer chart.*
- Independent Practice during Student Reading: *When you ask and answer a Who, Where, or What question, write the page number of the story and draw or write the answer on your Question/Answer chart.*

Lesson Wrap Up: Teacher reviews with students the Who, Where, and What questions and answers, emphasizing how asking and answering these questions have helped to increase understanding of the story.

Steps 3–5: Constructing a Macrostructure of the Story, Building a Situation Model, and Merging the Situation Model into World Knowledge. This sample lesson was designed to help students construct a microstructure (CI Model Step 1) of the story "Little Bear Goes to the Moon" from the book *Little Bear* (Minarik, 1957). The lesson, so far, has prepared these first-grade students to

	"Little Bear Goes to the Moon" from the book *Little Bear* by Else Holmelund Minarik (1957) CCSS ELA/Literacy Reading Standards for Literature #1-9, First Grade	
	Key Ideas and Details	
Standard 1	With prompting and support, ask and answer questions about key details in a text. *Teaching Suggestion: Demonstrate for students how to ask and answer questions about: a) why Little Bear decides to fly to the moon; b) what Little Bear does to fly to the moon; c) what happens to little bear when he tries to fly to the moon; and d) what does his mother say about him flying to the moon. Encourage students to ask and answer questions of their own.*	Microstructure
Standard 2	With prompting and support, retell familiar stories, including key details. *Teaching Suggestion: Demonstrate for students how to retell the story of "Little Bear Goes to the Moon" using the key details identified in Standard 1. Have students draw a series of pictures to retell the story in a comic strip frame format. Have students cut apart the pictures, reorder them, and retell the story to others.*	
Standard 3	**With prompting and support, identify characters, settings, and major events in a story.** ***Teaching Suggestion: Use Sample Lesson #1 on pp. ##***	Macrostructure
	Craft and Structure	
Standard 4	Ask and answer questions about unknown words in text. *Teaching Suggestion: Demonstrate for students what to do when the encounter an unknown word in a text. Encourage students to use the techniques shared. (Students are likely to know the meaning of all the words in the story "Little Bear Goes to the Moon.")*	
Standard 5	Recognize common types of texts (e.g., storybooks, poems). *Teaching Suggestion: Show students how the book Little Bear is a collection of short stories. Point out the title of the book and the titles for each of the stories. Have students identify other books that are a collection of short stories they have read or know about.*	Integration
Standard 6	With prompting and support, name the author and illustrator of a story and define the role of each in telling the story. *Teaching Suggestion: Identify the author and illustrator of the book Little Bear. Discuss how these two people worked together to create several children's books. Compare some of these books with Little Bear. Explain how the illustrator, Maurice Sendak, wrote and illustrated his own stories such as Where the Wild Things Are.*	
	Integration of Knowledge and Ideas	
Standard 7	With prompting and support, describe the relationship between illustrations and the story in which they appear (e.g., what moment in a story an illustration depicts). *Teaching Suggestion: Take students on a 'picture walk' through the story "Little Bear Goes to the Moon." Identify important events that do not have an illustration and draw illustrations for those events.*	
Standard 8	(Not applicable to literature)	
Standard 9	With prompting and support, compare and contrast the adventures and experiences of characters in familiar stories. *Teaching Suggestion: Use the book Moon Cake by Frank Asch (2014) to make these comparisons. Both books involve birthday events and the moon, but the content is very different.*	

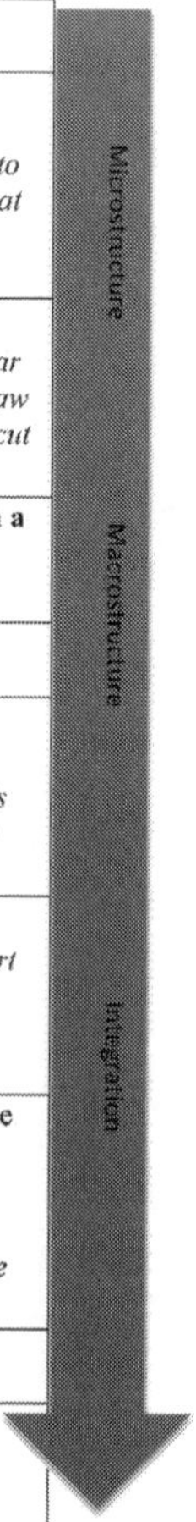

Figure 4.6 CI Theory Grounded Lesson Suggestions Using the Story "Little Bear Goes to the Moon"

delve more deeply into higher levels of the CI model: *Understanding Craft and Structure of this story* (CI Model Step 3) and *Integrating of Knowledge and Ideas from this story into their world knowledge* (CI Model Steps 4 and 5). Ms. Hicks will teach additional lessons based on the CI model with this story to build students' capacity to employ other evidence-based comprehension strategies and engage in higher-level discussions. Over time, these first-grade students will develop the capacity and propensity to employ a set of evidence-based comprehension strategies to process stories at multiple levels of the text comprehension processes described in the CI model. Figure 4.6 provides suggestions for CI model based reading comprehension lessons using the story "Little Bear Goes to the Moon" for addressing the CCSS ELA/Literacy Reading Anchor Standards for Literature #1-9 at the first-grade level (the bolded lesson is Sample Lesson #1).

PEDAGOGICAL IMPLICATIONS: USING CI THEORY AS A LENS FOR TEACHING THE CCSS INFORMATIONAL TEXT STANDARDS

Step 1: Selecting an Appropriately Complex Text. Mrs. Evets has selected an informational book *Lions and Tigers* (Brockman, 1986) to use in a comprehension lesson for a group of her second-grade students. Mrs. Evets considered four criteria in order to select a text at the appropriate level of complexity and within the appropriate grade band range. First, Mrs. Evets selected an informational text she thought might be of great interest to her students—an animal text. Learning about the different animals is fascinating for students of the age. Students have had a range of experience with lions and tigers discussed in the text. This book also supports the teaching of scientific concepts. Thus, the chosen topic lends itself well to multiple close readings. The use of photographs along with rich descriptions of the animals—lions and tigers—further enhances student interest. Second, Mrs. Evets employed the "Goldilocks principle" to select a text with a Lexile score in the range of 420L–820L. Because this book does not have a Lexile estimate, Mrs. Evets types the text of the book into the Lexile.com Analyzer. The results estimate the Lexile level of this particular text to be 660L, placing this book at the midpoint of the second-grade Lexile level "stretch" bandwidth suggested by the CCSS. Third, the book selected is from the information text genre. It lends itself well to teaching scientific concepts and it aligns with the comprehension standards for teaching information text. Finally, the qualitative aspects provided in this particular text include photographs and a descriptive text structure.

Step 2: Planning Comprehension Instruction to Construct a Macrostructure of an Informational Text. Mrs. Evets selected the information text *Lions and Tiger* for the purpose of helping these young children develop the reading comprehension skills as outlined in the second-grade CCSS for reading Informational Text as listed under the Standards Cluster #2: *Craft and Structure*. Mrs. Evet's lesson centers on anchor standard 5: *Know and use various text features (e.g. headings, tables of contents, glossaries, electronic menus, icons) to locate key facts or information in a text*. She selects two comprehension strategies to support this standard: *using text features to locate information* and *summarize* information presented in the text.

As students are guided to read the book *Lions and Tigers*, they are exposed to information about cat families, hunting habits, gender differences, adults and babies, and maturation. Making students aware of how authors organize information in text can help reveal to students the overall structure, which can in turn strengthen their comprehension. Mrs. Evets points out that this information text is not broken up into different sections so that it makes it more difficult for the reader to locate information. Being able to find information quickly and easily becomes more important as students begin to read longer and more complicated texts. Mrs. Evets talks about how authors often use headings and subheadings to point out the location of information within a text. Using various sized post it notes, Mrs. Evets invites her students to supply headings and subheadings in this information book to signal location of specific types of information about these large cats. Mrs. Evets then provides students with a blank graphic organizer and shows students how to place information located in headings and subheadings in circles around a central circle noting the topic of the book, Lions and Tigers. With this guided activity, Mrs. Evets enables her students to construct a coherent mental model or an overall picture of *Lions and Tigers* at a global level, called a *macrostructure*. This will enable students to recognize hierarchical relationships among various key ideas in text as they construct the organizational pattern in the graphic organizer. Authors employ a variety of text features to support the reader and standard 5 under the Anchor Standard 2: Craft and Structure provides an opportunity for the teacher to focus on and teach students about each of these text features used by authors to organize information. Attending to the different types of text features to support students in building an overall global structure or *macrostructure*. Without text features, readers must impose their own structure. Failure to identify or impose a structure on informational texts may cause students to learn and remember only unrelated lists of information, fragmented bits and pieces of information.

Using the lesson in figure 4.7 designed by Mrs. Evets, teachers can assist students to construct a *macrostructure* of the *Lions and Tigers* information text. Explicit instruction provides a great instructional framework where

CCSS Anchor Standard: Craft and Structure #5 (Second Grade) – *Know and use various text features to locate key facts or information in a text.* (This lesson will focus on identifying and recording text structure – descriptive text structure).

Materials: Copies of *Lions and Tigers* (Brockman, 1986) for teacher/each student, chart paper, marker

Lesson Objective/Explanation: *Today we will be learning how authors organize information so we can find and read it more easily. Learning to identify how books are organized can help you remember and understand the information the author is trying to tell you.*

Teacher Modeling: (Take a picture walk through the book *Lions and Tigers* and model for students to 'think aloud' about the contents of information shared on the page.) *On this page, I can see the author is telling me about the Lions and what they eat. I'm going to write the word 'hunt other animals and meat eater' on my chart and summarize the information I learned from this page. Oh look, now on the next two pages there is information about Lion family groups. Before I read on, I am going to picture in my what a Lion family or pride is. I'm going to write the word pride on my chart below the words 'Lion families.'* (Explain to students how information is organized on each page and that the author has done little to help the reader keep track of all of this information. Turn to the first two pages of the book and talk about what kind of a heading might be useful on this page. Help students to understand this first page was all about what lions eat. Make a sticky note heading – *Meat Eaters.* Create a "descriptive text structure" graphic organizer with Lions and Tigers in the center circle and arrays projecting out from the center circle to other circles: Lions and Tigers. Under each of these two circles create a list of facts about lions and tigers. The first fact under lions in this list is – *meat eater.*

Guided Practice (Scaffolding):

Now I am ready to have you help me. Let's look at the next two pages to see what the author is going to tell us about next about lions. Help students to understand this second two pages was all about lion family groups called prides. Make a sticky note heading and place it in the book – *Prides.*

Teacher records the word, 'pride' in the text structure graphic organizer under the circle - lions. Invite another student to read the next two pages. *Ask, can you see how the author is failing to help the reader by not providing organizing information like headings to make information easy to locate? What heading would we put on these next two pages?* Let children talk amongst themselves. Guide them to the heading of "King of Beasts." Put this on a sticky note in the book and record *King of Beasts* in the graphic organizer list of fact under the lion circle.

Independent Practice (Gradual Release): *You are now ready to try this on your own.* (Instruct the students to read the next two pages and to create a sticky note heading as well as put the new heading into the text structure graphic organizer list of facts about lions. Continue this process with facts about tigers.

Assessment: (Explain to the students that together you have read the book, learned how to use a make headings for books that do not have them to help readers locate and organize information. Have them study the graphic organizer and talk about how organizing information like this helps them to remember and store this information better in their brains. If time permits, have students close their eyes and picture the graphic organizer. Pair them up, and have them tell a partner three facts they learned from reading the book – *Lions and Tigers.*

Figure 4.7 Informational Book CI Model Macrostructure Lesson

teachers model, scaffold, and support the construction of their students' macrostructure (text understandings drawn from text features, structure, and literary devices). Research has shown that explicit instruction, modeling, and discussion to teach text structure and text features utilized in information texts

	"Lions and Tiger" by Alfred Brockman (1986) Second Grade
	Key Ideas and Details
Standard 1	Ask and answer questions about key details in text. *Teaching Suggestion: Spend time asking and answering questions with students after reading text. Some questions to consider: What do lions and tigers eat? What is the male and female lion and tiger called? How are lions and tigers alike?*
Standard 2	Identify the main topic and retell key details. *Teaching Suggestion: Use the title to determine main topic. Use each page to identify key details: habitat, adult vs. baby animals, female and male animals, family groups, tigress, etc.*
Standard 3	Describe the connection between two ideas or pieces of information. *Teaching Suggestion: Both lions and tigers are big cats. How are they alike/different?*
	Craft and Structure
Standard 4	Ask and answer questions to help determine or clarify the meaning of words and phrases. *Teaching Suggestion: Have discussions and ask and answer questions about the following words or phrases in text: king of beasts, mane, pride, cubs, Indian tiger, etc.*
Standard 5	**Know the various text features needed to key facts and information. *Teaching Suggestion: See explicit lesson p. x.***
Standard 6	Distinguish between information provided in pictures and those provided in text. *Teaching Suggestion: Do a picture walk with students and go through the book discussing with students the information that is shared through the photographs. Discuss how text enhances our understanding and provides information of topic. Discuss how photos reinforce the information the author is trying to share.*
	Integration of Knowledge and Ideas
Standard 7	Use the illustrations and details in a text to describe key ideas. *Teaching Suggestion: Do another close reading of the text asking students to pay attention this time to the photographs. Ask students to examine the photographs provided and discuss how these share additional information with the reader.*
Standard 8	Identify the reasons an author gives to support points in a text. *Teaching Suggestion: Read p. 21-22 with students and discuss how all tigers do not look the same.*
Standard 9	Identify basic similarities in and differences between two texts on same topic. *Teaching Suggestion: Use the book entitled "Who would win? Lion vs. Tiger" by Jerry Pollotta to make these comparisons between the two books. Similarities: photographs instead of illustrations used, both books discuss lions and tigers. Differences: Different facts about lions and tigers are introduced in these two books.*

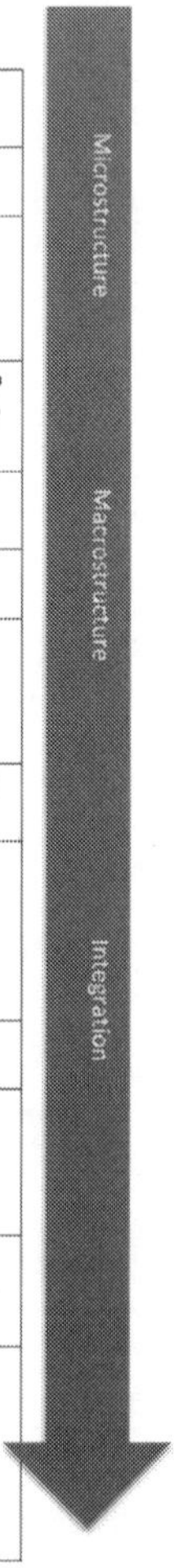

Microstructure
Macrostructure
Integration

Figure 4.8 CI Theory Grounded Lesson Suggestions Using the Informational Book "Lions and Tigers"

is quite effective (Cunningham & Allington, 1999; Pearson & Duke, 2002; Pearson & Fielding, 1994; Williams et al., 2004).

After teaching this particular lesson, Mrs. Evets will need to design other lessons that will continue to support her students in leWarning to construct a macrostructure of text. Teaching other *craft and structure standards* (anchor standards 4-6) will require additional close readings of the text with each close reading employing a lesson emphasizing a different level of the CI text comprehension process, different anchor standards for reading informational text, and selecting a new set of comprehension strategies to complement the comprehension process levels and new standards. Additionally, Mrs. Evets will need to teach more lessons that will require multiple close readings of the book *Lions and Tiger* with an emphasis this time on integrating the complex combination of the ideas represented in the *textbase* and the ideas created within the student's network of world and experiential background knowledge to form a situation model of the text as described in the CI model of text comprehension.

Finally, Mrs. Evets will teach additional lessons using the *Lions and Tigers* information text so as to complete the integration process. The integration process requires the reader to consciously integrate the contents of their situation model of the text held in working memory into their world knowledge network stored in long-term memory. What this means is that students with conscious, effortful linking of known world knowledge about these two types of big cats (stored in long-term memory) with new knowledge about these big cats from the *Lions and Tigers* text (held in working memory) is necessary for younger, less proficient readers—and even some more accomplished readers—to transfer the contents of a situation model into their world knowledge network stored in long-term memory. See figure 4.8 for lesson suggestions that correlate with each stage of Kintsch's *Construction-Integration Model of Text Comprehension*. All of these lesson suggestions are useful for implementation during multiple close readings of the book *Lions and Tigers* to support students' acquisition of multiple levels of comprehension processing as described in the CI model (see figure 4.8).

SUMMARY

Teaching the CCSS literature and informational text reading standards through the lens of Kintsch's *Construction-Integration Model of Text Comprehension* (Kintsch, 2013) helps teachers "to analyze texts in meaningful ways" recognizing the multiple levels of text processing in which students must engage successfully in order to comprehend a text well enough to increase their store of world knowledge (Kucan, Hapgood, & Palincsar, 2011, p. 76). Grounding comprehension instruction in a strong theoretical framework like that offered by Kintsch (2013) helps teachers to more fully understand the comprehension possibilities and problems that complex texts present their students. Knowing how to effectively analyze texts for comprehension obstacles and affordances helps teachers to formulate comprehension lessons that address the multiple levels of text processing their students need to accomplish and link appropriate CCSS reading standards to support them as they construct and integrate knowledge from the texts they read.

REFERENCES

Asch, F. (2014). *Mooncake.* New York, NY: Aladdin.

Brockman, P. (1986). *Lions and Tigers: An animal fact Book.* Mahwah, NJ: Watermill Press.

Calfee, R. (2009). Foreword. In S. E. Israel & G. G. Duffy (Eds.), *Handbook of research on reading Comprehension* (pp. xi–xv). New York, NY: Routledge.

Clyne, M., & Griffiths, R. (2005). *Sand.* Parsippany, NJ: Celebration Press – Pearson Education Group.

Cunningham, P. M., & Allington, R. L. (1999). *Classrooms that work: They can All Read and Write.* New York: Longman.

Dewitz, P., Jones, J., & Leahy, S. (2009). Comprehension strategy instruction in core reading programs. *Reading Research Quarterly, 44*(2), 102–26.

Duke, N. K., Halladay, J. L., & Roberts, K. L. (2013). Reading standards for informational text. In L. M. Morrow, T. Shanahan, & K. K. Wixson (Eds.), *Teaching with the Common Core Standards for English Language Arts, PreK–2* (pp. 46–66). New York: Guilford Press.

Duke, N. K., Pearson, P. D., Strachan, S. L., & Billman, A. K. (2011). Essential elements of fostering and teaching reading comprehension. In S. J. Samuels and A. E. Farstrup (Eds.), *What research has to say about reading instruction*, 4th ed. (pp. 51–93). Newark, DE: International Reading Association.

Durkin, D. (1993). *Teaching them to read, 6th edition.* Boston, MA: Allyn & Bacon.

Fielding, L., Kerr, N., & Rosier, P. (1998). *The 90% reading goal: 90% of our students will read at or above grade level by the end of third grade.* Kennewick, WA: New Foundation Press.

Graesser, A. C. (2007). An introduction to strategic reading comprehension. In D. S. McNamara (Ed.), *Reading comprehension strategies: Theories, interventions, & technologies* (pp. 3–26). New York, NY: Lawrence Erlbaum Associates.

Israel, S. E., & Duffy, G. G. (2009). *Handbook of research on reading comprehension.* New York, NY: Routledge.

Keene, E. O., & Zimmerman, S. (2013). Years later, comprehension strategies still at work. *The Reading Teacher, 66*(8), 601–06.

Kintsch, W. (2013). Revisiting the construction-integration model of text comprehension and its implications for instruction. In D. E. Alvermann, N. J. Unrau, and R. B. Ruddell (Eds.), *Theoretical models and processes of reading, 6th edition* (pp. 807–39). Newark, DE: International Reading Association.

Kintsch, W., & Kintsch, E. (2005). Comprehension. In S. G. Paris & S. A. Stahl (Eds.), *Children's reading comprehension and assessment* (pp. 71–104). Mahwah, NJ: Lawrence Erlbaum Associates.

Kucan, L. (2009). Engaging teachers in investigating their teaching as a linguistic enterprise: The case of comprehension instruction in the context of discussion. *Reading Psychology, 30*(1), 51–87.

Kucan, L., Hapgood, S., & Palincsar, A. S. (2011). Teachers' specialized knowledge for supporting student comprehension in text-based discussions. *The Elementary School Journal, 112*(1), 61–82.

Minarik, E. H. (1957). *Little Bear*. New York: HarperCollins.

National Institute for Literacy. (2008). *Developing early literacy: Report of the National Early Literacy Panel.* Jessup, MD: ED Publications.

National Institute of Child Health and Human Development. (2000). *Teaching children to read: An evidence-based assessment of the scientific research literature on reading and its implications for reading instruction* (NIH Publication No. 00-4769O). Washington, DC: U.S. Government Printing Office.

Pearson, P. D., & Duke, N. (2002). Comprehension instruction in the primary grades. In C. C. Block & M. Pressley (Eds.), *Comprehension Instruction: Research-based Best Practices* (pp. 247–58). New York: Guilford Press.

Pearson, P. D., & Fielding, L. G. (1994). Synthesis of research/reading comprehension: What works. *Educational Leadership, 51*(4), 62–68.

Pearson, P. D. (1974). Effects of grammatical complexity on children's comprehension, recall, and conception of certain semantic relations. *Reading Research Quarterly, 10(2)*, 155–92.

Perfetti, C., & Stafura, J. (2014). Word knowledge in a theory of reading comprehension. *Scientific Studies of Reading, 18*(1), 22–37.

Pollotta, J. (2016). *Who would Win? Lion vs. Tiger.* New York, NY: Scholastic, Inc.

Pressley, M. (2002). Improving comprehension instruction: A path for the future. In C. Collins-Block, L. B. Gambrell, & M. Pressley (Eds.), *Improving comprehension instruction: Rethinking research, theory, and classroom practice* (pp. 385–400). San Francisco, CA: Jossey-Bass.

Reutzel, D. R., Clark, S. K., Jones, C. D., & Kumar, T. (2016). The *Informational Text Structure Survey* (ITS^2): An Exploration of Primary Grade Teachers' Sensitivity to Text Structure in Young Children's Informational Texts. *Journal of Educational Research, 109 (1),* 81-98 .

Reutzel, D. R., Clark, S. K., Jones, C. D., & Gillam, S. L. (2016). *Young meaning makers: Teaching comprehension, grades K–2.* New York, NY: Teachers College Press.

Shanahan, T., Callison, K., Carriere, C., Duke, N. K., Pearson, P. D., Schatschnieder, C., & Torgesen, J. (2010). *Improving Reading Comprehension in Kindergarten through 3rd Grade: A Practice Guide* (NCEE 2010-4038). Washington, DC: National Center for Education Evaluation and Regional Assistance, Institute of Education Sciences, U. S. Department of Education. Retrieved from: http://ies.ed.gov/ncee.

Snow, C. E., Burns, M. N., & Griffin, P. (1998). *Preventing reading difficulties in young children.* Washington, DC: National Academy Press.

Williams, J. P., Hall, K. H., & Lauer, K. D. (2004). Teaching expository text structure to young at-risk learners: Building the basics of comprehension instruction. *Exceptionality*, *12*(3), 129–44. doi:10.1207/s15327035ex1203.

FURTHER READINGS

Duke, N. K., Pearson, P. D., Strachan, S. L., & Billman, A. K. (2011). Essential elements of fostering and teaching reading comprehension. In S. J. Samuels & A.

E. Farstrup (Eds.), *What research has to say about reading instruction*, 4th ed. (pp. 51–93). Newark, DE: International Reading Association.

Kintsch, W. (2013). Revisiting the construction-integration model of text comprehension and its implications for instruction. In D. E. Alvermann, N. J. Unrau, and R. B. Ruddell (Eds.), *Theoretical models and processes of reading, 6th Edition* (pp. 807–39). Newark, DE: International Reading Association.

Reutzel, D. R., Clark, S. K., Jones, C. D., & Gillam, S. L. (2016). *Young meaning makers: Teaching comprehension, Grades K–2*. New York, NY: Teachers College Press.

Chapter 5

Improving Metacomprehension with the Situation-Model Approach

Jennifer Wiley, Thomas D. Griffin, and Keith W. Thiede

ABSTRACT

Over the past fifteen years, research on improving students' monitoring of their own understanding while learning from text (*metacomprehension accuracy*) has led to the development of a theoretical framework called the *situation-model approach*. This approach has been motivated by the role that the situation model plays in comprehension, as well as the roles that online monitoring and the use of experience-based cues play in effective self-regulated study and learning. This work has elucidated how giving students a clear understanding of what it means to comprehend expository science text may be critical for effective self-regulation of study.

FRAMING THE ISSUE

Poor metacomprehension accuracy (i.e., the inability to judge one's own level of understanding from text) is a pervasive problem in the majority of college students (Baker, 1989; Pressley, 2002). Few students come to college equipped with the monitoring skills they need to engage in maximally effective self-regulated study behaviors that will in turn enable them to effectively comprehend and learn from expository texts (Ley & Young, 1998; Wandersee, 1998; Zimmerman, 2002). Many empirical studies have demonstrated that college students are quite poor at gauging how well they have understood what they have just read (Dunlosky & Lipko, 2007; Dunlosky & Metcalfe, 2009; Maki, 1998; Otero & Campanario, 1990; Thiede, Griffin, Wiley & Redford, 2009). The generally poor metacomprehension skills seen in most college students are unsurprising given the near total lack of attention given to developing these skills at any level of instruction in the United States. Yet, success in college depends to a considerable degree upon students' ability to engage in strategic reading of informational or expository texts. Simpson and Nist (2000) reported that 85 percent of college learning requires careful reading. Text is the primary source of information and students are required to study texts on their own. Despite the fact that the purpose and demands of reading in college are different from those in high school (Orlando et al., 1989), this is rarely made explicit to students, nor are they taught how to deal with the change in expectations.

To the extent that students do receive instruction, one approach to improving the study skills required for college-level reading is to provide guidance in strategic reading (Baker & Brown, 1984; Paris & Jacobs, 1984; Paris & Winograd, 1990, Pearson & Dole, 1987; Pressley & Afflerbach, 1995) which generally involves providing students with the knowledge of strategies they may use in the face of comprehension failures, particularly when reading to learn from expository science texts. This approach is based on observations that less skilled students fail to use effective reading strategies, and are limited in their knowledge of available strategies (Alexander & Murphy, 1998; Pressley, Yokoi, Van Meter, Van Etten, & Freebern, 1997). Work from this tradition has shown that that self-report inventories of study strategies and direct instruction on such strategies both predict text comprehension (Caverly, Nicholson, & Radcliffe, 2004; Mokhtari & Reichard, 2002; Moore, Zabrucky, & Commander, 1997; Pintrich, Wolters, & Baxter, 2000; Pressley, 2002; Schraw & Dennison, 1994; Zimmerman, 2002). However, while instruction emphasizing strategy knowledge can add tools to a reader's arsenal, strategy instruction alone is unlikely to maximize self-regulated learning (SRL) outcomes.

Instead, *accurate monitoring* of progress during ongoing learning episodes seems to be a critical ingredient for effective SRL (Flavell, 1979; Winne & Hadwin, 1998; Winne & Perry, 2000). Many models of effective SRL presume that accurate monitoring of ongoing learning is what allows for online regulation of cognitive processes during study (e.g., Griffin, Wiley & Salas, 2013; Metcalfe, 2009; Nelson & Narens, 1990; Thiede & Dunlosky, 1999; Thiede et al., 2009; Winne & Hadwin, 1998; Zimmerman, 2002). As such, accurate metacognitive monitoring is the gatekeeper for effective regulation of study (Winne & Perry, 2000), and correspondingly, comprehension monitoring accuracy has been demonstrated to relate positively to self-regulated learning outcomes from text (de Bruin, Thiede, Camp, & Redford, 2011; Griffin, Wiley, & Thiede, 2013; Thiede, Anderson, & Therriault, 2003; Thomas & McDaniel, 2007). The central premise that underlies the connection between monitoring and SRL, is that if a person does not accurately differentiate well-learned material from less learned material, he or she could waste time studying material that has already been mastered, or worse, could fail to restudy material that has not been adequately learned. Thus, improving metacomprehension accuracy can be seen as pivotal for effective SRL from text.

Pioneering studies by Maki and Berry (1984) and Glenberg and Epstein (1985) provided an early blueprint for the typical metacomprehension paradigm that is used to measure students' accuracy at monitoring of their own understanding to the present day. Participants are asked to study a set of passages, judge their comprehension for each, and then take a test of comprehension for each passage. In this paradigm, accuracy is operationalized as the intra-individual correlation between a person's comprehension ratings and his or her test performances; thus, greater comprehension monitoring accuracy is indexed by stronger positive correlations between predictive judgments and actual test scores. A standard term for this index is *relative metacomprehension accuracy* (Maki, 1998). This basic paradigm provides a good model for the actual SRL that students need to engage in on a daily basis, as students routinely have to complete assignments for multiple classes simultaneously, and they need regulate how much effort to devote to each topic.

MAKING THE CASE

Many years of research using this basic metacomprehension paradigm has demonstrated that typical levels of *relative metacomprehension accuracy* are quite low. For instance, Glenberg, Sanocki, Epstein, and Morris (1987) concluded, "Data from our laboratory has almost uniformly demonstrated poor calibration" (p. 120). Likewise, Maki (1998) reported that the mean intra-individual correlation between comprehension ratings and test performance across twenty-five studies from her lab was only .27. An analysis by Dunlosky across his lab's studies arrived at the same exact figure (Dunlosky & Lipko, 2007). Other reviews by Lin and Zabrucky (1998) and Weaver, Bryant, and Burns (1995) reached similar conclusions. In 2009, Thiede et al. completed a review of all published studies of relative metacomprehension accuracy that had been done in the previous thirty years, and also arrived at an average of $r = 0.27$ for the baseline conditions. Metacomprehension accuracy can be especially poor in less skilled, less able, or younger readers. An initial study in Griffin, et al. (2008) found that comprehension skill strongly predicted metacomprehension accuracy, with poorer comprehenders showing an inability to discriminate texts they understood well from those they understood poorly. A second study in Griffin, Wiley, and Thiede (2008) showed that proficient college readers with lower working memory capacity (WMC) also had poorer metacomprehension accuracy. Thiede, Griffin, Wiley, and Anderson (2010; Experiment 1) found that at-risk college readers had lower average metacomprehension accuracy than more proficient readers. Similarly, comprehension monitoring accuracy in younger readers (i.e., students in seventh and eighth grade) is so poor that sometimes it is observed to be negative (meaning that many younger students report understanding texts that they understood the least as texts that they understood the most; de Bruin et al.; Redford, Thiede, Wiley, & Griffin, 2011; Thiede, Redford, Wiley, & Griffin, 2012).

A prevailing explanation for inaccurate monitoring is that students typically use invalid cues to predict their comprehension. For example, the at-risk readers in Thiede et al. (2010) were found to rely more heavily on cues that were not tied to their representation of the text (such as the length of texts, or personal interest in the topic) when making their judgments of learning. Koriat's (1997) influential cue-utilization framework asserts that learners infer their level of learning and gauge likely future performance based upon two general types of cues: those tied to one's subjective experiences during learning and those tied to *a priori* assumptions about the task, materials, topic, one's abilities, or the presumed general effectiveness of the study strategies one has employed. Griffin, Jee, & Wiley (2009) mapped these cue types onto Flavell's (1979) distinction between meta-experiences and meta-knowledge, noting that the latter represents a heuristic route to deriving judgments of understanding, while the former are the cues that must be monitored during a learning episode. These *experience-based cues* more directly reflect the level of learning that has actually occurred and the quality of the mental representation one has constructed. It is upon these cues that accurate monitoring and effective ongoing regulation both depend.

However, not all experience-based cues are equally valid indicators of comprehension. Some cues reflect only surface memory or episodic memory for text, while other cues better reflect one's understanding of the concepts from the text, their relation to each other and to prior topic knowledge (Maki & Serra, 1992; Rawson, Dunlosky, & Thiede, 2000; Wiley, Griffin, & Thiede, 2005). Experience-based cues can be mapped onto the different levels of text-representation specified in the construction-integration model of text comprehension (Kintsch, 1998). In this model, text is concurrently represented at multiple levels including a lexical or surface level, a textbase level, and a situation model. The lexical level, containing the surface features of the text, is constructed as the words and phrases appearing in the text are encoded. The textbase level is constructed as segments of the surface text are parsed into propositions, and as links between text propositions are formed based on argument overlap. The construction of the situation model also involves linking propositions. However, the integration of propositions here involves connecting text information with the reader's prior knowledge (McNamara, Kintsch, Songer, & Kintsch, 1996) and making causal connections or inferences (Graesser & Bertus, 1998; Millis & Graesser, 1994; Trabasso & van den Broek, 1985; Wiley & Myers, 2003; Wiley & Voss, 1999). It is a person's situation-model that largely determines his or her performance on tests of comprehension (Kintsch, 1994; McNamara et al., 1996; Wiley, et al., 2005). Thus, it is experience-based cues related to the quality of one's situation model that are the most valid basis for making judgments of comprehension. The *situation-model approach* to metacomprehension recognizes the central role of valid cue use for accurate monitoring (Griffin et al.

Table 5.1 Relative Metacomprehension Accuracy by Instruction Condition across Studies.

Instructional Condition and Data Source	*Comparison*	*Instruction*
Delayed Keyword		
Thiede et al., 2003	0.38	0.70
Thiede et al., 2005, Exp 1	0.29	0.52
Thiede et al., 2005, Exp 2	0.16	0.55
Shiu and Chen, 2013	0.14	0.56
Delayed Summary		
Thiede and Anderson, 2003, Exp 1	0.28	0.60
Thiede and Anderson, 2003, Exp 2	0.28	0.61
Anderson and Thiede, 2008	0.20	0.64
Thiede et al., 2010, Exp 1	0.21	0.63
Concept Mapping while Reading		
Thiede et al., 2010, Exp 2	0.30	0.67
Self-Explanation during Re-reading		
Griffin et al., 2009, Exp 2	0.22	0.67
Self-Explanation from Diagrams		
Jaeger and Wiley, 2014	0.26	0.43
Test Expectancy		
Thiede et al., 2011	0.24	0.61
Wiley et al., 2008	0.15	0.43
Test Expectancy and Self-Explanation		
Wiley et al., 2008	0.15	0.56
Concept Mapping with Instruction (7th grade)		
Redford et al., 2011	−0.24	0.34
Delayed Keywords (7th grade)		
de Bruin et al., 2011	−0.02	0.27
Comprehension-based Curriculum (7th, 8th grade)		
Thiede et al., 2012, Exp 1	−0.26	0.43
Curriculum and Delayed Keyword (7th, 8th grade)		
Thiede et al., 2012, Exp 2	0.10	0.65
Delayed Diagram Completion (9th grade)		
van Loon et al., 2014	0.07	0.56

2009; Koriat, 1997; Rawson & Dunlosky, 2002) as well as the central role of the situation model in determining the validity of cues when engaged in learning from text (Kintsch, 1994; Rawson et al. 2000; Wiley et al. 2005). Work emanating from this approach has explored a number of conditions that may allow readers to use more valid cues when judging their own comprehension. As shown in table 5.1, there are now several studies that have been able to show a variety of contexts that can lead to sizable improvements in metacomprehension accuracy. These contexts can be classed into a few types (delayed generation tasks, generating explanations or concept maps while reading, and giving students a clear understanding of what it means to comprehend expository science text), and the benefits of each instructional approach are elaborated in the next section.

Pedagogical Implications

Benefits from Delayed Generation Tasks. Several studies have shown that activities that make the cues related to the situation model more *accessible* to students can improve their metacomprehension accuracy: Delayed Keyword Generation Tasks, Delayed Summarization Tasks, and engaging in explanation during reading. For example, in Thiede and Anderson (2003), accuracy was higher for students who wrote summaries of assigned readings after a delay, and then judged their performance, than for groups who either wrote a summary immediately after reading or wrote no summaries. Similarly, Thiede et al. (2003) showed that a delayed generation task, where students were asked to list keywords that captured the gist of assigned readings, also improved relative metacomprehension accuracy over a no-keyword-generation condition.

Why do delayed generation tasks improve relative metacomprehension accuracy? First, generating a summary or keywords may allow a reader to reflect on how successfully he or she is able to retrieve information during generation (cf. the modified feedback hypothesis described by Glenberg et al., 1987). Accordingly, a text may receive a high rating of comprehension if the person is able to retrieve a great deal of information about the text during generation; whereas, a text may receive a low rating of comprehension if the person struggles to retrieve information about the text. Second, the timing of the generation task is critical. Kintsch, Welsch, Schmalhofer, and Zimny (1990) showed that surface memory for text decays over time, whereas the situation model is robust to such decay. Thus, when writing a summary immediately after reading, a person may have easy access to their surface model (or episodic memory for the text) and can use this information to generate a summary. However, using this experience as a basis for a judgment of comprehension fails to improve accuracy because the performance on the immediate summary task and the later comprehension test are determined by different levels of representation. In contrast, when writing a summary after a delay, the findings by Kintsch et al. suggest that a person will likely have relatively greater access to the situation model of a text. Thus, using the experience of writing a summary after a delay as a basis of a judgment of comprehension improves accuracy because performance in both the delayed summary task and performance on the comprehension test are both based on the situation model. Thiede, Dunlosky, Griffin, and Wiley (2005) provided a test of this explanation for delayed generation effects by independently varying several different features of generation tasks. Consistent with the situation model approach, the critical feature for improving metacomprehension accuracy was a delay between reading and generation, because only this delay causes readers to have relatively greater access their situation models at the time of judgment. (Manipulation of other delays helped to rule out a Transfer Appropriate Processing explanation, as they did not improve accuracy.)

Delayed generation effects have been replicated several times across a number of studies (Anderson & Thiede, 2008; de Bruin et al., 2011; Lauterman & Ackerman, 2014; Shiu & Chen, 2013; Thiede & Anderson, 2003; Thiede et al., 2003, 2005, 2010, 2012). Delayed completion of diagrams can also result in improvements in metacomprehension accuracy (van Loon, de Bruin, van Gog, van Merrienboer, & Dunlosky, 2014).

Benefits from Explanation Tasks. While keyword and summary generation activities may need to be done at a delay to improve accuracy, other studies have explored the benefits of explanation-based activities that students can engage in during or immediately after reading. For example, prompting students to engage in self-explanation is intended to encourage access to situation-model cues during monitoring more directly. Based on previous work showing how explanation can help promote comprehension processes (Chi, 2000; Davey & McBride, 1986; King, 1994; McNamara, 2004), attempting to self-explain during reading should generate meta-experiences such as a subjective sense of how hard it is to generate an explanation, or how coherent an explanation seems, and this should in turn improve relative accuracy. To test this, Griffin et al. (2008) randomly assigned participants to one of three groups. One group read texts and then self-explained the connections between parts of each text as they read them a second time. Another group read the texts twice and a third group just read the texts once. The group that had attempted to explain connections to themselves experienced significantly better metacomprehension than the other groups. Similar benefits were seen by Jaeger and Wiley (2014) when readers were instructed to self-explain from illustrated texts.

Similarly, studies have begun exploring the use concept maps as learning activities and artifacts that might help to improve the metacomprehension accuracy of students with less advanced reading skills. Concept maps may help readers deal with the competing demands of reading and monitoring. Since the text is available during the activity, and the activity creates a visual representation of the situation model, concept mapping tasks may be especially appropriate for students who have limited processing resources (Stensvold & Wilson, 1990). Indeed, in a review of the literature, Nesbit and Adesope (2006) concluded that concept mapping tasks were the most effective activities for improving learning from text for younger, less skilled, or at-risk readers. In addition, constructing concept maps should help readers to have access to valid comprehension cues. Weinstein and Mayer (1986) suggested that instructing students to create concept maps of texts during reading helps them to identify the connections among concepts, which improves comprehension. From this perspective, concept mapping is similar to self-explanation, as both tasks should help readers to construct and pay attention to the underlying causal models of the subject matter. This can improve comprehension monitoring accuracy especially if readers are prompted to attend to causal connections when making their diagrams.

Thiede et al. (2010, Experiment 2) tested the effectiveness of a set of concept mapping activities using a within-subjects design where baseline relative metacomprehension accuracy was obtained by running participants through the standard paradigm. That is, students read a series of texts, judged their comprehension of each text, and then completed a comprehension test for each text. Participants, who were college students enrolled in a remedial reading course, then received extensive concept mapping instruction that included lessons on how to construct causal concept maps from short scientific texts. Then, the students completed the standard metacomprehension paradigm again, but this time they constructed concept maps while reading the texts. This improved both comprehension and relative metacomprehension accuracy. However, in another study with seventh graders, simply prompting students to generate concept maps did not lead to improvements in metacomprehension accuracy (Redford et al. 2011). Improvements were only found when readers were shown a good example concept map and were given explicit instruction in how to create and use concept maps for answering comprehension questions.

Benefits from Understanding What It Means to Comprehend a Text. Another set of studies has explored contexts that may help readers to *select* the most valid cues for comprehension monitoring from among those that are available, for example by giving students the expectancy that their comprehension will be assessed with inference tests rather than memory tests. This work takes as its starting point the premise that students need to understand what it means to "comprehend" an expository text in order to be able to monitor their own comprehension (Wiley, Griffin, & Thiede, 2008). Without specific instructions about what comprehension entails, what their goals for reading should be, and what comprehension tests will be like, students may evaluate their learning and make study choices based on memory cues instead of comprehension cues, and may read an expository text passively, or with the goal of trying to remember it, rather than trying to understand what it is saying.

Reading passively, or trying to store the exact ideas from a text into memory, may be the way students may generally approach reading for their classes. Reading with a goal of memorization is of course better than reading passively, and it can be an effective strategy if future tests ask for specific terms, details, or ideas directly stated by the text. Further, this behavior is certainly important for some subject matter and learning contexts. However, if tests require students to gain conceptual understanding, for example of scientific processes and phenomena from expository text, then it is important to prompt students to override the "passive reading" or "reading for memory" settings. Readers need to appreciate that their goal for reading is to try to understand how or why a phenomenon or process occurs, and that the questions they will be asked will depend on making connections and causal inferences across sentences, so that they can engage in monitoring of the correct behaviors. Instilling this learning goal may be particularly important when readers are tasked with understanding expository science texts.

There is a body of work that has shown how practice test questions can help to improve comprehension, especially when students are encouraged to engage in active processing of the text to answer the questions (c.f. Hinze, Wiley, & Pellegrino, 2013; Jensen, McDaniel, Woodard, & Kummer, 2014). There are now a couple of studies that test the idea that instilling appropriate reading goals and test expectances may be critical for accurate *meta*comprehension as well. One study used graduate students enrolled in a program in Educational Psychology (Thiede, Wiley, & Griffin, 2011). In this study, students were provided with an explicit statement about the nature of comprehension, an explicit statement about the nature of the final test items they should expect, and example inference test items. The manipulation was highly effective in this population. A second series of studies has further tested for this comprehension expectancy effect in first-year freshmen, varying the procedures in several ways to better understand the mechanisms underlying improved monitoring (Wiley, Griffin, & Thiede, 2008). Surprisingly, providing students with just a simple description about what they would be tested on ("memory of specific details for each text" vs. "comprehension and ability to make connections across different parts of the text") greatly impacted metacomprehension accuracy. It was also theoretically interesting that the effect emerged even when the test expectancy instruction was not given until *after* reading (but still before making monitoring judgments). This finding supports a cue-selection explanation rather than one that assumes expectancies may have their effects on monitoring by impacting text processing during reading of the texts, and therefore the benefits could have been attributed purely to improved cue access. Finally, when a self-explanation instruction was combined with comprehension expectancy instruction, the benefits to monitoring accuracy were additive, which supports the theoretical distinction between the two mechanisms (access and selection) as both being necessary for valid cue utilization and effective monitoring.

These instructional conditions have also been applied in a classroom context (Griffin, Wiley, & Thiede, 2013; Wiley, Griffin, Jaeger, Jarosz, Cushen, & Thiede, in press). College students enrolled in an introductory research methods course in Psychology were randomly assigned to receive the combined comprehension test expectancy and self-explanation instructional condition that was found to be effective in laboratory studies versus a no-instruction condition. Not only did students who received the combined test expectancy/self-explanation instruction have higher metacomprehension accuracy, they were also more likely to restudy the texts in a strategic manner (rather than just reread texts in order, or fail to reread texts altogether), and their restudy behavior was more effective in producing learning gains as evidenced by their quiz scores.

Benefits from Long-term Curricular Experiences. It has been argued that one main reason why students may experience poor metacomprehension accuracy is because they need a better understanding of what their goals should be when comprehending expository texts in different content areas. However, if prior instruction has already provided readers with this knowledge, then they should be in a better position to engage in accurate comprehension monitoring. Two recent lines of work suggest that differences in curricula can impact metacomprehension skills.

A cross-cultural study found that Chinese students have better metacomprehension accuracy than American students (Commander, Zhao, Li, Zabrucky, & Agler, 2014). The authors attributed these differences in accuracy to differences in instruction, and noted the lack of metacomprehension training in the United States, and the need to place more emphasis on the training of metacognitive skills (Hall, 2005; Nokes, 2010; Pintrich, 2002). Further, they note that content-area teachers often relegate teaching skills of comprehension and metacomprehension as being a part of "reading instruction" not content instruction (Hall, 2005), and therefore, "not their job." As a result, students in the United States are seldom taught how to learn a subject but, rather, are taught the content of the subject and generally left to figure out *how* to learn by themselves. This neglect continues at the college level, even as the quantity and complexity of information increases. On the other hand, the authors argue that supporting reading competence is a significant part instruction throughout earlier, middle and later grades as well as college in China, and that instruction routinely focuses on the use of comprehension and metacomprehension strategies.

In another study within the United States, Thiede, Redford, Wiley, and Griffin (2012) found that seventh- and eighth-grade students whose early literacy education focused on deep understanding and experience with inference tests were better able to access and select valid cues for judging comprehension, which supported dramatically better metacomprehension accuracy than was found in students coming from a more typical schooling experience. Moreover, superior monitoring accuracy led to better decisions about which texts to restudy, and produced significantly better overall comprehension. A potential explanation for this result is that prior experiences with inference tests, and a better understanding of what comprehension entails, allowed students to use more valid judgment cues when monitoring their own comprehension, and therefore more success at self-regulated study.

A SUMMARY OF IMPLICATIONS FOR INSTRUCTION

Based on the research reviewed above, the situation model approach makes several suggestions for instruction. In addition to encouraging readers to engage in comprehension monitoring, it also is important to help student to use valid cues to judge their own level of comprehension. One way of helping students is to have them participate in activities that make valid cues more *accessible.* A complementary approach is to be clear with students about what their goals for reading should be, and what kinds of test items they might expect, so that they may *select* the correct cues from among those that are available. Further, the more experience they have with comprehension-based activities and tests, the better they may become at judging their understanding from text.

In addition to these general recommendations, it seems likely that cognitive resource limitations of less skilled readers or younger readers will be important to keep in mind. Based on the finding that WMC was a strong predictor of metacomprehension accuracy, Griffin et al. (2008) suggested that students with limited attentional resources may be less able to attend to metacognitive cues while they are also processing a text. Resource limitations force students to rely on heuristic cues rather than on the more valid experience-based cues (Griffin et al. 2009). Thus, it is likely that resource limitations will need to be directly addressed for some populations of at-risk students (low reading skill, low WMC) to achieve accurate monitoring. Although WMC is not particularly malleable, learning activities can be designed to directly circumvent this constraint. Indeed, forcing all students to read each text twice, and self-explain only on the second reading, allowed even low-WMC students to show benefits from a self-explanation instruction (Griffin et al., 2008). Generating concept maps or completing diagrams may be other useful approaches that can help to support less skilled populations.

It also seems likely that many students may need explicit instruction in comprehension so they can better appreciate what it means to construct an understanding from expository text in specific disciplines. It has been argued that discipline-specific considerations for reading are rarely made explicit to students (Yore, Craig, & Maguire, 1998). Reading instruction in early grades is generally confined to the understanding of narrative texts, even though students are expected to eventually read for understanding from expository texts. This mismatch between basic literacy instruction using narratives, and the demands of college-level reading, may be particularly acute for at-risk students (Hall, 2004; Spence, Yore, & Williams, 1999). Thus, more exposure to expository science texts, and more explicit instruction on what it means to build understanding from expository science texts, may be essential for accurate goal setting and regulation of study behaviors. As demonstrated by the Thiede et al. (2012) study, students who have long-term exposure to a reading curriculum that emphasizes deep levels of comprehension throughout early schooling show more advanced comprehension-monitoring skills than students who acquire basic reading skills from a more typical curriculum. Providing more general knowledge about the genre of expository science texts, along with examples of comprehension test items, and articulating how these relate to what it means to comprehend expository text, should increase the likelihood that all students develop a portable set of metacognitive knowledge, skills, and goals to help them monitor their learning more accurately in contexts where there is no researcher or instructor there forcing them to perform particular tasks that happen to lead to more accurate judgements.

Over the past fifteen years, research on *metacomprehension accuracy* has led to the development of a theoretical framework called the *situation-model approach*. This approach has been motivated by the role that the situation-model plays in comprehension, as well as the role that online monitoring and the use of experience-based cues play in effective self-regulated study and learning. This work has led to the discovery of several contexts and conditions that have produced sizable improvements in comprehension monitoring accuracy. Further, this work has elucidated constraints that cognitive resources may impose on effective monitoring, and demonstrated how having an understanding of what it means to comprehend expository science text may be critical for engaging in effective self-regulation of study. The more general message of this work is that students may need explicit instruction and support in "what comprehension means" before they can attain the sophisticated understanding and monitoring skills that are now being emphasized as part of the new Common Core State Standards. With its adoption, research on how we can equip all students with the monitoring skills they need to effectively comprehend and learn from complex expository texts in content areas will become increasingly relevant for practitioners, policy-makers, and other stakeholders.

A final synopsis of the three main points for practitioners is (1) Be sure to telegraph what students are expected to know (i.e., what will be on the test and how it will be tested). This is especially important if the goal of the unit is for students to achieve real comprehension of concepts, and not just memorization of facts or definitions. (2) Be persistent in testing deeper comprehension and emphasizing deeper comprehension as a reading goal. As seen in the cross-cultural study (Commander, Zhao, Li, Zabrucky, & Agler, 2014) and the Thiede et al. (2012) middle school study, there is reason to believe that students with long-term exposure to curricula that stress deeper comprehension develop better comprehension-monitoring skills. (3) Emphasize comprehension and metacomprehension building activities when teaching reading. There are a number of possible activities (explanation, question-asking, concept mapping), and although they have not all been fully investigated yet, having students do things to work toward comprehension (connecting ideas across the parts of texts—and connecting new info with prior knowledge) seems to support both better comprehension and metacomprehension outcomes.

REFERENCES

Alexander, P. A., & Murphy, P. K. (1998). Profiling the differences in students' knowledge, interest, and strategic processing. *Journal of Educational Psychology, 90*, 435–47.

Anderson, M. C. M., & Thiede, K. W. (2008). Why do delayed summaries improve metacomprehension accuracy? *Acta Psychologica, 128*, 110–18.

Baker, L. (1989). Metacognition, comprehension monitoring, and the adult reader. *Educational Psychology Review, 1*, 3–38.

Baker, L., & Brown, A. L. (1984). Metacognitive skills and reading. In P. David Pearson (Ed.), *Handbook of reading research* (pp. 353–394). New York: Longman.

Caverly, D. G., Nicholson, S. A., & Radcliffe, R. (2004). The effectiveness of strategic reading instruction for college developmental readers. *Journal of College Reading and Learning, 35*, 25–46.

Chi, M. T. H. (2000). Self-explaining expository texts: The dual processes of generating inferences and repairing mental models. In R. Glaser (Ed.), *Advances in instructional psychology* (pp. 161–238). Hillsdale, NJ: Lawrence Erlbaum Associates.

Commander, N. E., Zhao, Y., Li, H., Zabrucky, K. M., & Agler, L. M. L. (2014). American and Chinese students' calibration of comprehension and performance. *Current Psychology, 33*, 655–71.

Davey, B., & McBride, S. (1986). Effects of question-generation training on reading comprehension. *Journal of Educational Psychology, 78*, 256–62.

de Bruin, A., Thiede, K. W., Camp, G., & Redford, J. R. (2011). Generating keywords improves metacomprehension and self-regulation in elementary and middle school children. *Journal of Experimental Child Psychology, 109*, 294–310.

Dunlosky, J., & Lipko, A. R. (2007). Metacomprehension: A brief history and how to improve its accuracy. *Current Directions in Psychological Science, 16*, 228–32.

Dunlosky, J., & Metcalfe, J. (2009). *Metacognition.* Thousand Oaks, CA: Sage Publications.

Flavell, J. H. (1979). Metacognition and cognitive monitoring: A new area of cognitive-developmental inquiry. *American Psychologist, 34*, 906–11.

Glenberg, A. M., & Epstein, W. (1985). Calibration of comprehension. *Journal of Experimental Psychology: Learning, Memory, and Cognition, 11*, 702–18.

Glenberg, A. M., Sanocki, T., Epstein, W., & Morris, C. (1987). Enhancing calibration of comprehension. *Journal of Experimental Psychology: General, 116*, 119–36.

Graesser, A. C., & Bertus, E. L. (1998). The construction of causal inferences while reading expository texts on science and technology. *Scientific Studies of Reading, 2*, 247–69.

Griffin, T. D., Jee, B. D., & Wiley, J. (2009). The effects of domain knowledge on metacomprehension accuracy. *Memory and Cognition, 37*, 1001–13.

Griffin, T. D., Wiley, J., & Salas, C. (2013). Supporting effective self-regulated learning: The critical role of monitoring. In R. Azevedo & V. Aleven (Eds.), *International handbook of metacognition and learning technologies* (pp. 19–34). Springer Science + Business Media, New York.

Griffin, T. D., Wiley, J., & Thiede, K. W. (2008). Individual differences, rereading, and self-explanation: Concurrent processing and cue validity as constraints on metacomprehension accuracy. *Memory & Cognition, 36*, 93–103.

Griffin, T. D., Wiley, J., & Thiede, K. W. (2013). Test expectancy effects on metacomprehension, self-regulation, and learning. *Proceedings of the 35th Annual Meeting of the Cognitive Science Society.* Austin, TX: Cognitive Science Society.

Hall, L. A. (2004). Comprehending expository text: Promising strategies for struggling readers and students with reading disabilities. *Literacy Research and Instruction, 44*, 75–95.

Hall, L. A. (2005). Teachers and content area reading: Attitudes, belief and change. *Teacher and Teacher Education, 21*, 403–14.

Hinze, S. R., Wiley, J., & Pellegrino, J. W. (2013). The importance of constructive comprehension processes in learning from tests. *Journal of Memory and Language, 69*, 151–64.

Jaeger, A. J., & Wiley, J. (2014). Do illustrations help or harm metacomprehension accuracy? *Learning and Instruction, 34*, 58–73.

Jensen, J. L., McDaniel, M. A., Woodard, S. M., & Kummer, T. A. (2014). Teaching to the test . . . or testing to teach: Exams requiring higher order thinking skills encourage greater conceptual understanding. *Educational Psychology Review, 26*, 307–29.

King, A. (1994). Guiding knowledge construction in the classroom: Effects of teaching children how to question and how to explain. *American Educational Research Journal, 31*, 338–68.

Kintsch, W. (1994). Learning from text. *American Psychologist, 49*, 294–303.

Kintsch, W. (1998). *Comprehension: A paradigm for cognition.* New York: Cambridge University Press.

Kintsch, W., Welsch, D., Schmalhofer, F., & Zimny, S. (1990). Sentence memory: A theoretical analysis. *Journal of Memory and Language, 29*, 133–59.

Koriat, A. (1997). Monitoring one's own knowledge during study: A cue-utilization approach to judgments of learning. *Journal of Experimental Psychology: General, 126*, 349–70.

Lauterman, T., & Ackerman, R. (2014). Overcoming screen inferiority in learning and calibration. *Computers in Human Behavior, 35*, 455–63.

Ley, K., & Young, D. B. (1998). Self regulation behaviors in underprepared (developmental) and regular admission college students. *Contemporary Educational Psychology, 23*, 42–64.

Lin, L., & Zabrucky, K. M. (1998). Calibration of comprehension: Research and implications for education and instruction. *Contemporary Educational Psychology, 23*, 345–91.

Maki, R. H. (1998). Test predictions over text material. In D. J. Hacker, J. Dunlosky & A. C. Graesser (Eds.), *Metacognition in educational theory and practice* (pp. 117–44). Hillsdale, NJ: LEA.

Maki, R. H., & Berry, S. L. (1984). Metacomprehension of text material. *Journal of Experimental Psychology: Learning, Memory, and Cognition, 10*, 663–79.

Maki, R. H., & Serra, M. (1992). The basis of test predictions for text material. *Journal of Experimental Psychology: Learning, Memory, and Cognition, 18*, 116–26.

McNamara, D. S. (2004). SERT: Self-explanation reading training. *Discourse Processes, 38*, 1–30.

McNamara, D. S., Kintsch, E., Songer, N. B., & Kintsch, W. (1996). Are good texts always better? Interactions of text coherence, background knowledge, and levels of understanding in learning from text. *Cognition and Instruction, 14*, 1–43.

Metcalfe, J. (2009). Metacognitive judgments and control of study. *Current Directions in Psychological Science, 18*, 159–63.

Millis, K. K., & Graesser, A. C. (1994). The time-course of constructing knowledge-based inferences for scientific texts. *Journal of Memory and Language, 33*, 583–99.

Mokhtari, K., & Reichard. C. A. (2002). Assessing student's metacognitive awareness of reading strategies. *Journal of Educational Psychology, 94*, 249–59.

Moore, D., Zabrucky, K., & Commander, N. E. (1997). Validation of the metacomprehension scale. *Contemporary Educational Psychology, 22*, 457–71.

Nelson, T. O., & Narens, L. (1990). Metamemory: A theoretical framework and new findings. In G. H. Bower (Ed.), *The psychology of learning and motivation* (pp. 125–41). New York: Academic Press.

Nesbit, J. C., & Adesope, O. O. (2006). Learning with concept and knowledge maps: A meta-analysis. *Review of Educational Research, 76*, 413–48.

Nokes, J. D. (2010). Preparing novice history teachers to meet students' literacy needs. *Reading Psychology, 31*, 493–523.

Orlando, V. P., Caverly, D. C., Swetnam, L. A. & Flippo, R. F. (1989). Text demands in college classes: An investigation. *Forum for Reading*, 21, 43–48.

Otero, J. C., & Campanario, J. M. (1990). Comprehension evaluation and regulation in learning from science texts. *Journal of Research in Science Teaching, 27*, 447–60.

Paris, S. G., & Jacobs, J. E. (1984). The benefits of informed instruction for children's reading awareness and comprehension skills. *Child Development, 55*, 2083–93.

Paris, S. G., & Winograd, P. (1990). How metacognition can promote learning and instruction. In B. F. Jones and L. Idol (Eds.), *Dimensions of thinking and cognitive instruction*. Hillsdale, NJ: Erlbaum.

Pearson, P. D., & Dole, J. A. (1987). Explicit comprehension instruction: A review of research and a new conceptualization of instruction. *Elementary School Journal, 88*, 151–65.

Pintrich, P. R. (2002). The role of metacognitive knowledge in learning, teaching, and assessing. *Theory Into Practice, 41*, 219–25.

Pintrich, P. R., Wolters, C. A., & Baxter, G. P. (2000). Assessing Metacognition and Self-Regulated Learning. In G. Schraw and J. C. Impara, (Eds.), *Issues in the measurement of metacognition* (pp. 43–97). Lincoln, NE: University of Nebraska-Lincoln.

Pressley, M. (2002). Metacognition and self-regulated comprehension. In A. Farstrup, S. J. Samuels (Ed.), *What research has to say about reading instruction*, 3rd Ed. (pp. 184–200). Newark, DE: International Reading Association.

Pressley, M., & Afflerbach, P. (1995). *Verbal protocols of reading: The nature of constructively responsive reading*. Hillsdale NJ: Erlbaum.

Pressley, M., Yokoi, L., Van Meter, P., Van Etten, S., & Freebern, G. (1997). Some of the reasons why preparing for exams is so hard: What can be done to make it easier? *Educational Psychology Review, 9*, 1–38.

Rawson, K., & Dunlosky, J. (2002). Are performance predictions for text based on ease of processing? *Journal of Experimental Psychology: Learning, Memory, and Cognition, 28*, 69–80.

Rawson, K., Dunlosky, J., & Thiede, K. W. (2000). The rereading effect: Metacomprehension accuracy improves across reading trials. *Memory & Cognition, 28*, 1004–10.

Redford, J. S., Thiede, K. W., Wiley, J., & Griffin, T. D. (2011). Concept mapping improves metacomprehension accuracy among 7th graders. *Learning and Instruction, 22*, 262–70.

Schraw, G., & Dennison, R. S. (1994). Assessing Meta-cognitive Awareness. *Contemporary Educational Psychology, 19*, 460–75.

Shiu, L. P., & Chen, Q. (2013). Self and external monitoring of reading comprehension. *Journal of Educational Psychology, 105*, 78–88.

Simpson, M. L., & Nist, S. L. (2000). An update on strategic learning: It's more than textbook reading strategies. *Journal of Adolescent & Adult Literacy, 43*, 528–41.

Spence, D. J., Yore, L. D., & Williams, R. L. (1999). The effects of explicit science reading instruction on selected Grade 7 students' metacognition and comprehension of specific science text. *Journal of Elementary Science Education, 11*, 15–30.

Stensvold, M. S., & Wilson, J. T. (1990). The interaction of verbal ability with concept mapping in learning from a chemistry laboratory activity. *Science Education, 74*, 473–80.

Thiede, K. W., & Anderson, M. C. M. (2003). Summarizing can improve metacomprehension accuracy. *Contemporary Educational Psychology, 28*, 129–60.

Thiede, K. W., Anderson, M. C. M., & Therriault, D. (2003). Accuracy of metacognitive monitoring affects learning of texts. *Journal of Educational Psychology, 95*, 66–73.

Thiede, K. W., & Dunlosky, J. (1999). Toward a general model of self-regulated study: An analysis of selection of items for study and self-paced study time. *Journal of Experimental Psychology: Learning, Memory, and Cognition, 25*, 1024–37.

Thiede, K. W., Dunlosky, J., Griffin, T. D., & Wiley, J. (2005). Understanding the delayed keyword effect on metacomprehension accuracy. *Journal of Experiment Psychology: Learning, Memory and Cognition, 31*, 1267–80.

Thiede, K. W., Griffin, T. D., Wiley, J., & Anderson, M. C. M. (2010). Poor metacomprehension accuracy as a result of inappropriate cue use. *Discourse Processes, 47*, 331–62.

Thiede, K. W., Griffin, T. D., Wiley, J., & Redford, J. S. (2009). Metacognitive monitoring during and after reading. In D. J. Hacker, J. Dunlosky, & A. C. Graesser (Eds.), *Handbook of metacognition and self-regulated learning* (pp. 85–106). Mahwah, NJ: Erlbaum.

Thiede, K. W., Redford, J. S., Wiley, J., & Griffin, T. D. (2012). Elementary school experience with comprehension testing may influence metacomprehension accuracy among 7th and 8th graders. *Journal of Educational Psychology, 104*, 554–64.

Thiede, K. W., Wiley, J., & Griffin, T. D. (2011). Test expectancy affects metacomprehension accuracy. *British Journal of Educational Psychology, 81*, 264–73.

Thomas, A. K., & McDaniel, M. A. (2007). Metacomprehension for educationally relevant materials: Dramatic effects of encoding-retrieval interactions. *Psychonomic Bulletin & Review, 14*, 212–18.

Trabasso, T., & van den Broek, P. (1985). Causal thinking and the representation of narrative events. *Journal of Memory and Language, 24*, 595–611.

van Loon, M. H., de Bruin, A. B., van Gog, T., van Merriënboer, J. J., & Dunlosky, J. (2014). Can students evaluate their understanding of cause-and-effect relations? The effects of diagram completion on monitoring accuracy. *Acta Psychologica, 151*, 143–54.

Wandersee, J. H. (1988). Ways students read texts. *Journal of Research in Science Teaching, 25*, 69–84.

Weaver, C. A., Bryant, D. S., & Burns, K. D. (1995). Comprehension monitoring: Extensions of the Kintsch and van Dijk model. In C. A. Weaver, S. Mannes, and C. Fletcher (Eds.), *Discourse comprehension: Essays in honour of Walter Kintsch* (pp. 177–93). Hillsdale, NJ: Lawrence Erlbaum Associates.

Weinstein, C. E., & Mayer, R. E. (1986). The teaching of learning strategies. In M. C. Wittrock (Ed.), *Handbook on research in teaching*, 3rd Ed. (pp. 315–27). New York: Macmillan.

Wiley, J., Griffin, T., & Thiede, K. W. (2005). Putting the comprehension in metacomprehension. *Journal of General Psychology, 132*, 408–28.

Wiley, J., Griffin, T. D., & Thiede, K. W. (2008). To understand your understanding one must understand what understanding means. In BC Love, K. McRae & VM Sloutsky (eds.), *Proceedings of the 30th Annual Conference of the Cognitive Science Society* (pp. 817–822). Austin, TX: Cognitive Science Society.

Wiley, J., & Myers, J. L. (2003). Availability and accessibility of information and causal inferences from scientific text. *Discourse Processes, 36*, 109–29.

Wiley, J., & Voss, J. F. (1999). Constructing arguments from multiple sources: Tasks that promote understanding and not just memory for text. *Journal of Educational Psychology, 91*, 301–11.

Wiley, J., Griffin, T. D., Jaeger, A. J., Jarosz, A. F., Cushen, P. J., & Thiede, K. W. (in press). Improving metacomprehension accuracy in an undergraduate course context. *Journal of Experimental Psychology: Applied.*

Winne, P. H., & Hadwin, A. F. (1998). Studying as self-regulated learning. In D. J. Hacker, J. Dunlosky, & A. C. Graesser (Eds.), *Metacognition in educational theory and practice* (pp. 277–304). Mahwah, NJ: Lawrence Erlbaum Associates.

Winne, P. H., & Perry, N. E. (2000). Measuring self-regulated learning. In M. Boekaerts and P. Pintrich (Eds.), *Handbook of self-regulation* (pp. 531–66). New York: Academic Press.

Yore, L. D., Craig, M. T., & Maguire, T. O. (1998). Index of science reading awareness: An interactive-constructive model, test verification, and grades 4-8 results. *Journal of Research in Science Teaching, 35*, 27–51.

Zimmerman, B. J. (2002). Becoming a self-regulated learner: An overview. *Theory into Practice, 41*, 64–72.

FURTHER READINGS

Dunlosky, J., & Metcalfe, J. (2009). *Metacognition: A textbook for cognitive, educational, life span, and applied psychology* (Chapter 9: Education). Thousand Oaks, CA: Sage.

Maki, R. H. (1998). Test predictions over text material. In D. J. Hacker, J. Dunlosky, & A. C. Graesser (Eds.), *Metacognition in educational theory and practice* (pp. 117–44). Hillsdale, NJ: LEA.

Thiede, K. W., Griffin, T. D., Wiley, J., & Redford, J. (2009). Metacognitive monitoring during and after reading. In D. J. Hacker, J. Dunlosky, and A. C. Graesser (Eds.), *Handbook of metacognition in education* (pp. 85–106). New York, NY: Routledge.

Chapter 6

The Reading-Writing-Thinking Connection

How Literacy and Metacognition Are Mutually Interdependent

Annamary L. Consalvo and Diane L. Schallert

ABSTRACT

This chapter considers ways in which metacognitive acts in writing can contribute to a fuller understanding of the scope of metacognitive processes in literacy. Entailing a brief history of the professional conversations; considerations of theories concerned with monitoring, communities, genre, and new/multiliteracies as well as relevant research; and discussion of implications for instruction, recommended themes for future inquiry include continued examination of affordances of multiliteracies, teacher stance, and for programs of writing based on principles and evidence that contribute to writers' development.

INTRODUCTION

Reading and writing are intimately connected literacy practices, with findings establishing that writing helps us be more effective readers (Graham & Hebert, 2011; Lee & Schallert, 2016). As Donald Murray (1982) stated, the writer is his or her own "first reader," a reader who also functions as a monitor. If the monitor, or first reader, is too harsh, too "metacognitive," we might say, the fluid writer shuts down, and instead, over-corrects and over-focuses on surface features rather than on content (Perl, 1979). We typically read so much more than we write of revised, edited, polished, and published prose, that *dis*satisfaction is a state with which we, as writers, must somehow make peace. By contrast, if the first reader or monitor is supportive or at least, temporarily suspends judgment, the writer may be able to get words onto a page. From the "shitty first draft" (LaMott, 1994), anything is possible.

From these initial ideas about the interrelationship of reading and writing grew our interest in what it would mean to add a consideration of writing processes to the discussion this volume has entertained on the connection between metacognition and reading comprehension. We hope to contribute to an appreciation of the necessarily metacognitive nature of reading processes by looking to the literature on another aspect of literacy, writing.

FRAMING THE CASE: DEFINITIONS AND EXPLANATIONS

We begin by considering the place that writing has taken in current views of literacy. There was a time when the two fields, reading and writing, were more clearly separated, with each reflecting a tradition with its own journals, yearly conference, and cited heroes (and villains), and housed in different parts of academic homes. Reading was often associated with teacher preparation at the elementary level, whereas writing was included as part of secondary preparation. The lines between these two fields were not always clean but it was quite possible to pursue academic interests in one area without becoming very knowledgeable about the other. When reading researchers' interest in comprehension processes flourished in the mid-1970s, one model soon dominated the descriptions we had for what was involved: Readers making sense of text by building mental scenarios or representations out of their existing schema knowledge, memories, and experiences (Anderson & Ortony, 1976; Anderson, Reynolds, Schallert, & Goetz, 1977; *situation models* in the language of van Dijk & Kintsch, 1983). In this view, the reader was always actively constructing meaning when interacting with a text, and from the start, this meaning-making was described as relying on metacognitive judgments of coherence and sense (Brown, 1980; Brown & Palincsar, 1982). Thus began the start of the constructivist era in educational research more broadly (Schallert & Martin, 2003).

As for the field of writing, the 1970s saw the start of the process movement, with the work of Emig (1971) presenting at first a lonely call for attention to what writers are actually doing as they write, as opposed to concentrating on the text as a product that has been written. The prolific work of Flower and Hayes (1979, 1981) soon intrigued writing researchers for what it offered them by way of a new codified way to study the writing process through the think-aloud protocol and by way of a new representation of these processes through a model depicting the writing process as a problem-solving space. Even though the model was soon enough critiqued (cf., Bizzell, 1982; Faigley, 1986; Flower, 1989), it remained intriguing for the position it ascribed to how a writer does the following: monitors the text that has been created so far; consults her existing knowledge of content, writing forms, and possible reactions of the intended audience; and evaluates the piece for how well it responds to the exigencies of the assignment, whether this assignment came from a teacher or outside source or from herself as a purpose acting as impetus for writing. Thus, in this model of writing, metacognitive processes were as important as text construction processes.

As reading researchers continued to take seriously the construction metaphor implied by their favorite description of reading comprehension, the language soon turned to how the reader was in fact constructing the text, not just meaning, with echoes of Fish (1980) who claimed that the text is in the reader's mind much more so than existing as mere words on a page. If the reader is making sense of a text by "writing" the text, why could not comprehension researchers learn from composition theorists like Emig (1971) and Flower and Hayes (1979, 1981) who were describing the writing process as a reflective, goal-directed, idea composing process? This is when we can date the start of the strong connection between the reading and writing fields, we might even claim, the beginning of *literacy* as a field.

In 1983, Tierney and Pearson wrote a seminal piece in *Language Arts* that proposed that reading is as much a process of composing meaning as is writing, and that much is gained by reading researchers looking to descriptions of what writing entails. In their theoretical description of reading as a composing process, several aspects evoke what is meant by metacognitive processes: reading involves a Planner that sets goals and that mobilizes relevant knowledge, an Aligner that determines ways to collaborate with the text author in attempting to see meaning from the author's perspective, and a Drafter that begins to make sense of the text by selecting possibly relevant background knowledge and attempting to fit textual cues into possible situation models. Most relevant, reading involves a Monitor that keeps track of whether initial drafts of meaning are making sense and are fulfilling the reader's goals and that then recruits a Revisor whenever the Monitor detects that sense-making is going awry. In its clear similarity to the writing process, reading as a composing process is saturated throughout with metacognitive processes.

We close this section by making explicit our definitions of the key terms we will use in this argument. For us, *reading* is a metacognitively driven design process of meaning making, of making sense of not only verbal print symbols but all sorts of semiotic signs (Kress, 2000). Thus, as used by the New London Group (1996), *literacy*, and here we make the jump that blurs the line between reading and writing, becomes extended to reading the world as much as reading the word, and thus, to multimodal meaning making. One process inherent in thinking of reading and writing as joined through their reliance on metacognition is the process of *reflection*, defined here as contemplating the meaning one is composing, either as a reader or as a writer, and revisiting and evaluating how well this meaning is fitting with the goals one has for the text. When one writes, it is not unusual that minutes will go by as the writer ponders whether "the text produced so far" (in the words of Flower & Hayes, 1981, p. 370) is on a trajectory to successful fulfillment of the writer's goals. As natural a subprocess of writing as it may seem, *reflection* is as useful when one is reading. Finally, *writing* itself, or more specifically, *process writing*, brings together the representation first created in Emig's (1971) call for attention to process and then modeled so brilliantly by Flower and Hayes as a thinking space, a problem-solving process by which a writer iteratively monitors whether a draft is developing well to fulfill the goals that initiated the writing in the first place.

MAKING THE CASE FROM EXTANT THEORETICAL AND EMPIRICAL WORK

Having framed the case for how intimately interrelated are the processes of reading, writing, and metacognition, we turn in this section to four specific areas of theory and research on key phenomena that we believe are helpful in providing direction to pedagogical implications: empirical studies of the reading-writing-metacognition connection; the work on communities of practice; the influence of genre theory and mentor texts; and the theoretical and empirical research from a New Literacies perspective.

Studies about the Reading-Writing-Metacognition Connection

There are several lines of work that provide evidence of the interesting connections among our three key constructs, reading, writing, and metacognition. First, there are studies showing correlational connections between students' scores on reading and writing measures, suggesting that these processes share some underlying process that is mutually beneficial, that projects itself into the reading and writing being measured (Shanahan, 1984; Shanahan & Lomax, 1986). For example, in an early study of the intercorrelations among several measures of subprocesses of writing and of reading, Shanahan reported that although there were several correlations across the two types of literacy, with some moderate to strong, there never was more than 43 percent of the variance in one form of literacy (reading or writing) accounted for by a subprocess of the other literacy. In a more rigorous test of the interconnection between reading and writing, Shanahan and Lomax tested the best fit of three models using data from a large sample of second and fifth graders who had been tested on several reading and writing subskills. Interestingly, the model with the best fit to the data was a fully interactive model that allowed for bidirectional influences across subskills of both literacies. Neither the reading-to-writing nor the writing-to-reading models were as good a fit with the data at both grade levels. Like Fitzgerald and Shanahan (2000) who outlined a complex perspective on the writing-reading connection as changing across skill development, we want to suggest that one of the underlying cognitive processes shared by both reading and writing is metacognition (what they called *metacognitive knowledge*).

Second, there is work focused on the processes invoked when students read in order to write. Initiated by Spivey (1990; Spivey & King, 1989), this research looked at how students compose from sources, on how their writing is influenced by the texts they access as they compose their own reports to reflect their understanding of a topic. Similarly, in a study of students undertaking a seven-month-long research project on some aspect of World War II, Many, Fyfe, Lewis, and Mitchell (1996) reported that students had different visions for what it meant to research a topic, approached their reading in one of several ways, and then wrote a final paper that reflected to varying degrees how they could uptake the sources they encountered and transform their understanding into text form. As Noll and Fox (2003) described, it is helpful to new scholars in a field to notice from their immersion in their discipline's literature all the ways that writers make their arguments. Learning a discipline's ways of knowing, doing, and writing in the words of Carter (2007) is the focal task of undergraduate education. Finally, Kwon and Schallert (2016) reported on ten advanced biliterate readers, graduate students in several fields, who used metacognitive processes as they read for the purpose of writing important pieces in their training (dissertation proposals or manuscripts for publication).

Third, there have been intervention studies that have investigated how reading can help students' writing, and vice versa. In laying the groundwork for their own intervention study of middle school students learning English in Korea, Lee, and Schallert (2016) reviewed several studies of the effects of reading on both reading and writing, and the effects of writing on both reading and writing, including studies that involved readers/writers in their native language as well as in second/foreign language classrooms. Their own study was a year-long implementation of once-per-week lessons in one of three versions: extensive reading, extensive writing, or the more usual type of English class translation activities, the latter acting as a control group. Results indicated that extensive writing led to improved posttest scores on a reading test as well as on a writing task even though the students in the writing group did not engage in extensive reading. Students in the extensive reading group showed improvement in writing (as well as in reading) even though they were engaged in no extra writing as compared to the control group. The authors concluded that, moderated by a certain level of proficiency in the language, reading and writing in a second/foreign language can be improved by engaging frequently in either literacy process.

Writing as an Act of Community Membership

No literacy act ever occurs in isolation. We gesture, speak, read, and write because of, through, and in response to others, whether in local contexts or in the larger context of culture (Bakhtin, 1981; Vygotsky, 1978; Wertsch, 1991). One construct that we believe may be particularly useful to our consideration of how reading and writing are connected is that of *communities of practice* and its associated learning mechanism of *legitimate peripheral participation,* introduced by Lave and Wenger (1991; but see Consalvo, Schallert, & Elias, 2015 for a critique of the (mis)use of this construct). These two key ideas refer to the *practices*, that is, the practiced ways of engaging in any kind of culturally legitimated, bounded process, that established members of a group have developed and that are introduced gradually to newcomers as they are inducted into the community. Learning happens, in this view, when newcomers are tolerated, allowed, and to varying degrees welcomed to participate in the activities of a given community. To the degree that experts deem them able, newcomers are eventually given or take up more central aspects of the community's practices. This path to membership may be strewn with obstacles such as failures, small and large, by the novice and the witting or unwitting path-blocking maneuvers of insiders, to name but two. As a different way to think about the practices into which individuals are drawn, Gee (2005) introduced the idea of *affinity spaces*, both face-to-face and virtual, and more recently extended the concept to *passionate affinity spaces* (Gee & Hayes, 2011) in which participants engage in passion-driven learning. Affinity spaces, as the name suggests, have a magnetic quality and are locations where individuals converge, however temporarily, based upon shared interest, and where, as in communities of practice, these same individuals may be at differing levels of expertise.

It is interesting to consider, given the social nature of learning, how writing within and for a given community (as disciplines or fields can be conceptualized) emphasizes ways in which writers (authors/communicators) consider their own particular audiences. In fact, it is the community into which one is permitted access and/or is mentored (and we all are members of multiple such collectives) where members learn and use particular "ways with words" (Heath, 1983). The particular ways with words of a given community, or *D*iscourse (versus small-d discourse, which refers to everyday interactions) is the "language plus being the 'right' *who* and saying the 'right' *what*. . . . What is important is not [just] language, and surely not grammar; but *saying* *(writing)-doing-being-valuing-believing combinations*" (Gee, 1996, p. 127, italics original). Indeed, disciplinary writing highlights how newcomers to a field must learn to read the texts of the practice or the discipline in order to understand and acclimate to the thinking/cultural models of the group into which they are seeking to reposition themselves (Shanahan & Shanahan, 2015). In many ways, anyone who undertakes entry into a new field is a learner of a new language. As a learner of new ways with words, attention to the communicative efficacy of one's speech, deportment, and means of inscription become critical to one's sense of whether (or not) one belongs, and is (or is not) legitimated, into a community.

That a community of practice reads various texts of interest is a given, whether those texts are alphabetic, visual, aural, or three-dimensional objects or places. It is through the social, situated processes of literacy learning that members of a community take up the ways with words of the group (Rowe, 2008; Smagorinsky, Cook, & Reed, 2005). Through such social processes, newcomers come to internalize the voices of community experts (Vygotsky, 1978), and these voices act as metacognitive guides to how texts should be read, how one should scribe within the community to embody its purposes more fully.

Genre Theory and Mentor Texts

Another literature that informs the connection we are making between reading, metacognition, and writing is the work that has explored the ways in which mentor texts serve as the sanctioned genres of a given community or discipline. These mentor texts lend structural visibility to writers and, thereby, support metacognitive awareness of novices and experts alike. In any given community, there exist codified ways of communicating. It is interesting to us that the word *ways* connotes both habitual behaviors and trodden paths. Ways with words become behaviors/pathways or speech genres through adoption and repeated use by actual, living people going about their lives: "*Verbal communication can never be understood and explained outside of this connection with a concrete situation*" (Volosinov, 1929/86, p. 95, original emphasis). If speech comes before writing, it makes sense that some literary genres grow from speech genres: "Like all other speech acts genres arise from the codification of discursive properties" (Duff, 2014, p. 202). The move to written inscription into the cultural bedrock, however, is not a predictable, formulaic, or linear process. According to the *Oxford Dictionary of Literary Terms* (Baldick, 2008), "A literary genre is a recognizable and established category of written work employing such common conventions as will prevent readers or audiences from mistaking it for another kind" (p. 140).

Using the accepted and respected texts of a field as proxy-teachers is one way to help students grow into degrees of expertise so that the learner becomes a text-maker within the field. The term "touchstone texts," by Calkins (1994), was used as a descriptor of exemplar texts that a writer could emulate. Similarly, "mentor texts" (Dorfman & Cappelli, 2007; Gainer, 2013) are those texts that act as an expert tutor for a writer: "Writing mentors are for everyone—teachers as well as students" (Dorfman & Cappelli, 2007, p. 2). To treat a text *as* a mentor text requires a meta-reading of that text: it calls for textual analysis to unlock how the text is put together, how arguments and positions are forwarded, and it depends on continuous realistic self-assessment of the degree to which a reader/writer is more and less able to control features of the text (Kruger & Dunning, 1991). The use of mentor texts in classrooms is a way that teachers can bring in authors' voices, choices, and sensibilities into the lives of student-writers and a way to bolster and support the classroom's disciplinary curriculum. Hillocks (1987) supported the use of mentor texts when he pointed out that "writers need knowledge of discourse structures traditionally provided by the study of model pieces of writing" (p. 81). To treat a text as a mentor text is a metacognitive act.

New Literacies

For a scholarly collection devoted to the connection between reading and metacognition, a final argument for the need to consider writing is what many have called the *digital turn* marking twenty-first-century perspectives on literacy. It is still difficult to know how transformative the advent of the Internet age will eventually be viewed, but even in the scant years since its inception, literacy researchers have recognized the special affordances that were created with the Web. Now, readers read and respond as a matter of course everywhere and at every moment, now writers write so as to be read by a public both known and unknown, and now, getting readers to write a response becomes the point of social literacy acts. Thus, in a digital age, it is difficult to separate reading from writing from reading again. Where some decried the computer early on because it seemed to draw young people away from text, millennials today continuously and seamlessly combine communicating with others, finding answers to their questions by "googling," and arranging their lives through web interfaces as they reserve tickets for flights and music shows, apply for graduate school, buy coffee, and pay for traffic citations. Life in the twenty-first century is a text-rich experience.

Marking this amalgamated experience of digital reading and writing are at least three scholarly developments worthy of mention. First, a new theoretical model of literacy was offered that positioned text interactions under an umbrella of socially situated discourse acts that expanded what we now view as literacy to include nonlanguage based "texts." As Kress (2000) stated, "The multimodal texts/messages of the era of Multiliteracies need a theory which deals adequately with the processes of integration/composition of the various modes in these texts: both in production/making and in consumption/ reading" (p. 149). This theory, usually referred to as a New Literacies framework, encompasses at least two separate perspectives but shares the idea that our conceptions of the literacies of the twenty-first century need to include digital and multimodal forms of communication acknowledging the sociocultural context in which meaning-making inherently exists (Kress, 2000; New London Group, 1996).

Second, descriptions of what is involved when individuals access the Internet have put metacognitively sophisticated strategies at the heart of successful Internet use. As Afflerbach and Cho (2010) described, even simply finding the proper texts that will fulfill one's purpose is a complex process that challenges readers as they navigate the Web. Strategies are involved in such a process orchestrated by all the metacognitive decision-making described for any kind of reading. With the advent of a Web 2.0 world, Internet readers have become text producers as much as consumers, and the strategies necessary to become a successful presence online involve as much reading as writing. Here, we are reminded of the description of young people who have created a blogging presence through their online writings, of how they have learned to read and respond to fellow bloggers in order to receive back enough response that their own blogs become popular (Roach, 2015).

Finally, in classroom use of online discussion, students read and write as they communicate with peers, all the while addressing a goal of making meaning of course readings and concepts. Such use of online discussion has been described by Vogler et al. (2013) as providing users the chance to engage in the following practices:

> (a) Participants can read at their own pace their group members' messages, pondering those that intrigue them and skimming over those that are less interesting or too difficult to deal with in the moment; (b) having read several messages, a student can begin to formulate a response to reflect emerging ideas created from what has been read; (c) the student can then engage in composing processes with a goal to make clear and to communicate an idea that is still new, triggered by an earlier posting; (d) once posted, a message takes on a life of its own as it now becomes part of the collaboratively created text influencing any other student who reads it; and (e) all of these processes can occur in different orders. (p. 235)

Clearly, in online discussion, metacognitive processes of "pondering" and "reflecting" as students read and write to make sense together are practiced in one literacy event that cements reading, writing, and metacognitive processes.

PEDAGOGICAL IMPLICATIONS

Having set the stage by recounting seminal scholarship on metacognition, revisiting research on metacognition in reading and writing, considering how being a part of a community of readers and writers underpins literate practices, reviewing how New Literacies Studies continues to open avenues for reconceptualizing literacy theory and practice, and discussing how an understanding of genre as ways with words, we now turn our attention to pedagogical considerations of how these conversations converge within and between teachers' practices.

Stance

Teachers' knowledge, understandings, and beliefs are at play in determining what gets taught and how. Teaching is a complex, value-laden, historically contested profession that Hargreaves (2001) has argued demands significant emotional labor from its members. A teacher's knowledge, understandings, and beliefs contribute to her/his positioning, or stance, as a way of being in the teaching world. In everyday usage, *stance* refers to physical placement or position; here, we use *stance* as a metaphoric navigational compass with its cardinal points alluding broadly to professionalism, philosophical orientation, affect concerning relationships with others and feeling for and about the disciplines, and ethics. To elucidate this idea, we draw from Cochran-Smith and Lytle's (1991) conceptions about teacher knowledge and how those "knowledges" interact to contribute to a teacher's positioning. First is "knowledge-*for*-practice" which emphasizes teachers "knowing more" about their content, theory, pedagogy, and strategy awareness (pp. 243–54). This conception foregrounds formal knowledge, directly taught. Second, is "knowledge-*in*-practice" (Schon, 1983) in which "the emphasis is on knowledge in action: what very competent teachers know as it is expressed or embedded in the artistry of practice, in teachers' reflections on practice, in teachers' practical inquiries, and/or in teachers' narrative accounts of practice" (Cochran-Smith & Lytle, 1991, p. 262). At the heart of knowledge-*in*-practice as a construct is the valuing of exemplary teacher case knowledge and practices, including deep and active reflection and collaborative study. Third, "knowledge-*of*-practice" values the efforts of teachers to trouble their understandings of teaching itself: "The knowledge-*of*-practice conception turns on the assumption that the knowledge teachers need to teach well emanates from systematic inquiries about teaching, learners and learning, subject matter and curriculum, and schools and schooling" (p. 274). Taken together, this tripartite model of teacher knowing contributes to a teacher's stance about the practice of teaching.

It is the practitioner identity of a teacher of literacy, of reading and of writing, that interests us. If an educator were to concur with our chapter up to this point, we would conclude that he or she would value student choice, student interests outside of school, classroom talk, inquiry, enough time for students to read and write, and creating a classroom environment that supported independent literacy activities. If practitioners esteemed and used these teaching practices, they would likely have to negotiate their practices with differing school or district mandates, as "administration and/or the value of high-stakes exams have power over the instructional preferences of teachers and students" (Vetter, Myers, & Hester, 2014, p. 12). Acknowledging those difficulties and complexities in the professional life of a literacy teacher, we move to a discussion of what a stance that would value the combination of reading, writing, and metacognition might look like in practice.

In considering teaching and learning as a social or constructivist endeavor, effective literacy teachers create environments that are conducive to learning. Holding that talk as exploration was essential to learning well, Barnes (1993) identified four prerequisites:

> First, a sense of who the students are and what kinds of activities they are likely to be able and willing to engage in. Second, there must be conscious or tacit views about how children learn. Third, linked to these views the teacher will have a repertoire of classroom relationships and activities likely to support such learning. . . . Fourth, the course of a lesson will also be shared by the teacher's sense of what is important for her students to experience and understand. (p. 17)

Teachers of writing offer students many and varied opportunities to write and believe that students learn to write *by* writing. Their educational and/or experiential backgrounds afford them an appreciation that oral language, reading, and writing are inextricably bound (Shanahan, 2006). We concur with the National Council of Teachers of English (2004, pp. 2–3) that teachers appreciate that people, including students, can and should have writing in their lives both in and outside of school; that teachers adopt and adapt structures supportive of writing such as conferring with individual students, formatively assessing writing in progress and offering instruction based on that evaluation; and, that educators intentionally build a classroom culture of safety and respect to foster the building of a positive classroom community that includes talk, choice, and degrees of supported autonomy. Foundationally, it is essential for teachers to believe that they and their students have lives and stories worth sharing through writing and that writing for an authentic audience can help students build agency as writers. In sum, teachers' stances matter a great deal when considering whether and how they provide an environment conducive to, and opportunities for students to engage in productive metacognitive acts.

Literacy in Formal and Nonformal Contexts

Reading-like-a-writer is a metacognitive turn on reading in which a newcomer to a field attempts to learn how to use the coin-of-the-realm, how to traffic in and conduct exchanges of ideas and goods in the ways of the desired group. In fact, learning to produce a text (broadly defined) that is recognized by the group as fitting into the conversation and desired actions of the group is a systemic signifier of status within said group. It is the newcomer's desire to join a particular group that serves as the engine, or motivator, for this work to move forward. Students can be guided in how to read mentor texts to unlock the secrets of text-making in their chosen field (see, e.g., Noll & Fox, 2003).

Informal and affiliation groups hold promise for the teaching and learning of this sort of text-making, this sort of new "language acquisition." For example, youth all over the world, write, comment, and collaborate in fan fiction forums (Black, 2009; Guzzetti & Gamboa, 2005), extending the stories of, for example, Harry Potter, Twilight, Hunger Games, and hundreds of others across media (see https://www.fanfiction.net). These forums are governed by an ethos of community and take a protective stance toward newcomers as they seek to add their voices. Used by native English speakers and by those who desire to improve their writing in English, fan fiction forums provide many youth with support, through a dedicated online community of readers and writers. As well, they provide motivation through shared passionate interest in the particular storyworld chosen by the forum. Fan fiction writing depends on the careful consideration of the original text and as carefully created imitative text, fostering in its "fans" a meta-awareness of text.

Finally, discussion that takes place online, through synchronous chatting or asynchronous postings, blurs the lines between reading, writing, and thinking (Vogler et al., 2013). Such hybrid literate acts not only require an individual to read in order to respond, but also to write in order to express one's incipient thinking, and to look for connections between ideas that have been expressed in the written discussion. Because writing slows down the thinking and enhances the noticing process, it makes a person consider what is being said, word-by-word. This slowing-down process is a natural form of metacognition.

Writing Programs and Modes of Instruction

Modes of writing and evidence-based recommendations. Identifying four modes of writing instruction, Hillocks (1984) in a meta-analysis of research, named the "presentational mode" as the most common, and one that is teacher led and controlled (p. 143). The "natural process mode" (p. 143), by contrast, is relatively unstructured, with the teacher acting as facilitator, and with emphasis on peer feedback; however, students did not study model texts and received little in the way of feedback directed at improvement. The "environmental mode" (pp. 144–46) reflects what is known as a *workshop* model with the teacher structuring instructional time with pertinent mini lectures, the use of model or mentor texts, ample time to write, peer and teacher feedback, and multiple drafts being hallmarks of this mode. Last, the "individualized mode" (pp. 146–47) describes a combination of writing program materials and tutorials for instruction. This mode is highly idiosyncratic and variable. Of all these modes, Hillocks found that the environmental mode was, by far, the most effective.

More recently, Graham (2010) undertook a meta-review of writing instruction practices, offering several recommendations based on his findings. First, echoing Hillocks' (1987) commendation of the environmental mode, Graham reported that "the process approach to writing is an evidence-based practice that provides teachers with a framework to create a supportive classroom writing environment, with flexible classroom routines, where both writing and writing instruction can be anchored" (p. 130). Two key factors are that teachers dedicate large chunks of time to writing, and that writing is taught as a process of planning, drafting, revising, editing, and publishing or sharing. Secondly, teachers help students become "strategic writers" (p. 132). This recommendation echoes metacognitive internalization of the process of writing through which students learn to plan, monitor, revise, and summarize (p. 132). Graham then offered the advice to "teach basic text transcription skills to mastery" (p. 133), referring to the necessity of teaching handwriting and spelling. However, he noted that these skills are best taught in the context of actual writing. Fourth, Graham recommended that teachers "foster students' interest, enjoyment, and motivation to write" (p. 135), specifically, by encouraging student effort, setting high expectations, maintaining contagious enthusiasm and encouragement, and inviting students into thoughtful activities that, unlike rote activities, challenge them and help to foster motivation. Lastly, teachers whose students improve their writing "increase students' knowledge about writing" (p. 134). This recommendation supports the use of mentor texts as models for students' writing, graphic organizers as organizational aids for students, and the careful structuring of inquiry projects to support student interest and the acquisition of competencies associated with writing.

Packaged writing programs. Packaged curricula tend to appear as quick-fix panacea for perceived difficulties of a particular subject area or skill set. Writing instruction is no exception. For example, there is the Collins Writing Program, developed by John Collins and launched by his self-published book (1992/2007). With distilled and re-shaped principles of writing instruction, the core of the program is what is casually referred to as the "five types of writing," implying on first glance five meta-genre categories but instead, referring to the renamed stages of the writing process. The website offers scant research that supports the program. Similarly, the Jane Schaffer Writing Program offers teachers a simplified way to think about writing instruction. Wiley (2000), a composition expert, critiqued this program as an example of a commercial program, the successes of which "well conceal aspects of writing instruction crucial to students' *further* development" (p. 61 italics original). Not a substitute for ongoing and deep professional development for teachers, it helps teachers help students internalize a usable four-paragraph writing structure. Many teachers are left with no idea as to what directions their writing instruction should take once this initial structure is taught: "Unfortunately, there is no *next* in the Schaffer approach" (Wiley, 2000, p. 63).

Viable programs of writing. The current interest and scholarship in disciplinary literacy, and in particular, writing can be traced at least partially to what is called writing across the curriculum or WAC, the intention of which is to foster a culture of writing in college campuses with an underlying assumption that writing leads to deeper learning. More recently, there has been increasing interest in supporting writing within the situatedness of the discipline in which it occurs (e.g., lab report writing in science). Disciplinary literacies show the cultural nature of their arenas of study. For just two examples, the field of mathematics strives to find what is true and the study of history foregrounds the importance of corroboration across multiple sources for any historical claim (Shanahan & Shanahan, 2008). Lyles and Anson (2012) provided a long range review of how WAC has been effectively working within the disciplines. That writing should be seen as a kind of disciplinary knowing has received recent attention with scholars addressing misconceptions of one-size-fits-all strategy-based writing: "Rather, we need to be able to conceptualize writing in the disciplines in a way that is grounded in the disciplines themselves, a viable alternative to an understanding of writing as universally generalizable" (Carter, 2007, p. 387). Many states now require courses in secondary teacher preparation programs for all prospective middle-and high- school teachers with names like *Literacy in the Content Areas*, with the aim of encouraging future teachers both to teach the writing of their disciplines and to use writing as an aid to disciplinary learning.

Finally, there is the National Writing Project, a nationwide network of local university-school partnerships that provide educators with professional development about writing. Using a flexible, local needs-based model, professional development opportunities center on three broad principles that include encouraging local teachers to become writing leaders; offering specifically customized workshops and in-service programs to local schools; and "providing continuing education and research opportunities for teachers" (NWP,

2016, p. 2). The centerpiece of each site is the several weeks long Summer Institute in which teachers come together and study, write, and inquire about the teaching of writing under the guidance of the site's leaders. A recent, national study showed "a positive, statistically significant effect on the four attributes of student argument writing—content, structure, stance, and conventions—measured by the National Writing Project's Analytic Writing Continuum for Source-Based Argument. In particular, . . . students demonstrated greater proficiency in the quality of reasoning and use of evidence in their writing" (Gallagher, Woodworth, & Arshan, 2015, p. 1). Research has shown that NWP professional development leads to increased teacher retention with over 90 percent of respondents saying their work has been influenced by their Summer Institute attendance. And, in a study that looked at twelve sites, the improvement in students' writing in several measures (e.g., content, organization, stance, sentence fluency, and diction) was statistically significant in half of those sites (LeMahieu, 2008).

CONCLUDING THOUGHTS

The purpose of this chapter has been to consider and draw connections about metacognition between reading and writing and to highlight ways in which writing brings, to a literate life, its own set of metacognitive problems to be solved. We looked at ways in which the digital turn, through Internet velocity, audience responsiveness, and affinity groups and communities of various sorts, contributes to increasing and changing metacognitive processes. We hope that, in some ways, this chapter addresses some of what Moje (2009) called for in terms of "theorizing and analyzing the new and for positioning it in relation to the *old*" as well as for "clarification of terms and concepts without narrowing, ossifying, or dichotomizing" (*p. 359*) the conception of new, multimodal, and traditional literacies. As literacy scholars, we look to ways that educators can better teach students to self-regulate, make effective authorial decisions, and pursue their own interests and for their own purposes, and we see this volume and our own contribution to it as providing some thoughts on how these goals might be fulfilled. After all, if our goal is to both become and help create teachers who value the knowledge, life worlds, and sensibilities that students bring with them into learning contexts, a curriculum with students at the center is one worth working for: "Being recognized with respect as the person you are, and then being given the space to take seriously the complex work in front of you: that is an approach to curriculum in which each individual can create an identity, where they can affiliate with the groups that matter to them and cooperate with other groups" (Bomer, 2011, p. 310).

REFERENCES

Afflerbach, P., & Cho, B. (2010). Determining and describing reading strategies: Internet and traditional forms of reading. In H. S. Waters & W. Schneider (Eds.), *Metacognition, strategy use, and instruction* (pp. 201–25). New York, NY: Guilford Press.

Anderson, R. C., & Ortony, A. (1975). On putting apples into bottles – A problem of polysemy. *Cognitive Psychology, 7*(2), 167–80.

Anderson, R. C., Reynolds, R. E., Schallert, D. L., & Goetz, E. T. (1977). Frameworks for comprehending discourse. *American Educational Research Journal, 14*, 367–82.

Bakhtin, M. M., & Holquist, M. (1981). *The dialogic imagination: Four essays*. Austin: University of Texas Press.

Baldick, C. (2008). *The Oxford dictionary of literary terms*, 3rd ed. New York: Oxford University Press.

Barnes, D. (1993). Supporting exploratory talk for learning. In K. M. Pierce & C. J. Gilles (Eds.), *Cycles of meaning* (pp. 17–34). Portsmouth, NH: Heinemann.

Bizzell, P. (1982). Cognition, convention, and certainty: What we need to know about writing. *PRE/TEXT, 3*, 213–43.

Black, R. (2009). English-language learners, fan communities, and 21st century skills. *Journal of Adolescent and Adult Literacy, 52(*8), 688–97.

Bomer, R. (2011). *Building adolescent literacy in today's English classrooms.* Portsmouth, NH: Heinemann.

Brown, A. L. (1980). Metacognitive development and reading. In R. J. Spiro, B. C. Bruce, & W. F. Brewer (Eds.), *Theoretical Issues in Reading Comprehension* (pp. 453–81). Hillsdale, NJ: Erlbaum.

Brown, A. L., & Palinscar, A. S. (1982). Inducing strategic learning from texts by means of informed, self-control training. *Topics in Learning and Learning Disabilities, 2*(1), 1–17.

Calkins, L. M. (1994). *The art of teaching writing.* Portsmouth, NH: Heinemann.

Carter, M. (2007). Ways of knowing, doing, and writing in the disciplines. *College Composition and Communication, 58*(3), 385–418.

Cochran-Smith, M., & Lytle, S. L. (1991). Relationships of knowledge and practice: Teacher learning in communities. *Review of Research in Education, 24*, 219–305.

Collins, J. (1992/2007). *Improving student performance through writing and thinking across the curriculum.*West Newbury, MA: Collins Educational Associates.

Consalvo, A., & Schallert, D. L., & Elias, E. M. (2015). An examination of the construct of legitimate peripheral participation as a theoretical framework in literacy research. *Educational Research Review, 16*, 1–18. http://dx.doi.org/10.1016/j.edurev.2015.07.001.

Dorfman, L. R., & Cappelli, R. (2007). *Mentor texts: Teaching writing through children's literature, K–6.* Portland, ME: Stenhouse.

Duff, D. (2014). *Modern genre theory.* New York: Routledge. Retrieved from https://books.google.com/books?id=zXV_BAAAQBAJ&dq=speech+genre+as+origin+of+literary+genres&source=gbs_navlinks_s.

Emig, J. (1971). *The Composing Process of 12th Graders*. Urbana, IL: National Council of Teachers of English.

Faigley, L. (1986). Competing theories of process: A critique and a proposal. *College English, 48*(6), 527–40.

Fish, S. (1980). *Is there a text in this class? The authority of interpretive communities.* Cambridge, MA: Harvard University Press.

Fitzgerald, J., & Shanahan, T. (2000). Reading and writing relations and their development. *Educational Psychologist, 35*(1), 39–50.

Flower, L. (1989). Cognition, context, and theory building. *College Composition and Communication, 40*(3), 282–311.

Flower, L., & Hayes, J. R. (1981). A cognitive process theory of writing. *College Composition and Comprehension, 32*(4), 365–87.

Gainer, J. (2013). 21st-Century mentor texts: Developing critical literacies in the information age. *Journal of Adolescent and Adult Literacy, 57*(1), 16–19.

Gallagher, H. A., Woodworth, K. R., & Arshan, N. L. (2015). *Impact of the National Writing Project's College-Ready Writers Program on teachers and students.* Menlo Park, CA: SRI International.

Gee, J. P. (1996). *Social Linguistics and Literacies: Ideology in Discourses*, 2nd ed. New York: Routledge Falmer.

Gee, J. P. (2005). Semiotic social spaces and affinity spaces: From the age of mythology to today's schools. In D. Barton & K. Tusting (Eds.), *Beyond communities of practice: Language, power and social context* (pp. 214–32). Cambridge: Cambridge University Press.

Gee, J. P., & Hayes, E. R. (2011). *Language and learning in the digital age.* New York: Routledge.

Graham, S. (2010). Facilitating writing development. In D. Wyse, R. Andrews, & J. Hoffman (Eds.), *The Routledge international handbook of English, language, and literacy teaching* (pp. 125–36). New York: Routledge.

Graham, S., & Hebert, M. (2011). Writing to read: A meta-analysis of the impact of writing and writing instruction on reading. *Harvard Educational Review, 81*(4), 710–44.

Guzzetti, B., & Gamboa, M. (2005). Online journaling: The informal writing of two adolescent girls. *Research in the Teaching of English, 40*(2), 168–206.

Hargreaves, A. (2001). Emotional geographies of teaching. *Teachers College Record, 103*(6), 1056–80.

Heath, S. B. (1983). *Ways with words: Language, life, and work in communities and classrooms.* Cambridge, England: Cambridge University Press.

Hillocks, G., Jr. (1984). What works in teaching composition: A meta-analysis of experimental treatment studies. *American Journal of Education, 93*(1), 133–70.

Hillocks, G., Jr. (1987). Synthesis of research on teaching writing. *Educational Leadership,* (May), 71–82.

Kress, G. (2000). Design and transformation: New theories of meaning. In B. Cope & M. Kalantzis (Eds.), *Multiliteracies: Literacy learning and the design of social futures* (pp. 153–61). London: Routledge.

Kruger, J., & Dunning, D. (1991). Unskilled and unaware of it: How difficulties in recognizing one's own incompetence lead to inflated self-assessments. *Journal of Personality and Social Psychology, 77*(6), 1121–34.

Kwon, H., & Schallert, D. L. (2016). Understanding translanguaging practices through a biliteracy continua framework: Adult biliterates reading academic texts in their two languages. *Bilingual Research Journal, 39(2)*, 138–151.

LaMott, A. (1994). *Bird by bird.* New York: Anchor.

Lave, J., & Wenger, E. (1991). *Situated learning: Legitimate peripheral participation.* New York: Cambridge University Press.

Lee, J., & Schallert, D. L. (2016). Exploring the reading-writing connection: A year-long classroom-based experimental study of middle school students developing literacy in a new language. *Reading Research Quarterly, 51*(2), 143–164.

LeMahieu, J. (2008). Putting the quality into professional development: Data from NWP research. Congressional briefing [Power Point slides]. Retrieved from http://www.nwp.org/swf/articulate/congressional_briefing/player.html.

Lyles, K., & Anson, C. M. (2012). The intradisciplinary influence of composition and WAC, Part 2. *The WAC Journal, 22*, 7–19.

Many, J. E., Fyfe, R., Lewis, G., & Mitchell, E. (1996). Traversing the topical landscape: Exploring students' self-directed reading-writing-research processes. *Reading Research Quarterly, 31*, 12–35.

Moje, E. B. (2009). A call for new research in new and multiliteracies. *Research in the Teaching of English, 43*(4), 348–62.

Murray, D. M. (1982). Teaching the other self: The writer's first reader. *College Composition and Communication, 33*(2), 140–47.

National Council of Teachers of English (NCTE). (2004). *NCTE beliefs about the teaching of writing.* Retrieved from http://www.ncte.org/positions/statements/writingbeliefs.

National Writing Project (NWP). (2016). *What sites do.* Retrieved from http://www.nwp.org/cs/public/print/doc/nwpsites/what_sites_do.csp.

New London Group. (1996). A pedagogy of multiliteracies: Designing social futures. *Harvard Educational Review, 66*(1), 60–93.

Noll, E., & Fox, D. L. (2003). Supporting beginning writers of research: Mentoring graduate students' entry into academic discourse communities. *Yearbook of the National Reading Conference, 52*, 332–44.

Perl, S. (1979). The composing processes of unskilled college writers. *Research in the Teaching of English, 13*(4), 317–36.

Roach, A. K. (2015). *Learning to write in public(s): A study of children's digital delivery in networked publics.* Unpublished diss., University of Texas, Austin, TX.

Rowe, D. W. (2008). The social construction of intentionality: Two-year-olds' and adults' participation at a preschool writing center. *Research in the Teaching of English, 42*(4), 387–434.

Schallert, D. L., & Martin, D. B. (2003). A psychological analysis of what teachers and students do in the language arts classroom. In J. Flood, D. Lapp, J. R. Squire, & J. M. Jensen (Eds.), *Handbook of research on teaching the English language arts* (pp. 31–45). Mahwah, NJ: Erlbaum.

Schon, D. (1983). *The reflective practitioner.* San Francisco: Jossey-Bass.

Shanahan, T. (1984). Nature of the reading-writing relation: An exploratory multivariate analysis. *Journal of Educational Psychology, 76*(3), 466–77.

Shanahan, T. (2006). Relations among oral language, reading, and writing development. In C. A. MacArthur, S. Graham, & J. Fitzgerald (Eds.), *Handbook of writing research* (pp. 171–83). New York: Guilford.

Shanahan, T., & Lomax, R. G. (1986). An analysis and comparison of theoretical models of the reading-writing relationship. *Journal of Educational Psychology, 78*(2), 116–23.

Shanahan, T., & Shanahan, C. (2008). Teaching disciplinary literacy to adolescents: Rethinking content-area literacy. *Harvard Educational Review, 78*, 40–59.

Shanahan, T., & Shanahan, C. R. (2015). Disciplinary literacy comes to middle school. *Voices from the Middle, 22*(3), 10–13.

Smagorinsky, P., Cook, L. S., & Reed, P. M. (2005). The construction of meaning and identity in the composition of an architectural text. *Reading Research Quarterly, 40*(1), 70–88.

Spivey, N. (1990). Transforming texts: Constructive processes in reading and writing. *Written Communication, 7*, 256–87.

Spivey, N. N., & King, J. R. (1989). Readers as writers composing from sources. *Reading Research Quarterly, 24*, 7–26.

Tierney, R. J., & Pearson, P. D. (1983). Toward a composing model of reading. *Language Arts, 60*(5), 568–80.

van Dijk, T. A., & Kintsch, W. (1983). *Strategies of discourse comprehension.* New York, NY: Academic Press.

Vetter, A., Myers, J., & Hester, M. (2014). Negotiating ideologies about teaching writing in a high school English classroom. *The Teacher Educator, 49*(1), 10–27.

Vogler, J. S., Schallert, D. L., Park, Y., Song, K., Chiang, Y. H. V., Jordan, M. E., . . . & Sanders, A. J. (2013). A microgenetic analysis of classroom discussion practices: How literacy processes intermingle in the negotiation of meaning in an online discussion. *Journal of Literacy Research*, *45*(3), 211–39.

Volosinov, V. N. (1929/86). *Marxism and the philosophy of language*, trans. L. Matejka & I. R. Titunik. Cambridge, MA: Harvard University Press (Original work published in 1929).

Vygotsky, L. S. (1978). *Mind in society: The development of higher psychological processes*. Cambridge, MA: Harvard University Press.

Wertsch, J. V. (1991). *Voices of the mind: A sociocultural approach to mediated action.* Cambridge, MA: Harvard University Press.

Wiley, M. (2000). The popularity of formulaic writing (and why we need to resist). *English Journal*, (September), 61–67.

Chapter 7

Improving Adolescents' Reading Comprehension and Engagement through Strategy-based Interventions

Susan Chambers Cantrell, Janice F. Almasi, and Margaret Rintamaa

ABSTRACT

In this chapter, we share lessons learned from two statewide evaluations of supplemental strategy-based reading interventions for adolescent readers. We first describe the interventions and provide a synthesis of research findings, including both quantitative student outcomes and perspectives on student engagement drawn from interviews with students themselves. Based on these lessons, we offer critical foundational elements of strategy-based interventions for students in middle and high schools. These insights, supported by our own work as well as the extant literature on strategy-based instruction, provide practical guidance for literacy educators and classroom teachers who wish to engage in strategy-based instruction as a curricular intervention.

INTRODUCTION

The ability to read, understand, and apply complex text is critical for success in postsecondary education and in the workforce; yet significant numbers of youth are not able to meet the challenges of school reading. Most recent results on the National Assessment of Educational Progress (NAEP) show that more than one quarter of eighth-grade students do not reach basic levels of achievement on NAEP and do not demonstrate basic abilities to locate information, identify the main idea, theme, or purpose of a passage, make simple inferences or interpret word meanings from text. Similarly, just 36 percent of eighth-grade students who participated in NAEP scored at or above the proficient level and demonstrated strong abilities to read, infer, and analyze complex texts (National Center for Education Statistics, 2013). Although these assessment results are concerning, they represent some improvements nationwide over previous assessment years. In the past decade, policy-makers and educators have focused greater attention on reading at the secondary level, funding programs and implementing practices to improve youth's reading achievement. Strengthened emphases on preparing more students for college, reducing the need for college remediation, and raising the dropout age in many states has caused secondary schools to develop systems of interventions for students who do not meet certain benchmarks in reading at particular points in their secondary schooling (Mellard, McKnight, & Jordan, 2010). Still, implementing interventions at the secondary level can be quite challenging, due to many constraints and considerations ranging from scheduling to meeting the wide-ranging needs of secondary students (Brozo, 2009/2010; Fuchs, Fuchs, & Compton, 2010; King, Lemons, & Hill, 2012).

In our own work, we have been involved with the federally funded Striving Readers program, which initially was created as a research-focused initiative designed to study targeted interventions for middle- and high-school students who were reading at lower levels as measured by standardized assessments. As evaluators of two Striving Readers interventions in one state, we learned a great deal about supplemental interventions for middle- and high-school students, and we present the models we evaluated and the results of those evaluations in this chapter. The recommendations we make are grounded, in part, in what we learned from those Striving Readers studies. In addition, they are informed by Susan's more recent work on the Culturally Responsive Instruction Observation Protocol (CRIOP), a framework for instruction in culturally diverse classrooms (Powell, Cantrell, & Rightmyer, 2013; Powell, Cantrell, Correll, & Malo-Juvera, 2016) and Janice's development, with her colleagues, of a narrative comprehension intervention for students at risk of attention-deficit hyperactivity disorder (Lorch, Milich, Almasi, van den Broek, Charnigo, & Hayden, 2012), and Margaret's work preparing middle school and secondary teachers. This chapter represents our collective knowledge about metacognition, comprehension, and engagement.

FRAMING THE ISSUE: ACHIEVEMENT AND ENGAGEMENT IN TWO STRATEGY-BASED INTERVENTIONS

Researchers have identified comprehension-based interventions as most effective in improving adolescents' reading achievement (Edmonds et al., 2009; Slavin, Cheung, Groff, & Lake, 2008). In particular, interventions geared toward students' strategy development are most often recommended for increasing comprehension abilities (Biancarosa & Snow, 2004; Conley,

2008). Strategies are cognitive, metacognitive, and behavioral processes that a reader uses to understand and apply texts in ways that serve the reader's purposes (Almasi & Fullerton, 2014; Graesser, 2007; Hacker, 2004; Paris, Lipson, & Wixson, 1983; Pressley, Borkowski, & Schneider, 1989). As students learn to employ strategies, such as summarizing, questioning, self-monitoring, connecting to prior knowledge, and constructing mental images, they are better able to create meaning and solve problems they may encounter during the reading process. Teachers can facilitate this learning by teaching these strategies to students in combination through explicit instruction and application opportunities (National Reading Panel, 2000). A goal of strategy instruction is making students more metacognitive, or aware and in control of their own thinking processes during reading. In learning how to think about their reading and to employ strategies as needed to achieve the goals of particular literacy tasks, students are better equipped to meet the demands of challenging academic reading.

To achieve high academic performance, students not only must be metacognitive strategy users, but they must also be motivated to read, comprehend, and to enact the strategies to achieve high levels of understanding. They must be willing to engage in and persist with challenging reading texts and tasks. Such levels of reading engagement are associated with reading achievement (Becker, McElvany, & Kortenbruck, 2010; Guthrie et al., 2013; Morgan & Fuchs, 2007; Mucherah & Yoder, 2008; Organisation for Economic Co-operation and Development [OECD], 2009). In their comprehensive research review on reading motivation (a key component of reading engagement), Schiefele, Schaffner, Moller, and Wigfield (2012) found interwoven and reciprocal relationships between motivation and reading competence. In simple terms, the more motivated a person is to read, the more s/he reads. The more a person reads, the better s/he gets at reading. The better a person is at reading, the more motivated s/he is to read. In this way, students' reading engagement fuels their competence, and in turn, increasing competence fuels reading engagement. These reciprocal relationships between motivation and reading competence have been the foundation of many strategies-based comprehension interventions such as the Learning Strategies Curriculum.

THE LEARNING STRATEGIES CURRICULUM

The Learning Strategies Curriculum is a strategy-based intervention for students who have difficulties with school reading. Initially developed for students with learning disabilities, this intervention has been used with students with and without disabilities (Tralli, Colombo, Deshler, & Schumaker, 1996). In the Learning Strategies Curriculum, students are taught strategies for understanding and solving problems with text. Strategies are categorized into three different strands. One strand focuses on *acquisition* of information during reading using strategies geared toward word identification, making mental pictures of what is read, paraphrasing text as it is read, and asking questions or making predictions during the reading process. A second strand focuses on *storage* of information or studying the information once it has been acquired. Strategies in this strand include helping students use mnemonics and other memorization tools, as well as techniques for understanding new vocabulary. The third strand focuses on *expression,* and strategies are geared toward strengthening students' skills in writing, monitoring for errors, and taking tests. The instructional approach is highly structured: students progress through eight instructional stages as they learn each strategy taught as part of the Learning Strategies Curriculum. Each strategy is taught through well-defined instructional stages that include explicit instruction with modeling, opportunities for guided and independent practice with both instructional-level and grade-level texts, and pre- and post-assessment. Once students have mastered a strategy, a concerted effort is made to draw students' attention to how they might use the strategy in other contexts and courses.

The research we conducted on the Learning Strategies Curriculum in our state showed positive results when it was implemented with sixth- and ninth-grade students who were reading two or more grade levels below grade level (Cantrell, Almasi, Rintamaa, & Carter, 2016). Students took a supplemental reading class in the place of an elective for an entire year, in addition to their regular English class. Using a randomized treatment-control group design, we compared achievement and motivation outcomes for 605 sixth-grade students who participated in the intervention with 530 students who did not participate and 593 ninth-grade students who participated in the intervention with 535 students who did not participate. After one year of intervention, we found significant impacts on reading motivation for both sixth- and ninth-grade students. In terms of reading achievement, we found significant impacts of the intervention for ninth-grade students but not for sixth-grade students after just one year of intervention. However, a follow-up study showed that sixth-grade students who were still low achieving after one year of intervention seemed to benefit from a second year of instruction in the Learning Strategies Curriculum. This led us to conclude that the Learning Strategies Curriculum was indeed beneficial, but that some students may need more than one year of intervention to see meaningful improvements on standardized measures. Later in this chapter, we will provide specific examples of the ways teachers in the project we evaluated used the Learning Strategies Curriculum to improve their reading comprehension and how aspects of instruction facilitated motivation.

In addition to student achievement outcomes, we examined teachers' implementation of the intervention and their sense of self-efficacy as they implemented the intervention over time. Over the course of our four-year evaluation, teachers grew in implementation of the intervention. Implementation fidelity was relatively low during the first year of implementation, but it improved to high levels by the end of the project. Interestingly, after the first year of implementation, we found that teachers' self-efficacy for literacy teaching was more important than implementation fidelity when it came to student achievement outcomes (Cantrell, Almasi, Carter, & Rintamaa, 2013). Students of teachers who felt confident about their abilities to teach literacy were more successful, despite teachers' lack of adherence to the Learning Strategies Curriculum model. As the years passed, teachers became more comfortable with the model and with managing their responsibilities as literacy leaders in their buildings (Cantrell, Madden, Rintamaa, Almasi, & Carter, 2015). Teachers needed more than one year to become comfortable with strategy instruction, especially if they did not have strong backgrounds in the area of literacy teaching.

KENTUCKY'S COGNITIVE LITERACY MODEL

Another strategy-based intervention we have experienced is Kentucky's Cognitive Literacy Model (KCLM). This intervention was developed by the state's Department of Education as an alternative to commercial programs that, to KCLM developers, sometimes seemed to marginalize teachers' expertise and minimize student engagement. A major intention behind KCLM is for schools to integrate the supplemental course into its system of interventions in ways that reduce student perceptions of KCLM as a remedial course and to use the course as an academic seminar of sorts. KCLM places student engagement at the center and addresses engagement through four primary instructional components: motivation, strategic processing, instructional strategies, and communication. Instruction in the four components is linked by content-related themes such as success, the environment, and problem-solving. Teachers work with students to investigate these themes through related topics, texts, and projects that embed explicit instruction in the four key KCLM components.

The KCLM addresses each key component in integrated ways as students investigate topics. The first component, *motivation,* focuses on utilizing instructional techniques that will cause students to want to engage in literacy tasks and to persist with those tasks. To motivate students, teachers ground instruction in real-world issues and engage students in project-based learning around those issues. Teachers use varied instructional formats (whole-group, small-group, partner work) and integrate technology and media in students' reading, writing, and research tasks. The second component, *strategic processing,* involves providing explicit comprehension strategy instruction in key strategies, such as making connections to prior knowledge, inferring and predicting, asking questions, summarizing, visualizing, and comprehension monitoring. Teachers focus on instruction through modeling, explanation, practice, and reflection. The third component, *content learning,* focuses on using tools for comprehension and vocabulary learning. As students engage in learning content around the focal themes, teachers embed vocabulary instruction through visual, auditory, physical, or emotional experiences. Teachers take time to explain and give examples of new, key terms and give students opportunities to use their own words or nonlinguistic representations to define new words. Students learn to use tools to support their comprehension in content learning, such as double entry journals, anticipation guides, and mind mapping. The fourth component, *communication,* focuses on strengthening students' oral and written communication skills. Students write collaboratively and independently to demonstrate learning, communicate in authentic ways as part of project-based learning, and reflect on and evaluate their own learning processes and products. Teachers engage students in pre-, during-, and post-text–based discussion strategies. They provide explicit instruction in writing strategies as well as foundational writing skills.

Funding for the federal Striving Readers research program was eliminated before we could complete our evaluation of the impacts of KCLM, but our work in schools during the two years that we collected data enabled us to conduct interviews with approximately seventy students who participated in KCLM and their teachers. These interviews provided a great deal of insight into the ways in which KCLM supported students' reading comprehension and engagement. From the perspectives of the students themselves, we were able to discern practices that students found engaging, and we were able to see which practices were less engaging for students. In short, the most important factors in promoting students' reading engagement within the context of the supplemental intervention class were *texts, topics, strategies,* and *relationships* (Cantrell, Pennington, Rintamaa, Osborne, Parker, & Rudd, in press). Students responded positively to relevant texts and topics and felt they had greater access to texts in their intervention class. But it wasn't just exposure to texts and opportunity to read them, the topics of the texts were critically important in engaging students. Students liked books that related to their lives and to which they could connect on a personal level. Texts with topics such as teen suicide, teen pregnancy, and drinking and driving were meaningful to students and engaging to them. Students also were motivated by digital texts and communicated their enthusiasm for conducting research and creating media such as public service announcements and blogs associated with content themes. Students' engagement waned, however, when they were asked to perform decontextualized tasks such as reading duplicated articles and completing related skill and vocabulary activities. Strategy instruction was a large component of KCLM, and in interviews students often articulated how they were learning to use specific strategies or were becoming more strategic, in general, in their reading both in and outside the intervention class.

PEDAGOGICAL IMPLICATIONS: THE FOUR "RS" OF READING INTERVENTIONS FOR ADOLESCENTS

Adolescence, as a period of developmental transition, is a time of change (Petersen, 1988). However, the notion that adolescence is chaotic, tumultuous, or a "normative disturbance" (Steinberg & Morris, 2001, p. 85) is not supported by developmental research (Petersen, 1988; Steinberg & Morris, 2001). Most adolescents make it through the biological, social, emotional and cognitive changes fairly well, and the most recent analyses of adolescents' reading achievement indicate increased performance by eighth graders from 2011 to 2013 and long-term substantive gains made by adolescents since 1971, particularly during the time period of 2008–2012 (Kena et al., 2015). As well, high school graduation rates have increased substantially from 74 percent in 1990 to 81 percent in 2012, and dropout rates have decreased from 12 percent in 1990 to 7 percent in 2012. However, reading achievement, graduation, and dropout rates vary by race and gender, with males performing worse than females and Black and Hispanic adolescents performing worse than white adolescents. Thus, a proportion of adolescents experience gradual declines in academic achievement, motivation, and engagement beginning in early adolescence that places them at risk, particularly during school transitions (Anderman, 2013; Eccles et al., 1993). Although research has not supported the notion that adolescents' academic and motivational decline is related to developmental changes, it does suggest that educators must design learning environments and contexts that match adolescents' developmental needs better (Anderman, 2013; Eccles Midgley et al., 1993; Eccles & Roeser, 2011). The aforementioned research syntheses suggest learning environments for adolescents should: (1) foster *relationships* between teachers and students that are more personal and positive; (2) offer instructional *routines* that take into account adolescents' increasing levels of cognitive sophistication wherein content is challenging but not competitive; (3) be *relevant*, taking advantage of adolescents' interests and affording opportunities for student decision-making, goal setting, and choice; (4) be *responsive* to students' needs.

Based on our evaluations of the two supplemental interventions implemented in Kentucky as part of Striving Readers, and on other work we have done in the areas of metacognition, comprehension, and engagement for students placed at risk and those who are already experiencing difficulty with school reading, we can offer a number of lessons we have learned about

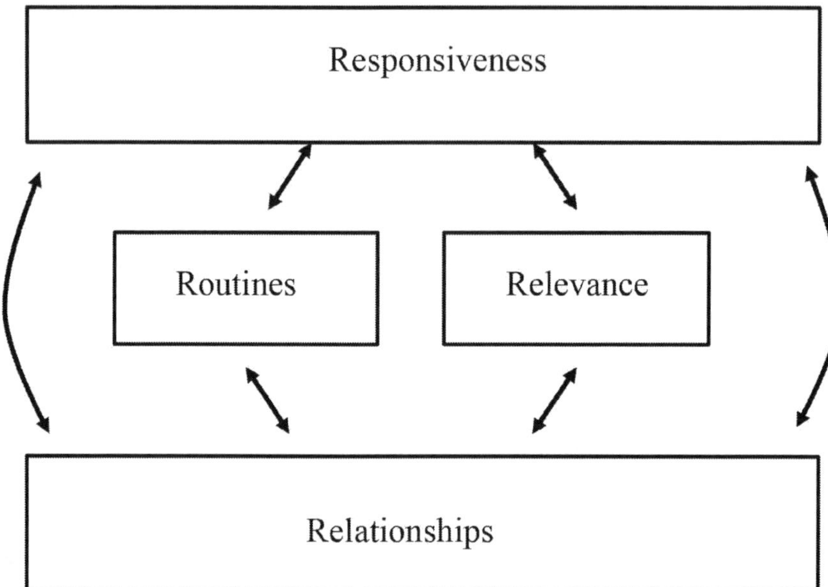

Figure 7.1 Four Rs of Supportive Reading Interventions for Adolescents

implementing strategy-based interventions for students. From these lessons and from the research on optimal learning environments for adolescents cited above, we have identified four critical components that we call "the four Rs" of reading interventions for adolescents: relationships, routines, relevance, and responsiveness. Figure 7.1 shows the ways in which we conceptualize these pedagogical concepts as interrelated and working in conjunction with one another within effective interventions for adolescents. In describing these concepts, we begin from the bottom, or foundation, and work upward, all the while recognizing the variety of contexts and external forces that influence the ways in which interventions are implemented.

RELATIONSHIPS

In many reading interventions for adolescents, the focus is primarily on cognitive dimensions of learning. However in our work, we have come to believe that classroom relationships are foundational to successful secondary reading interventions. Social relationships are at the heart of adolescents' lives both in and outside of school, and relationships with both adults and peers are primary in shaping students' identities. Student-teacher relationships play a pivotal role in student engagement, and as a result, these relationships influence student learning (Pianta, Hamre, & Allen, 2013). In our own research, one of the most critical factors in fostering engagement and learning in a supplemental reading intervention course was classroom relationships (Cantrell, et al., in press). In our evaluation of KCLM, students' relationship with the teacher was a key factor in students' perceptions of the class. If the students reported liking the teacher, they were likely to speak positively about the class. When we asked about the class, students often responded in terms of what the teacher did as opposed to the content of the class or class activities. The students perceived text and activity selection as a primary function of the teacher, and the extent to which they appreciated the texts, activities, and assignments directly related to their respect for the teacher. Equally important was the extent to which the supplemental intervention class provided a space in which teachers could develop relationships with students who had negative histories in the school setting.

When middle and high school students believe their teachers care about them personally, they are more likely to be engaged and to achieve academically (Pianta et al., 2013; Ryan & Patrick, 2001). We found this to be true in the predominantly rural settings in which we conducted our evaluations, and it is true for urban youth, as well. In their work with youth through the National Urban Alliance, Jackson, and Cooper (2007) reported that relationships with teachers were most vital to students' engagement. Specifically, they identified:

- Relationships that they believe appreciate their identity and honor them as individuals;
- Relationships that are built on genuine dialogue in which students and teachers communicate what's meaningful and relevant to them both; and
- Relationships in which teachers demonstrate the ardent belief in the potential of their students by bridging required content to students' personal frame of reference (p. 246).

To build relationships, teachers must get to know students in the whole of their lives in terms of students' cultural identities so they can make important curricular and instructional connections to students' lives. It is these connections that are especially important for students from historically underserved groups, including English Learners (Powell et al., 2013).

How do teachers establish positive relationships in an intervention setting? One of the key conditions for engagement in an intervention setting is support for student autonomy (Assor, 2013). Teachers can support student autonomy by providing choice in materials, texts, activities, and mode of expression. The more that teachers can minimize control, the higher level of autonomy students will experience. This often can be a difficult task for secondary teachers who are accustomed to traditional classroom structures and routines, which place the teacher at the center (O'Brien, Stewart, & Moje, 1995). We found it especially difficult for teachers in an intervention setting in which teachers worried that minimizing control might lead to behavior problems among students who had experienced failure in school. However, once positive classroom relationships are established and supported, students are likely to respond to autonomy and minimized control with higher engagement and learning.

Another key condition in supporting student-teacher relationships is having empathy and showing respect for students' feelings and perspectives, especially when students disagree with the teacher (Assor, 2013). As one student in our KCLM evaluation said about her teacher, "She lets me speak my mind." Creating contexts in which students can interact with the teacher in an atmosphere of mutual respect lays the foundation for an effective intervention.

ROUTINES

Instruction for adolescents should focus on challenging, higher-level cognitive strategies, but such instruction should not overwhelm to the point of frustration. Critical thinking and creativity should permeate lessons. In addition to a focus on cognitive processes, well-designed lessons that meet adolescents developmental needs include challenging content that requires critical thinking and permits creativity. However, that challenging content should be delivered using classroom and instructional routines that provide stability. Routines become very important in designing and implementing comprehension interventions, particularly for students who struggle to comprehend. "Routine" refers broadly to regular patterns used to organize instruction within a lesson and across the school day. For some students who struggle with comprehension, regularity within lessons provides predictability. When students are able to anticipate and predict what will occur next in a lesson or throughout the school day, it enhances engagement, helps them understand time allotment, and reduces stress, anxiety, and behavior problems (Kern & Clemens, 2007; Martella & Marchand-Martella, 2015). This is not to suggest that instruction should be rote or repetitious, instead we are suggesting that a predictable pattern for activities within a lesson is helpful.

In addition to regular patterns, "routine" refers to an "integrated set of practices" (Duke & Pearson, 2002, p. 225). Examples of such instructional routines include integrated sets of comprehension strategies such as the Learning Strategies Curriculum or reciprocal teaching. Hinchman (2006) points out that simplicity is key in helping students learn and apply strategies in a range of contexts: "Explicit instruction should be straightforward and brief. Yet it must include information on how a strategy can be used, as well as a model of such use within the context of a variety of texts" (p. 127). Supported and independent practice should follow explicit instruction, with teachers continuously assessing and scaffolding student learning and application through responsive coaching until students use the strategies independently and flexibly. When teachers implement reading interventions that support this gradual release of responsibility through structured routines, they provide a framework for learning that reduces the cognitive load for students. For example, in the Learning Strategies Curriculum, each strategy is taught through eight instructional stages: pretest and commitments, describe, model, verbal practice, controlled practice and feedback, posttest and commitments, and generalization. Students quickly become familiar with this structure and know what to expect as they learn and integrate the strategies.

Students at risk of attention-deficit hyperactivity disorder (ADHD), in particular, benefit from classroom and instruction routines in that these students tend to have difficulty with working memory. For students with attentional issues, their ability to store and retrieve complex information and organize it for recall it is compromised (Barkley, 1997). Thus, comprehension and strategic processing are particularly difficult for these students. Predictable instructional routines such as those used in explicit instruction, or in particular interventions such as the Learning Strategies Curriculum are helpful. Instructional aids such as graphic organizers or mnemonics that facilitate storage and retrieval of text are necessary supports.

In the Learning Strategies Curriculum classrooms in which we observed, teachers tended to follow a predictable routine. Each class period usually began with a review of the steps of the prior day's focal strategy. The class would then progress through one or two of the eight instructional stages during the class session. For example, on one day a teacher began her class with a discussion of the visualization strategy known by the mnemonic SCENE (see appendix A). She asked for volunteers to say what each of the letters stood for, and to provide examples as each step was named (verbal practice). On a prior day, the students had created foldables that provided a visual of each of the steps, and once the review was complete, the students used this tool in pairs or small groups to practice the SCENE strategy with a play that they were preparing to read (controlled practice). In another example, the teacher began the class period discussing the questioning strategy ASKIT (see appendix A). Students volunteered what each letter stood for, and the teacher reminded them about each of the steps. The teacher then read aloud from the novel *Number the Stars* (Lowry, 1989), modeling the ASKIT strategy as she read (modeling). Then she had the students read to themselves and practice the strategy (controlled practice).

As depicted by the arrows in figure 7.1, routines can affect classroom relationships and vice versa. Routines can provide a sense of structure and safety for students that enable students to take cognitive and social risks to improve engagement and learning. Once well established, these routines also can give teachers a sense of security in allowing students more autonomy in decision-making or in collaborative work. Similarly, strong classroom relationships can affect routines as teachers learn to evoke more engage responses from students during intervention routines as classroom relationships deepen.

RELEVANCE

Researchers who have made recommendations for improving adolescent literacy based on compiled research identify student engagement as an essential dimension for reading and literacy interventions and point to the importance of attention to students' motivation. (Alverman, 2001; Biancarosa & Snow, 2004; Kamil et al., 2008). In our own work with literacy interventions, we have found this emphasis on students' engagement and motivation to be well placed. In our evaluation of KCLM, we found student growth was greater in classrooms in which students were actively participating and persisting with challenging tasks than when students were passive and inattentive.

In our research, students have told us that they are most engaged by relevant texts, topics, and tasks. Students want to read diverse and interesting texts about topics that directly relate to their lives. These texts can be modern young adult novels, and they also can be classic texts as long as students can relate to the characters and their problems. In the KCLM intervention, students were engaged by popular novels such as *The Hunger Games* (Collins, 2008), and they also mentioned classic texts such as *To Kill a Mockingbird* (Lee, 1960). In addition to novels, students used electronic and internet-based texts to conduct research and explore difficult issues such as bullying, teen pregnancy, and drinking and driving. Further, teachers utilized video and other visual images to encourage thinking and learning about these relevant issues. When texts were too difficult for students to read completely on their own, teachers read aloud parts of the text to students to scaffold students' comprehension. Teachers anticipated new vocabulary and potentially challenging concepts in advance of the reading and supported students' comprehension by discussing these more difficult aspects of the text prior to reading. Strategies were practiced in the context of these texts as teachers modeled during read-alouds and as students practiced independently during silent reading.

In an intervention setting for adolescents, the work that students do needs to be contextualized within students' lives and what is important to them. Real-world issues, including socio-political ones, are motivating for students. At times in KCLM, teachers had students read duplicated articles that included vocabulary activities and comprehension questions to accompany the articles. However, in our observations and interviews of students who participated in KCLM, we found reading and writing for real purposes and audiences was

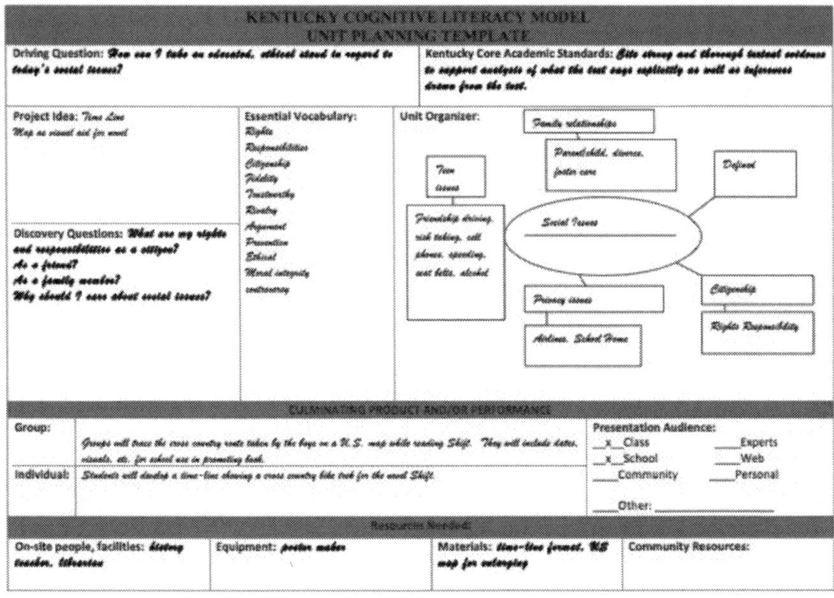

KENTUCKY COGNITIVE LITERACY MODEL
UNIT PLANNING TEMPLATE

Driving Question: *How can I take an educated, ethical stand in regard to today's social issues?*

Kentucky Core Academic Standards: *Cite strong and thorough textual evidence to support analysis of what the text says explicitly as well as inferences drawn from the text.*

Project Idea: *Time Line Map as visual aid for novel*

Discovery Questions: *What are my rights and responsibilities as a citizen? As a friend? As a family member? Why should I care about social issues?*

Essential Vocabulary: *Rights, Responsibilities, Citizenship, Fidelity, Trustworthy, Rivalry, Argument, Prevention, Ethical, Moral integrity, controversy*

Unit Organizer:

CULMINATING PRODUCT AND/OR PERFORMANCE

Group: *Groups will trace the cross country route taken by the boys on a U.S. map while reading Shift. They will include dates, visuals, etc. for school use in promoting book.*

Individual: *Students will develop a time-line showing a cross country bike trek for the novel Shift.*

Presentation Audience:
__x__Class ____Experts
__x__School ____Web
____Community ____Personal
____Other: __________

Resources Needed:

On-site people, facilities: *history teacher, librarian*

Equipment: *poster maker*

Materials: *time-line format, US map for enlarging*

Community Resources:

Adapted from *The Unit Organizer Routine* (Edge Enterprises, 1994); *PBL Starter Kit* (The Buck Institute for Education, 2009); "How to Develop a Standards-Based Unit of Study" (Kentucky Department of Education, 2007); and *High Schools That Work and Making Middle Grades Work Summer Institute* (Southern Regional Education Board, 2008).

READING STRATEGIES	TEACHING TOOLS: Increasing Comprehension	TEACHING TOOLS: Expanding Vocabulary
☐ **PK** Making connections to/activating prior knowledge; developing schema X **I/P** Inferring and predicting ☐ **Q** Asking questions ☐ **S** Determining important ideas and summarizing X **V** Visualizing ☐ **S/R** Synthesizing and retelling ☐ **M/C** Monitoring/clarifying understanding of text *The letters in bold indicate an abbreviation each reading strategy. The strategies are coded to the comprehension and/or vocabulary teaching tools that support them.	Cues, Questions and Advance Organizers X Anticipation/Reaction Guide (PK, Q, M/C) ☐ Question/Answer/Relationship (PK, I/P, Q, S, M/C) ☐ Skimming (PK, I/P, V, S/R) Non-linguistic Representations ☐ Pattern Organizers (S, V) ☐ Mind Mapping (Q, V, S/R, M/C) X Pictograph (PK, V) Identifying Similarities and Differences ☐ Comparison Matrix Chart (PK, S) ☐ Comparison Guide Map (PK, S, V, S/R, M/C) ☐ Graphic Organizer for Analogies and Metaphors (I/P, S, V) ☐ Student or Teacher-Generated Classification Graphic Organizer (dependent on graphic organizer) Summarizing and Note taking ☐ Cornell Notes (Q, S, MC) ☐ Note Taking Using Both Sides of the Brain (PK, S, V, M/C) X Summary Frame (Dependent on frame) ☐ Rule-Based Strategy (Q, S, M/C)	Vocabulary Activities X Word Storm (PK, I/P) ☐ Closed /Open Word Sort (PK, Q, S, V, S/R) ☐ Three-Way Tie (PK, I/P, Q, V, M/C) ☐ Connect the Words (PK, I/P, Q, V, S/R, M/C) ☐ LitFig (PK, I/P, Q, V, M/C) X Four Square Vocabulary Map/Frayer Model (PK, V, M/C) ☐ Word Questioning (PK, I/P, Q, S, V, S/R, M/C) X Text Impressions (PK, I/P, Q) ☐ Cinquain (PK, S, V, S/R, M/C) ☐ Rate Your Knowledge (P/K, I/P, Q/ M/C) ☐ Vocabulary Tree (PK, M/C) Vocabulary Games ☐ Password (PK, I/P, V, S/R) ☐ Memory (PK, MC) ☐ Most Important Word (PK, I/P, Q, S) X **Key word match –Smart Board**

COMMUNICATION	ASSESSMENTS	
Writing	**Formative**	
X Writing to Learn: emphasizes the students' thinking in an informal form (e.g. any KCLM teaching tool that requires writing). ☐ Writing to Demonstrate Learning: intended to assess learning of content or ability to complete a task (e.g. exit slips, rough drafts, student-generated graphic organizer). ☐ Writing for Authentic Purposes: intended to develop skills in communication and to promote learning and thinking (e.g. articles, letters, editorials, written projects, blogs, web pages).	☐ Student Goal-setting ☐ Journal/Learning Log X Graphic Organizers ☐ Rough Drafts ☐ Checklists (Introducing, Progressing, Mastering, etc.) X Review Games/Activities X Teacher Questioning X Exit Slips/Activities ☐ Student Practice Activities/Exercise	X Student Partner Talk (Think-Pair-Share; Turn & Talk) X Preliminary Plans/ Outlines/ Prototypes PBL Progress Work Report : Individual ☐ PBL Progress Work Report: Group ☐ Practice Presentation X Quizzes/Tests ☐ Teacher's Anecdotal Notes ☐ Role-Playing X One-on-one Student/Teacher Conference ☐ Other ________
Speaking	**Summative**	
X Paired Discussion X Group Discussion X Presenting to an Audience	☐ Written Project, with Rubric ☐ Oral Presentation, with Rubric ☐ On Demand Writing X Test	☐ Peer Evaluation X Self-Evaluation ☐ Other ________

Adapted from *The Unit Organizer Routine* (Edge Enterprises, 1994); *PBL Starter Kit* (The Buck Institute for Education, 2009); "How to Develop a Standards-Based Unit of Study" (Kentucky Department of Education, 2007); and *High Schools That Work and Making Middle Grades Work Summer Institute* (Southern Regional Education Board, 2008).

Figure 7.2 Kentucky Cognitive Literacy Model Unit Planning Template

much more engaging for students than reading passages printed on worksheets and doing related vocabulary and comprehension exercises. We found students were much more enthusiastic about creating public service announcements or brochures on relevant topics such as bullying, teen pregnancy, or drinking and driving. They were engaged in conducting the research to strengthen their authentic products. This is an example of theme-based learning in which students explore real-world issues engages students in literacy learning.

Figure 7.2 shows an example of a Unit Planning Template from KCLM in which teachers built instruction around a relevant theme for students. Each component of the intervention is addressed using materials, resources, and activities related to that particular theme. Not only does this approach facilitate cross-curricular content learning, but it also provides rich opportunities for authentic language use and literacy practice to support students' literacy engagement and achievement. On the second section of the template, teachers select the reading strategies that will be taught or re-enforced as part of the unit.

The ways in which students are encouraged to approach their work can make a difference in the extent to which students find their learning relevant in an intervention setting. Digital technologies are essential elements in adolescents' lives outside of school, and they appreciate opportunities to utilize digital tools inside the classroom, as well. Internet-based texts, videos, music, electronic texts are motivating to students and build upon the knowledge they already have. These opportunities provide adolescents who have been labeled as "struggling" with different ways to demonstrate their abilities in ways that not only support students' self-efficacy for literacy tasks, but also reconceptualize competence for adolescents who have been unsuccessful with more traditional school-based literacy tasks (O'Brien, 2007). Adolescents also appreciate opportunities to work collaboratively to create projects and discuss texts. The following excerpt from an interview with a student from a KCLM classroom illustrates the difference that relevance can make for students:

> *I:* The last time I was here you were working on a brochure about . . . I think you were doing teen pregnancy?
>
> *S:* Yeah. I liked doing that 'cause you got to do something different. Like work on the computer and iPads and get your information. And I don't know. I just liked doing it.
>
> *I:* So did you guys all agree on [pause] did you talk about a topic or how did you pick . . . how did you guys pick that topic?
>
> *S:* I guess because it's so big around here, teen pregnancy and [pause] I don't know. I guess we just wanted to do something that we know about. Stuff we know about.

In supplemental reading intervention classrooms that really engage students, teachers provide regular and multiple opportunities for students to be active in their own literacy learning. Alvermann and McClean (2007) label literacy instruction that is grounded in students' interests and engages students in taking an active role in their learning as "participatory instruction" (p. 7). In participatory classrooms, students set and monitor progress toward their long- and short-term goals, and they openly discuss and learn about issues of importance. Rather than assuming students who have experienced school reading failure are incapable or disengaged, Alvermann and McClean call for an approach in which teachers validate the literacy practices in which students already engaged both in and out of school. They describe a participatory approach in which students

> read for multiple purposes from trade books, textbooks, magazines, newspapers, student-generated texts, digital texts, hypermedia productions, visuals, artistic performances, and the like . . . teachers create opportunities to engage actively in meaningful subject matter learning that extends and elaborates on the literacy practices they already own and value. (p. 8)

We agree these practices really are best for engaging students in literacy learning and improving their literacy achievement. However, we also believe these are not the kinds of experiences that students who struggle with school reading are often provided, particularly in a reading intervention setting. By increasing the use of these participatory practices within the reading intervention classroom, teachers can make interventions more relevant and meaningful to students.

As shown by the arrows in figure 7.1, relevance is reciprocally related to classroom relationships. Teachers must come to know students personally to understand what is relevant to students. Before teachers can make curricular and instructional connections to students' lives and experiences, they must have a strong sense of their students' cultural identities. In turn, as teachers work to make intervention content, texts, and activities more relevant to students, classroom relationships will deepen.

RESPONSIVENESS

An overarching element essential for an effective secondary reading intervention is responsiveness. Teachers who implement reading interventions for adolescents must be responsive to the specific needs of each learner, because adolescents' requirements for success vary widely. One of the factors that must be considered in implementing strategy-based interventions is the time it takes for students to internalize and apply reading strategies in a variety of contexts. One of the findings from our study of the Learning Strategies Curriculum was that strategies can take a long time to learn, and some struggling readers need extended time to learn them (Cantrell et al., 2013). Although short-term interventions can be effective for very young children who are experiencing difficulties learning to read (Schwartz, 2005), middle and high school students may benefit more from interventions that span a whole school year or even longer. Through regular progress monitoring, teachers can evaluate how much students have improved and can identify students who may need additional time and instruction in the intervention.

Teachers also must demonstrate responsiveness in the ways in which they teach strategies and scaffold students' flexible strategy use. In the most effective interventions, teachers focus on introducing and practicing strategies individually but then facilitate application for integrated use of the strategies in a variety of contexts (Edmonds et al., 2009). For example in the Learning Strategies Curriculum, teachers introduce a visualizing strategy by describing and modeling the steps of the strategy using a mnemonic (SCENE). They engage students in various stages of guided and independent practice, provide opportunities to use the strategy in both instructional-level and grade-level texts, and encourage use of the visualization strategy in a variety of contexts. Although teachers introduced each strategy sequentially through an eight-stage process, strategies were continually reviewed and integrated. In one Learning Strategies Curriculum classroom that we observed, students were instructed to find a place where they could use a strategy for identifying an unknown word and to use the SCENE strategy for visualization during silent reading of a self-selected text. Teachers showed responsiveness by scaffolding students' strategy use as they encountered difficulties with reading. Teachers used prompts and reminders as key tools during the scaffolding process. In one classroom we observed, the teacher had many strategies posted on the bulletin board that had been introduced through the Learning Strategies Curriculum. During one class session, she gave the students an article and asked students to select a strategy from the bulletin board to practice as they read the article. The teacher demonstrated responsiveness to students' needs by allowing the students to select a strategy to practice based on students' self-assessment of their goals and progress toward strategy acquisition.

Responsiveness to adolescents' developmental needs means that teachers must be keen observers, make use of assessments that can actually inform instruction, and select instructional interventions that are matched to students' social, cognitive, and motivational needs. In their descriptive case study of the manner in which four school districts implemented Response to Intervention in its first year, Almasi, Edwards and Hart (2011) found that teachers and administrators were uncertain and confused about the manner in which RTI should be implemented. This confusion meant that schools scrambled to find adequate resources and materials to meet students' needs. Ultimately, schools relied on what Wanzek and Vaughn (2007) refer to as "standardized interventions," or interventions that are already developed and that have determined in advance, what reading skills or strategies that are taught, the order in which they are taught, and often featured scripted lessons that insure fidelity to the program. Under some dimensions of this definition, the Learning Strategies Curriculum might be considered a standardized intervention. The problem in Almasi, Edwards and Hart's (2011) study, however, was that schools indiscriminately placed all students who needed tier 2 instruction into the same intervention regardless of individual needs. As students completed these interventions, school personnel found students were not successful and began to realize that the standardized interventions were not meeting students' needs. In other words, the selected intervention and the subsequent instruction were not responsive to students.

This is not to suggest that standardized interventions are not helpful, but they are developed in research settings and are affiliated more with research than practice (Fuchs & Fuchs, 2006). Thus, in order to be effective and responsive to students' needs, it is essential to examine the population of students for whom a standardized intervention was designed and implement it with fidelity as it was intended in order to reap the social, cognitive, or motivational benefits found in the original research.

When considering the entire learning environment, responsiveness is overarching because, as shown by the arrows in figure 7.1, it is integrally linked to the other three essential elements. Moje (2008) suggests responsiveness "requires (1) knowledge of young people, (2) knowledge of the disciplines and/or the secondary school subject areas, and (3) knowledge of the texts and literacy practices that are valued and privileged in both" (p. 60). If relationships are a foundational element of effective interventions for adolescents in the ways in which teachers know and respect students, then responsiveness is the way in which teachers utilize their knowledge of students' lives, interests, experiences, and needs to expand students' knowledge and abilities. At the same time, secondary reading intervention teachers must be attune to and adjust instruction for the content and literacy practices that both will enable students to be successful in school and will resonate with students as relevant. Responsiveness even plays out in intervention routines as teachers consistently assess students' needs and adjust their instruction in accordance with those needs.

CONCLUSION

The lessons we have learned about reading interventions for secondary students are drawn from two very different supplemental interventions and from work that has taken us in even more disparate directions since we evaluated the interventions we described in this chapter. The Learning Strategies Curriculum and KCLM interventions reflect different views of literacy (the first more cognitive, the second more social), yet both offer important opportunities for students when implemented within a supportive setting that considers the varied goals, knowledge, experiences and identities that adolescents bring to the intervention context. Reading interventions can accelerate the reading achievement of middle and high school students, but educators should take caution not to assume intervention practices that work for younger children will accelerate the progress of older readers in those same ways (Wanzek, Vaughn, Scammacca et al., 2013).

Based on our work we know that relationships, relevance, routines and responsiveness are critical in engaging adolescent readers and improving reading comprehension in strategy-based intervention settings. However, often there are factors outside of a teacher's control that impact the ability to create each of these in an intervention classroom. Budget constraints can lead to larger class sizes in which it is more difficult to develop strong relationships with each student, thereby affecting teacher responsiveness and instructional relevance. At the same time, policy mandates and assessment pressures can lead to widespread adoption of packaged "one-size-fits-all" interventions that fail to consider the particular needs of the students who may be placed in those interventions. Teachers sometimes have limited access to professional learning opportunities and training to implement the intervention, yet we know teachers need a clear understanding of and support for establishing routines that will maximize learning.

Despite these challenges, we have seen expert teachers who focus on relationships, routines, relevance, and responsiveness in the context of sound strategy-based reading instruction make a positive difference in adolescents' reading comprehension and engagement. However, more research is needed that examines the efficacy of strategy-based interventions in a variety of classroom contexts with a wide range of student populations so educators can better predict for whom a particular intervention might work best. Similarly, research is needed that highlights ways to better utilize and be responsive to students' cultural and adolescent identities within the intervention setting to maximize student learning and improve the ways in which interventions are implemented.

REFERENCES

Almasi, J. F., Edwards, P., & Hart, S. (2011, December). *Waiting for special education: Intended and unintended influences of RTI on literacy instruction*. Paper presented at the 61st Annual Meeting of the Literacy Research Association (formerly the National Reading Conference). Jacksonville, FL.

Almasi, J. F., & Fullerton, S. K. (2012). *Teaching strategic processes in reading*, 2nd ed. New York: Guilford.

Alvermann, D. E. (2001). *Effective literacy instruction for adolescents.* Paper Commissioned by the National Reading Conference. Chicago, IL: National Reading Conference.

Alvermann, D. E. & McClean, C. A. (2007). The nature of literacies. In L. S. Rush, J. Eakle, & A. Berger (Eds.), *Secondary school literacy: What research reveals about classroom practice.* Urbana, IL: National Council of Teachers of English.

Anderman, E. M. (2013). Middle school transitions. In J. Hattie & E. M. Anderman (Eds.), *International Guide to Student Achievement* (pp. 176–78). New York: Routledge.

Assor, A. (2013). Allowing choice and nurturing an inner compass: Educational practices supporting students' need for autonomy. In S. L. Christenson, A. L. Reschly, & C. Wylie (Eds.), *Handbook of research on student engagement* (pp. 421–40). New York: Springer.

Aukerman, M. (2013). Rereading comprehension pedagogies: Toward a dialogic teaching ethic that honors student sensemaking. *Dialogic Pedagogy: An International Online Journal, 9*(1), A1–30.

Becker, M., McElvany, N., & Kortenbruck, M. (2010). Intrinsic and extrinsic reading motivation as predictors of reading literacy: A longitudinal study. *Journal of Educational Psychology, 102*, 773–85.

Biancarosa, G., & Snow, C. E. (2004). *Reading next – A vision for action and research in middle and high school literacy: A report from the Carnegie Corporation of New York.* Washington, DC: Alliance for Excellent Education.

Brozo, W. G. (2009/10). Response to intervention or responsive instruction? Challenges and possibilities of response to intervention for adolescent literacy. *Journal of Adolescent & Adult Literacy, 53,* 277–81. doi:10.1598/JAAL.53.4.1.

Cantrell, S. C., Almasi, J. F., Rintamaa, M., & Carter, J. C. (2016). Supplemental reading strategy instruction for adolescents: A randomized trial and follow-up study. *Journal of Educational Research, 109*(1), 7-26.

Cantrell, S. C., Almasi, J. F., Carter, J. C, & Rintamaa, M. (2013). Reading intervention in middle and high schools: Implementation fidelity, teacher efficacy, and student achievement. *Reading Psychology, 34*, 26–58.

Cantrell, S. C., Madden, A., Rintamaa, M., Almasi, J. F., & Carter, J. C. (2015). The development of literacy coaches' efficacy beliefs in a dual-role position. *Journal of School Leadership*, 25(4), 562-591.

Cantrell, S. C., Pennington, J., Rintamaa, M., Osborne, M., Parker, C., & Rudd, M. (in press). Supplemental literacy instruction in high school: What students say matters for reading engagement. *Reading and Writing Quarterly.*

Collins, S. (2008). *The hunger games.* New York: Scholastic.

Conley, M. W. (2008). Cognitive strategy instruction for adolescents: What we know about the promise, what we don't know about the potential. *Harvard Educational Review, 78*, 84–106.

Duke, N. K., & Pearson, P. D. (2002). Effective practices for developing reading comprehension. In A. E. Farstrup & S. J. Samuels (Eds.), *What research has to say about reading instruction*, 3rd ed. (pp. 205–42). Newark, DE: International Reading Association.

Eccles, J. S., Midgley, C., Wigfield, A., Buchanan, C. M., Reuman, D., Flanagan, C., & MacIver, D. (1993). Development during adolescence: The impact of stage-environment fit on young adolescents' experiences in schools and families. *American Psychologist, 48*(2), 90–101.

Eccles, J. S., & Roeser, R. W. (2011). Schools as developmental contexts during adolescence. *Journal of Research on Adolescence, 21*(1), 225–41.

Edmonds, M. S., Vaughn, S., Wexler, J., Reutebuch, A. C., Tackett, K. K., & Schnakenberg, J. W. (2009). A synthesis of reading interventions and their effects on reading comprehension outcomes for older struggling readers. *Review of Educational Research, 79*, 262–300.

Fuchs, D., & Fuchs, L. S. (2006). Introduction to Response to Intervention: What, why, and how valid is it? *Reading Research Quarterly, 41*(1), 93–99.

Fuchs, L., Fuchs, D., & Compton, D. (2010). Rethinking response to intervention at middle and high school. *School Psychology Review, 39*(1), 22–28.

Graesser, A. C. (2007). An introduction to strategic reading comprehension. In D. S. McNamara (Ed.), *Reading comprehension strategies: Theories, interventions, and technologies* (pp. 3–26). New York: Lawrence Erlbaum Associates.

Guthrie, J. T., Klauda, S. L., & Ho, A. N. (2013). Modeling the relationships among reading instruction, motivation, engagement, and achievement for adolescents. *Reading Research Quarterly, 48*, 9–26.

Hacker, D. J. (2004). Self-regulated comprehension during normal reading. In R. B. Ruddell & N. J. Unrau (Eds.), *Theoretical models and processes of reading*, 5th ed. (pp. 755–79). Newark, DE: International Reading Association.

Hinchman, K. A. (2006). I want to learn to read before I graduate: How sociocultural research on adolescent literacy struggles can shape classroom practice. In L. S. Rush, J. Eakle, & A. Berger (Eds.), *Secondary school literacy: What research reveals for classroom practice.* Urbana, IL: NCTE.

Jackson, Y. & Cooper, E. J. (2008). Building academic success with underachieving adolescents. In K. Beers, R. E. Probst, & L. Rief (Eds.), *Adolescent literacy: Turning promise into practice*. Portsmouth, NH: Heinemann.

Kamil, M, L., Borman, G. D., Dole, J., Kral, C. C., Salinger, T. S., & Torgesen, J. (2008). *Improving adolescent literacy: Effective classroom and intervention practices.* Washington, DC: U.S. Department of Education, Institute of Education Sciences, National Center for Education Evaluation and Regional Assistance.

Kena, G., Musu-Gillette, L., Robinson, J., Wang, X., Rathbun, A., Zhang, J., Wilkinson-Flicker, S., Barmer, A., & Dunlop Velez, E. (2015). The Condition of Education 2015 (NCES 2015-144). Washington, DC: U.S. Department of Education, National Center for Education Statistics. Retrieved May 27, 2015 from http://nces.ed.gov/pubsearch.

Kern, L., & Clemens, N. H. (2007). Antecedent strategies to promote appropriate classroom behavior. *Psychology in the Schools, 44*(1), 65–75.

King, S. A., Lemons, C. J., & Hill, D. R. (2012). Response to intervention in secondary schools: Considerations for administrators. *NASSP Bulletin, 96*, 5–22.

Lee, H. (1960). *To kill a mockingbird.* New York: Grand Central Publishing.

Lorch, E. P., Milich, R., Almasi, J. F., van den Broek, P., Charnigo, R., & Hayden, A. (2012). *A narrative comprehension intervention for elementary school children at-risk for attention-deficit hyperactivity disorder.* Retrieved from http://ies.ed.gov/ncer/projects/grant.asp?ProgID=5&grantid=1272.

Lowry, L. (1989). *Number the stars.* New York: Sterling.

Martella, R. C., & Marchand-Martella, N. E. (2015). Effective instruction: An illustrative program example using SRA FLEX Literacy. *Education and Treatment of Children, 38*(2), 241–72.

Mellard, D., McKnight, M., & Jordan, J. (2010). RTI tier structures and instructional intensity. *Learning Disabilities Research and Practice*, 25, 217–25.

Morgan, P. L., & Fuchs, D. (2007). Is there a bidirectional relationship between children's reading skills and reading motivation? Exceptional Children, 73, 165–83.

Mucherah, W., & Yoder, A. (2008). Motivation for reading and middle school students' performance on standardized testing in reading. *Reading Psychology, 29*, 214–35.

National Center for Education Statistics (2013). *The Nation's Report Card: A First Look: 2013 Mathematics and Reading* (NCES 2014-451). Washington, DC: Institute of Education Sciences, U.S. Department of Education.

National Reading Panel (2000). *Teaching children to read: An evidence-based assessment of the scientific research literature on reading and its implications for reading instruction* (Report of the Subgroups). Washington, DC: U.S. Department of Health and Human Services, Public Health Service, National Institutes of Health, and the National Institute of Child Health and Human Development.

O'Brien, D. G., Stewart, R. A., & Moje, E. B. *(*1995*).* Why content literacy is difficult to infuse into the secondary curriculum: Strategies, goals, and classroom realities. Reading Research Quarterly, 30, 442–63.

O'Brien, D. G. (2007). "Struggling" adolescents' engagement in multimediating: Countering the institutional construction of incompetence. In D. E. Alvermann, K. A. Hinchman, D. W. Moore, S. F. Phelps, & D. R. Waff (Eds.), *Reconceptualizing the literacies in adolescents' lives (2nd edition)* (pp. 29–46). Mahwah, NJ: Lawrence Erlbaum Associates.

Organisation for Economic Co-operation and Development. (2009). *PISA Results (Volume III), Learning to Learn: Student engagement strategies and practices. Reading for change—Performance and Engagement across Countries.* Paris: OECD. http://browse.oecdbookshop.org/oecd/pdfs/browseit/9810091E.PDF.

Paris, S. G., Lipson, M. Y., & Wixson, K. K. (1983). Becoming a strategic reader. *Contemporary Educational Psychology, 8*, 293–316.

Petersen, A. C. (1988). Adolescent development. *Annual Review of Psychology, 39,* 583–607.

Pianta, R. C., Hamre, B. K., & Allen, J. P. (2013). Teacher-student relationships and engagement: Conceptualizing, measuring, and improving the capacity of classroom interactions. In S. L. Christenson, A. L. Reschly, & C. Wylie (Eds.), *Handbook of Research on Student Engagement* (pp. 365–86). New York: Springer.

Powell, R., Cantrell, S. C., Malo-Juvera, V., & Correll, P. (2016). Operationalizing culturally responsive instruction: Preliminary findings of CRIOP research. *Teacher's College Record, 118,* 1-46.

Powell, R., Cantrell, S. C., & Rightmyer, E. (2013). Teaching and reaching all students: An instructional model for closing the gap. *Middle School Journal, 44,* 22–30.

Pressley, M., Borkowski, J. G., & Schneider, W. (1989). Good information processing: What it is and how education can promote it. *International Journal of Educational Research, 13,* 857–67.

Ryan, A. M., & Patrick, H. (2001). The classroom social environment and changes in adolescents' motivation and engagement during middle school. *American Educational Research Journal, 38*, 437–60.

Schiefele, U., Schaffner, E., Moller, J., & Wigfield, A. (2012). Dimensions of reading motivation and their relation to reading behavior and competence. *Reading Research Quarterly, 47*, 427–63.

Schwartz, R. M. (2005). Literacy learning of at-risk first-grade students in the Reading Recovery early intervention. *Journal of Educational Psychology, 97,* 257–67.

Slavin, R. E., Cheung, A., Groff, C., & Lake, C. (2008). Effective reading programs for middle and high schools: A best-evidence synthesis. *Reading Research Quarterly, 43*(3), 290–322.

Steinberg, L., & Morris, A. S. (2001). Adolescent development. *Annual Review of Psychology, 52*, 83–110.

Tralli, R., Colombo, B., Deshler, D. D., & Schumaker, J. B. (1996). The Strategies Intervention Model: A model for supported inclusion at the secondary level. *Remedial and Special Education, 17*(4), 204–16.

Wanzek, J., Vaughn, S., Scammacca, N. K., Metz, K., Murray, C. S., Roberts, G., & Danielson, L. (2013). Extensive reading interventions for students with reading difficulties after grade 3. Review of Educational Research, 83, 163–95.

FURTHER READINGS

Kentucky Department of Education (2015). Kentucky Cognitive Literacy Model, http://education.ky.gov/curriculum/conpro/engla/Pages/Kentucky-Cognitive-Literacy-Model.aspx.

This website includes training modules and key resources for planning and implementing the Kentucky Cognitive Literacy Model intervention.

Kansas University Center for Research on Learning (2015). Learning Strategies Curriculum, http://www.kucrl.org/sim/strategies.shtml.

This website provides foundational information on the Learning Strategies Curriculum. Links to background information and professional development opportunities for each Learning Strategies Curriculum strategy are embedded.

APPENDIX A

Sample Learning Strategies Curriculum Mnemonics

SCENE:
S: Search for picture words
C: Create or Change the scene
E: Enter lots of details
N: Name the parts
E: Evaluate your picture

ASKIT:
A: Attend to clues as you read
S: Say some questions
K: Keep predictions in mind
I: Identify the answers
T: Talk about the answers

Chapter 8

Preparing College Students to Learn More from Academic Texts through Metacognitive Awareness of Reading Strategies

Richard L. Isakson and Marné B. Isakson

Many college students struggle to learn from academic texts. Research indicates that academic reading can be improved when students become more metacognitively aware as they read. A two-credit course was created to teach academic reading strategies, and these were taught within an atmosphere of metacognitive awareness permeating every lesson, every explanation, demonstration, practice session, debriefing time, record-keeping experience, and assessment. The outcomes of this approach showed significant improvement in metacognitive awareness, comprehension, reading rate, and attitudes toward academic reading. In this chapter metacognitive awareness is defined in the context of college reading, the need for it is established, a model is described for learning well from academic text, and a college reading course is presented that uses this model.

INTRODUCTION

Too many college students struggle to read their academic texts. Even though 86 percent of high schools students taking the ACT indicated they aspired to post high school education, 69 percent actually enrolled, but only forty-four percent were ready for college-level reading (ACT, 2014). Furthermore, our experience at a competitive university (where students enter with an average ACT reading score of 28.6 and a high school GPA of 3.82) suggests that even "44% ready for college reading" are challenged to complete their heavy reading assignments and to learn well from them. For some this is the first time they have been faced with a significant amount of academic reading. How do they cope? Only about 30 percent of college students consistently read their assignments before going to class (Baier, Hendricks, Warren-Gorden, Hendricks, & Cochran, 2011; Clump, Bauer, & Bradley, 2004; University of California Board of Regents, 2008). A full 16 percent of the students admit to never reading their assignments (Pecorari, Shaw, Irvine, Malström, & Mezek, 2012). Too many college students who do the reading start on the first word and plow through to the end of a reading assignment using low-level strategies such as rereading, locating information, and memorizing (Nist & Holschuh, 2000). This gap between the demands of college reading and the abilities of some students to read their college texts has been called the "great divide" (Springer, Wilson, & Dole, 2014). According to Nist and Simpson (2000), learning how to study academic texts is not taught in high school and college instructors assume students already know how. Thus, knowing how to study academic texts becomes the hidden curriculum—and it should not be hidden.

The Problem

Though most college students can "read" in terms of decoding, word recognition, and basic comprehension, many come ill-equipped to meet the demands of academic reading where "approximately 85% of all college learning involves reading" (Nist & Simpson, 2000, p. 648).

A Solution

As we see it, to improve academic reading, college students need the following: (1) they need to be taught a set of proven academic reading strategies; (2) this needs to occur within a pervasive atmosphere of metacognitive awareness; (3) students must practice using the strategies until they are well learned; and (4) this practice must occur using the texts for their own classes so they learn to adapt the strategies for actual text situations. This is our model of improving academic reading.

In this chapter we define metacognitive awareness in the context of college reading, establish the need for it, describe a college reading course that uses our model for improving academic reading, and present the outcomes showing that college readers can improve as academic readers. In presenting the above points, we show how we envelop college students in metacognitive awareness from start to finish, in every lesson, every explanation, demonstration, practice session, debriefing time, record-keeping experience, and assessment.

CONCEPTS CENTRAL TO HELPING COLLEGE STUDENTS IMPROVE AS ACADEMIC READERS

The following terms are defined in the context of college reading.

Academic Reading

Academic reading is learning from a text for an educational purpose as opposed to leisure reading which has little accountability. Successful academic reading demands reading proficiency, knowledge of reading strategies to use as needed, motivation to persist in reading, and the metacognitive awareness to recognize if reading goals are being met and what to do about it if not.

Metacognitive Awareness in Reading to Learn

The construct of metacognitive awareness, a term first coined by Flavell (1976), has been studied for over a century (e.g., Dewey, 1910; James, 1890; Thorndike, 1917) but did not capture the interest of literacy researchers until cognitive psychologists began looking at the processes of learning. Flavell was interested in a person's consciousness of their experience while performing a mental task and the use of that consciousness to bring about desired outcomes. Metacognition in the context of academic reading involves thinking about the reading act before, during, and after processing a text (Pressley & Gaskins, 2006) and regulating and controlling this reading process including purposefully selecting from a repertoire of strategies to accomplish an accurate representation of the text's ideas (Nist & Holschuh, 2000). From the writings of numerous researchers (e.g., Baker & Brown, 1984; Maki, 1998; Mokhtari & Reichard, 2002; Veenman, Van Hout-Wolters, & Afflerbach, 2006), we learn that metacognitive knowledge in the context of reading includes (1) *recognizing* the influences on one's reading task such as purposes for reading, the demands of the text, the importance of the reading task, and strategies for processing the text given these constraints; (2) *monitoring* the state of one's own processing, whether or not one is understanding and remembering what is being read and detecting most of the trouble spots; (3) *knowing* when and how to use the strategies to address the difficulties and then regulating and adeptly integrating this declarative, procedural and conditional knowledge to remedy the break down in understanding and to co-construct the meaning of the text with the author; and (4) *evaluating* if the reading act has accomplished the reading purpose, judging the adequacy of one's learning.

Furthermore, in academic reading, the reader must enter the conversations of a discipline, and that involves the metacognition to recognize its discourses and choose reading strategies appropriate for the discipline (Shanahan, Shanahan, & Misischia, 2011; Simpson & Nist, 2002) because reading an epic poem demands some different processing than does an engineering text.

Strategies for Academic Reading

Reading strategies are behaviors intentionally used by readers to guide the processing of information in a text for the purpose of facilitating their learning. A reading strategy is "a deliberate, conscious, metacognitive act" prompted by the reader's vague sense that they are not understanding (Afflerbach, Pearson, & Paris, 2008, p. 368). A skill becomes a strategy when the learner moves from an automatic reading behavior to an intentionally chosen plan for processing information, knowing why, when, where, and how to use it (Armbruster, Echols, & Brown, 1983). These strategic and metacognitive actions are essential for learning from academic text (Alexander & Jetton, 2000). Otherwise, using a strategy without metacognitive awareness can lead to a lock-step, unproductive attempt to learn from a text.

THE NEED FOR METACOGNITIVE AWARENESS IN COLLEGE READERS

"Good readers are massively strategic before, during, and after reading" (Pressley & Gaskins, 2006, p. 100), but novice academic readers are not (Baker & Brown, 1984). Some college readers do not recognize the lack of their own understanding (Dunlosky & Rawson, 2012; Thiede, Anderson, & Therriault, 2003), have a limited repertoire of strategies to draw upon (Nist & Holschuh, 2000; Sheorey & Mokhtari, 2001), may have illusions of having comprehended well (Snyder & Pressley, 1990), may seem satisfied with surface learning and not go beyond to think critically (Ku & Ho, 2010; Magno, 2010), do not adapt their processing strategies well for their reading purpose (Linderholm, 2006), do not know what to do when comprehension breaks down (Hacker, 1998), and so are unable to remedy the situation for better comprehension of the text. Adding to this frustration of underdeveloped metacognitive awareness is this problem: "By the time students enter college, they are expected to possess metacognitive skills. Professors have little sympathy for students who say they did poorly because they thought they understood the materials but did not, studied the wrong information, or felt ready for a test when they really were not" (Holschuh & Aultman, 2009, p. 122).

In the above review of literature we have attempted two things: (1) to define fundamental aspects of academic reading and (2) to point out the need for and importance of metacognitive awareness in college readers. We now describe our model of how we teach college students to be more metacognitively aware as they read and thereby boost their abilities for and positive attitudes toward academic reading.

FACILITATING METACOGNITIVE AWARENESS IN COLLEGE READERS

This section presents what we know about teaching metacognitive awareness, shares our experience helping college students become effective academic readers, and tells how we engaged students in metacognitive processing throughout instruction and helped them realize the benefits of strategic reading of their own academic texts.

Teaching Metacognitive Awareness

The literature validates that metacognitive awareness can be taught (Caverly, Nicholson, & Radcliffe, 2004; Hong-Nam & Leavell, 2011; Van Blerkom & Van Blerkom, 2004), and that without it, strategy instruction is minimally useful. The literature also supports the contention that substantial reading improvement comes by students practicing on the assigned texts for their courses. The relevance and immediacy of this practice increases the likelihood of transfer beyond the reading course (Nist & Simpson, 2000; Pacello, 2014). Practicing on their own text motivates students to use the strategies from an expectation that the strategies will them help learn more from their reading (Maier & Richter, 2014). Moreover, we find that students like to read their own texts during a reading improvement course—to be able to read their texts is why they took the course. For this reason we chose not to use any of the popular texts for improving academic reading with their large number of strategies and abundant passages for practice. It seemed these programs omitted or did not focus on relevant practice using students' own texts. Instead, we wrote our own handbook (Isakson with Isakson, 2016) for students to learn only twenty-eight strategies and then practice them extensively on texts for their own classes.

The best instructional approaches are those that explicitly teach strategies with emphasis on when, why, and how to use them, and how to evaluate them (Duke & Pearson, 2002; Zohar & David, 2009), in other words, with emphasis on the metacognition underlying the use of the strategies. For the acquisition of metacognitive awareness, instruction must be embedded in content, must include encouragement to try the strategies, and must involve prolonged practice to ensure smooth use of the strategies (Veenman, Van Hout-Wolters,

& Afflerbach, 2006). Nist & Holschuh (2000) give four steps for direct strategy instruction: modeling, providing examples, practicing strategy use, and evaluating strategy use. They argue that college students must understand a strategy's underlying processes if they are to continue using it.

For effective strategy use, the learner must first understand the strategy based on declarative, procedural, and conditional knowledge (Fenstermacher, 1994) about the strategy. Metacognitive awareness, as the key ingredient for effective strategy use, must be engaged if the reader is to assess and manage the immediate text situation (Weinstein, Acee, & Jung, 2011), to learn the select the appropriate strategy, integrate it with other strategies (Pressley & Gaskins, 2006), and modify it for the reading purpose and text type (Caverly, et al., 2000).

Helping College Students Become Effective Academic Readers

Students who completed our reading course at Brigham Young University in Provo, Utah, improved significantly as academic readers as shown by self-reports and by significant pre/post differences on outcome measures. Below we show how we accomplished this with our model.

The Course. Because of her years of experience as a reading specialist, the second author was employed as an adjunct professor in the Counseling and Career Center to develop an academic reading course to serve the needs of students who were overwhelmed and stressed by their heavy reading loads. The course was taught on a trial basis beginning in 2007 and was refined over seven years with much input from others. The course, *Advanced Reading Strategies for College Success (ARS),* is a two-credit semester-long course held twice a week.[1]

The Students. The students who enroll in the course are mostly juniors and seniors, predominantly men. These students are not poor readers, having an average college GPA of 3.7 and an average ACT Reading Score of 26.8. Many had taken AP classes in high school, had received scholarships, and were determined learners. We realized that if these "good readers" were feeling overwhelmed by their reading loads, we could suppose a real need for such a course in higher education. An important point here is that college students with good reading scores and grades can benefit from instruction in strategic reading. Other universities also see this need for reading help that is beyond remedial (e.g., Boise State University, 2013; Dartmouth, 2015; Harvard Bureau of Study Counsel, 2013; University of Georgia, 2015) but most of the help is in the form of two-week or weekend courses, reading skills labs, or websites with resource materials rather than our in-depth credit-course offering (Brigham Young University, 2015).

These offerings give credence to the view that even proficient readers may need help learning to read difficult texts.

The Instructors. Because multiple sections were offered, the course developer trained instructors using a two-part method: (1) Instructors who volunteered to teach the course sat through her class, experiencing it as a student. (2) Those in training met in a weekly staff meeting with current instructors to debrief the recent lessons and to go over the upcoming ones. We think both aspects, taking the course and attending staff debriefing meetings, make an effective training method for course instructors.

The Content of the Course. The two questions asked while developing the course were (1) What do expert readers do as they read academic texts? (2) What do novice academic readers do as they read? By answering these, we hoped to see where college students currently are as academic readers, where they could go as readers, and what they needed to learn to be able to read more like expert readers who read with engagement, solid understanding, critical insight, and in a time-efficient manner.

Since metacognitive awareness is highly apparent in expert readers but only dimly present in novice academic readers, the basic tenet of the course is to imbue every activity in and out of class with metacognitive processing to facilitate substantial rather than superficial learning. The next priority is to teach reading in multiple layers because expert readers prepare themselves *before* reading to glean what they want from the text, constantly monitor and control their understanding *during* reading, and *after* reading make sure that they had learned what they wanted from the reading. After reading they also process the ideas beyond the text to extend and critique their understanding and to use the author's ideas as a catalyst for new thinking. Additionally, we emphasized the following principles observed in expert academic reading: be an active reader (connect, infer, wonder, demand understanding, probe beyond the obvious, etc.), co-construct the text by infusing questions and ideas with the author's, embrace reading challenges, and have the intellectual stamina to stay with the task until the goal is met. To this list, we added daily practice using the reading strategies and keeping records of the reading, including reflective thinking and self-assessment of progress.

We selected key strategies for the course from our review of the literature, especially Pressley and Afflerbach's (1995) meta-analysis of thirty-eight expert-reader studies, from our research of professors across seventeen disciplines on how they read their academic texts (Isakson & Isakson, 2013 December), and from the course developer's forty years of teaching reading. Over several semesters we refined a set of academic reading strategies, using them with students, obtaining student and instructor feedback, returning to the literature, and adding some and deleting

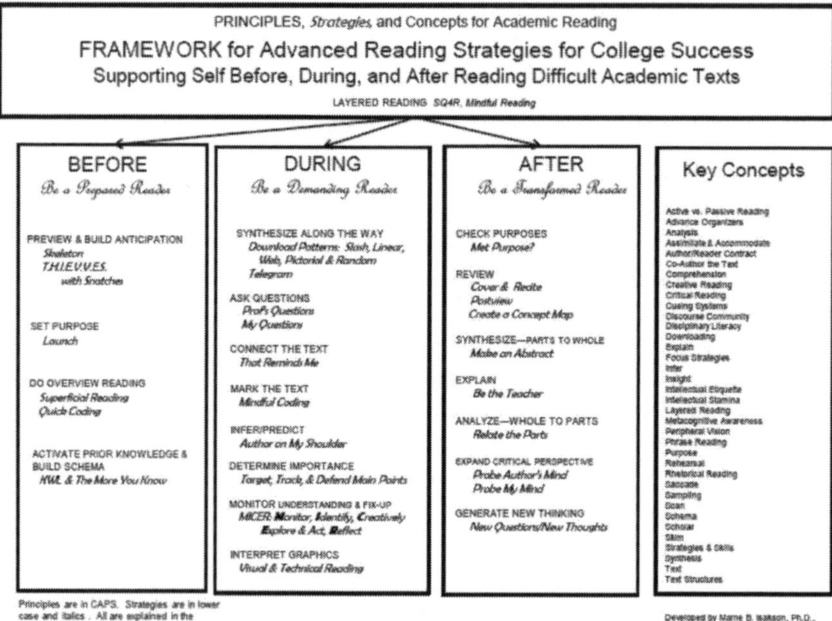

Figure 8.1 The Framework of Strategies and Key Concepts Taught in the ARS Course. Used by permission of the authors.

others. The twenty-eight resulting strategies, displayed in figure 8.1, can be categorized within three layers of reading: Before, During, and After.

Within this framework there are nineteen *principles,* the general overarching established ways of reading an academic text that are key to lifelong learning from reading. Four of these principles can be used *before reading* and include six specific strategies to become a Prepared Reader. Eight principles are used *during reading* and include ten specific strategies to become a Demanding Reader. Seven principles are used *after reading* and include ten specific strategies to become a Transformed Reader. For each of these principles of academic reading, the student learns what it is, why it is important, how to apply it in a general sense, and then how to use the specific strategies related to each principle.

Here are examples, one from each category of strategies taught. The Before strategy, *T.H.I.E.V.V.E.S. with Snatches*, helps students quickly preview the text for content, "What am I going to learn from this text?" The acronym stands for steps in a strategy originally developed by Manz (2002) and modified by us for college use: Title, Headings, Introduction, Every first sentence of a paragraph or section, Visuals, Vocabulary, Every author-generated question, and Summary. A During strategy, *Telegram*, has the reader pause periodically while reading to synthesize by writing in the margins the essence of what was just learned, "In a phrase, what is the message of this part?" An After strategy, *Be the Teacher*, has the student explain to someone else what was just learned. In going beyond retelling, the "teacher" supplies original examples, analogies, drawings, underlying principles, etc. "How can I best explain this concept to someone else so they can understand it?" The strategy fosters deeper understanding and awareness of possible gaps in the "teacher's" understanding the text.

Procedures for Teaching. *Advanced Reading Strategies for College Success (ARS)* uses a "flipped classroom model" (Tucker, 2012) teaching twenty-eight reading strategies (sixteen strategies deemed essential for understanding and retaining of text information and twelve advanced strategies for deeper critical and creative processing of text), and ten drills for speeding up academic reading. In the flipped classroom, the learning of the information is to occur before class instead of during class and the practice homework is done in class so the instructor can give immediate help, can coach students, and can clear up misconceptions before they become entrenched.

Before class, students read the assigned pages in the course handbook about the designated strategy, watch an online demonstration of it (via video or PowerPoint Presentation), and try it on a text for another class as guided by what we term a ThinkSheet, which is a list of steps to guide the reader when first using the strategy. During class time, in small groups they debrief their learning and experiences with the strategy while sharing their ThinkSheets, collaborate as a whole group to clarify and form a list of essential actions regarding that strategy, then practice it independently with coaching by the instructor and with a student mentor (who had completed and done well in the course earlier), and debrief that reading experience with the whole class. After class, they again practice the strategy on their own text, combining it with other strategies to learn well from their own texts for authentic, important reasons. They record and reflect on the experience.

The Results of the Course. The measured outcomes of the course were collected from over 400 students across six semesters and show highly significant gains in metacognitive awareness (*Metacognitive Awareness Reading Strategy Inventory*, Mokhtari & Reichard, 2002), attitudes toward college reading (*College Students Attitudes toward Reading*, Isakson, 2010), comprehension, and reading rate (*Nelson-Denny Reading Test*, Brown et al., 1993; *Line Read Rate Test,* Isakson, 2007). The results are displayed in table 8.1. Qualitative results, including an anonymous survey one to four semesters after having completed the course, indicated that students had transferred the strategies they learned to their course work in

Table 8.1 Pretest–Posttest Differences for Eight Measures of Effects of the Advanced Reading Course

		Pretest		Posttest		M			
Measure	n	M	SD	M	SD	Difference	t	p	d
NDRT Comp	417	228.51	16.19	231.74	11.81	03.23	04.82	0.000	0.23
NDRT Rate	417	208.37	24.71	275.88	32.28	67.51	42.70	0.000	1.52
MARSI GLOB	417	2.86	0.58	3.96	0.52	01.10	34.98	0.000	1.41
MARSI PROB	417	3.44	0.59	4.02	0.49	00.58	19.07	0.000	0.95
MARSI SUP	417	2.39	0.60	3.34	0.60	00.95	30.07	0.000	1.24
MARSI TOTAL	417	2.89	0.53	3.80	0.45	09.91	33.84	0.000	1.35
LRR	400	25.44	10.20	55.52	20.78	30.09	31.82	0.000	1.35
ATTITUDE	417	29.98	5.63	39.01	5.39	09.03	28.36	0.000	1.27

Note: NDRT Comp, Nelson–Denny Reading Test, comprehension subtest; NDRT Rate, Nelson–Denny Reading Test, reading rate subtest; MARSI, Metacognitive Awareness of Reading Strategies Inventory; GLOB, global strategies; PROB, problem-solving strategies; SUP, support-reading strategies; TOTAL, overall MARSI score; LRR for Narrative, informal assessment of line read rate for two passages from the same narrative text; ATTITUDE, College Student Attitudes toward Reading survey.

the disciplines, that they continue to use the strategies over time, and that they are now completing their assigned readings for their courses (Isakson & Isakson, 2013 November). As one student said, "This is the most important course I have taken in college because it helped me do well in all my other classes."

An especially gratifying result of the course is measured by our survey of attitudes toward academic reading. A student's emotional response to reading is a central factor in the successful reading of an academic text. Attitude toward reading "causes the learner to approach or avoid a reading situation" (Alexander & Filler, 1976, p. 1). Negative attitudes toward academic reading can be altered when students learn to use strategies for reading academic texts with metacognitive awareness and realize the payoff of this effort (Isakson & Isakson, 2013 August). If students are learning strategies but not seeing improvement in their reading from using the strategies, their attitudes toward reading are unlikely to improve. Therefore, we chose to measure changes in attitude toward academic reading, using an instrument we created for our course (Isakson, 2010)[2] at the same time that we measured changes in metacognitive awareness. The results from the attitude survey indicated that students were much more positive toward academic reading and were more likely to comply with their reading assignments for their other classes by the end of the course than at the beginning. For example, students were asked to tell the degree to which they agreed or disagreed with this statement on the attitude survey: "When I receive a college reading assignment, I am able to accomplish the reading efficiently and on time." On the pre-survey, 40 percent agreed or strongly agreed, but on the post-survey 90 percent agreed or strongly agreed.

Now we show how metacognitive awareness permeated all the activities, homework, and assessments of the course.

Envelop Students in Metacognitive Thinking

Metacognitive awareness is developed through three main avenues: (1) explicit teaching of the strategies with metacognitive processing questions asked and solicited throughout, (2) mindful practice of the strategies, and (3) assessments created to engage metacognitive thinking.

How Metacognitive Awareness is Involved in the Explicit Teaching and Mindful Practice of Reading Strategies. Learning is infused with metacognitive awareness before, during, and after class. Participation in small groups is set up for metacognitive thinking: "Share what you did. How did it work? How do you know? Why did or didn't it work?" In whole group discussions, little didactic teaching takes place; rather students are guided to awareness and prodded through questions and demonstration. Before coached practice, they synthesize their learning about the why's, how's, and when's of using a strategy then collaborate to state succinctly what the strategy is and list the essential aspects of using it well. During the coached practice, they refer to the list as needed and try the strategy again while the coach roves and asks metacognitive questions: "How are you using the strategy with your text? Is it working? What questions do you have?" After practicing,, students share new insights in a debriefing session about using the strategy, "What do you now understand that you didn't understand earlier? What is becoming clear to you about this strategy?" Students also learn much from each other.

Since metacognitive questions are constantly asked of students, they soon learn to ask the questions of themselves and classmates and ultimately to internalize metacognitive awareness as a way of being with a text. Table 8.2 shows some of the formats into which metacognitive questions are asked across the lesson.

How Metacognitive Awareness Is Developed through Assessment. Our assessments measure the desired learning outcomes and contribute to pre- and post-evaluations using formative and summative information to see if students are moving toward more expert-like reading behaviors. Furthermore, the assessments also are learning tools to cultivate metacognitive awareness. In table 8.3 we present six of our assessments, describe them, and explain how metacognitive awareness is enhanced when students do the assessments. Across the semester the formative assessments methodically nudge students into building habits of metacognitive thinking through required practice and reflecting on the processes used (Pacello, 2014). Such

Table 8.2 Suggestions for Instructors to Use Metacognitive Awareness Questioning within the Flipped Classroom Structure.

DEBRIEFING TIME#1: (about 3 to 7 min)

New strategy is studied and practiced before class. Have students display ThinkSheets to show practice with the new strategy. Do one or several of these:

1. One-Minute Share: In small groups students share their experiences with the strategy with their own texts. Tablemates push them to higher levels of understanding.
2. Ask Me: "What we don't fully get is . . ." (Answer their lingering questions. Students are to realize that being metacognitive in adapting the strategy is the expectation.)
3. Whole Group Synthesis: "What essential principles about the strategy can be extracted from the learning experiences? What do we want to keep in mind now as we try it on a new text?"

PRACTICE TIME ON OWN TEXT: Have students execute the strategy with support. (about 20 to 25 min)

Rove through the entire class, coaching and cheerleading as needed, perhaps keeping a chart of who is coached to be sure every student is coached as often as possible.

Mini-Conferences for Metacognitive Awareness: Systematically "interrupt" a student for metacognitive thinking: 30-second to 2-minute conferences. Ask any, all of these, or different questions:

1. "Where are you right now? What is going on in your mind to learn from this text? Why are you doing this? Is it working? How do you know?
2. "Why is it important to do a strategy such as this? What does it do for you as a reader?
3. "How are you adapting it for this text and your purpose? What might you do differently?
4. "What is your goal for reading this text? Are you meeting your purpose? How do you know?"
5. Tailor-make the metacognitive questions to fit the strategy.

Interruptions for Thinking. Occasionally, briefly interrupt the whole class (<2 min.) to share an observation, solve a common problem, process an insight, or clarify a procedure.

Prime the Pump: As you observe what students are doing and the insights they are having as you coach, ask several students to share later with the whole group.

DEBRIEFING TIME#2: (about 10 to 15 min). Do one or more of these on any one day. Sometimes the discussion is in small groups, sometimes with a partner, but some of it often is as a whole class.

1. Text Variety: "I saw this strategy being used on a ___, ___, and ___ text. How did it work? What did you do differently than you might have done with another text? How did you adapt the strategy?"
2. Text Situations: "Sam, will you present your text situation? What did you do and why? Let's discuss how to approach the text given this situation and how to adapt the strategies to best read this text. What insights and suggestions do the rest of you have?"
3. The Bottom Line: "What are the distinctive, defining attributes of the strategy and the importance of this strategy and its underlying principle for academic reading?"

Table 8.2 Suggestions for Instructors to Use Metacognitive Awareness Questioning within the Flipped Classroom Structure. (continued)

4. Partner Boost: "Tell a partner how far you are already in your text, which steps you are on for that strategy, and which aspects of the strategy you are going to think more about and explore for the text you started in class today." Partners, question "Why? How are you adapting it?"

INDIVIDUAL SYNTHESIS TIME: (about 2 to 5 min).

Take Away Message: "Write what insights you gained today about the strategy? What is your Take-Away Message about it? Because of your learning before class and during class, what are the essential things you are going to remember and apply when choosing to use this strategy?" Use a sheet they write on each time and keep in their folder.

assessments let them see what they are picking up from the course and feed their motivation to keep using the strategies. In our summative evaluation, part of the final exam involves an Analysis of Progress activity in which students are given all their pre/posttests, are asked to react to them and explain their growth or the lack thereof, and give anecdotal evidence to substantiate their claims. Also on the final we asked students to consolidate what they are taking away from the course by asking them to tell us which strategies they will continue to use in their major and why. We also asked them to tell which few strategies they would most recommend to a freshman struggling with reading and give reasons why.

In this section we have shared how we help students use strategies with metacognitive awareness. Basically we involve students in highly interactive and engaging activities where they (1) gain declarative, procedural, and conditional knowledge of the strategies, (2) spend a large part of the class time actually practicing the strategies with coaching on a text they need for another class and then debrief the experiences in intense discussions about using and modifying the strategies for maximum learning effect, and (3) participate in assessment performances that draw on metacognitive awareness and cause students to think about and justify their decisions about the reading actions they take.

The learning we have described in this chapter can be instrumental in helping to solve the problem in higher education of too many students having poor attitudes toward academic reading and avoiding reading their assignments. At stake is the quality of their education. They can and need to approach academic texts in ways that lead to enthused inquiry and deep learning. Because of what is now known about facilitating academic reading, students who want to improve need no longer be limited by a lack of metacognitive awareness and strategic resources and by superficial approaches

Table 8.3 A Sampling of the Course Assessments to Exemplify the Integral Role of Metacognitive Awareness in Assessing Student Progress.

Instrument	*Purpose*	*When used*	*When scored*	*Description*	*How the Assessment Cultivates Metacognitive Awareness*
Reading Log	Formative	Almost daily	Weekly	A log of academic reading for other classes. Student gives purpose for reading a specific text, the strategies used to accomplish the purpose, and a reflection on how using at least one of the strategies was adapted to contribute to meeting the purpose. Once a week, the reader considers all the entries and reading experiences of the week and writes a short self-evaluation.	The reading log, more than any other activity for the class, nudges students into tailor-made reading based on decisions about the nature of the text, their professor's expectations, the students' motivations for learning from the text, and procedures they intend to use to decide their reading purposes and how to meet them. The reflection box for each reading causes readers to learn about themselves as a reader, what insights they gained about when, why, and how to use at least one particular strategy. The reading log helps insure that the student will practice on his or her own important texts and will reflect on the use of the strategies which increases the power and results of that practice. Moreover, the instructor's feedback on the returned Reading Log enhances students' metacognitive experiences.
ThinkSheet	Formative	At least twice per week	weekly	This is a set of instructions that guide the student through the steps as they are learning how to do the strategy.	Its purpose is to walk them through processes that may be new to them or may not have seemed useful or important to them earlier when reading academic texts. They follow the steps carefully and thoughtfully the first few times to build a foundation of knowledge upon which innovation and adaptation build. After they are confident they know how to do the strategy with full benefit for learning from difficult texts, they stop using the ThinkSheet and can now mold the strategy to fit their needs.

Reading Interview	Formative	Once	Beginning of course	This interview is administered as a take-home written interview with six questions and several sub-questions. It has the students analyze themselves as readers of academic text.	A sample of its metacognitive questions follow: When textbook reading is difficult for you, what are some of the reasons? What do you do to . . . a. Focus your attention? To refocus when your mind wanders? b. Be sure you understand the text? c. Use the information and ideas in the text as a springboard for your own thinking? Explain what if anything you do: d. Before you begin reading a textbook assignment? e. While you are reading the assignment? f. After you finish reading the assignment? How do you adapt your reading strategies to different types of texts?
Demonstration of Progress	Formative	Once	Midterm	An essay at midterm in which students consider their progress since the beginning of the semester in reading their academic texts for other classes. They are to address "What observable, measureable pieces of evidence indicate your progress along a continuum of being successful in reading your college texts? Explain your progress or the lack thereof as a reader of your academic texts."	Metacognitive Awareness occurs while students analyze their evidence, reflect on it, and convey their observations. They are to give evidence along three dimensions: 1. Read Well. Evidence could include tests, quizzes, projects, levels of preparation for class discussions, self-observation from Reading Log reflections, etc. 2. Reading Rate. Evidence could include changes shown on Speeding Up Charts, in being able to read assignments in a timely manner, observations by self and others about reading speed, etc. 3. Other Aspects of Academic Reading Abilities. Evidence could include their self-reports of engagement, confidence, stress levels, and changes in attitudes, procrastination, and avoidance of reading academic texts.

(*Continued*)

Table 8.3 A Sampling of the Course Assessments to Exemplify the Integral Role of Metacognitive Awareness in Assessing Student Progress. (continued)

Instrument	*Purpose*	*When used*	*When scored*	*Description*	*How the Assessment Cultivates Metacognitive Awareness*
PAMA Performance Assessment of Metacognitive Awareness	Formative Summative	Mid Final	Mid-term, self-scored Final Instructor-scored	This test was created to simulate the Verbal Protocol Analysis procedures used by Ericsson and Simon (1984) and Pressley and Afflerbach (1995) in the attempt to access the mental processes of the student while reading. We had students write their processing strategies while reading a challenging text.	This test is the culmination of the course for it clearly shows students' abilities to read a challenging text with numerous metacognitive decisions along the way. Students monitor, regulate, and evaluate their decisions and processes throughout the test. It is exciting to witness students' realization that they have indeed become metacognitive and strategic readers. For more information see Isakson and Plummer (2016).
Analysis of Progress	Summative	Once	Final	As part of the final exam, students are given a packet of all their tests (excluding the Nelson-Denny protocol where they only see their scores). They are asked to read, react, and explain the differences from where they were at the beginning of the course to where they are now, at the end of the course.	The explanations require recall of their processing strategies across the semester and recognition of changes in their metacognitive awareness abilities. For the Reading Interview which is administered only at the beginning of the semester, they read their original answers to the questions and react to how they have changed as a reader since then, and account for growth or the lack thereof. For the other outcome measures they react to their scores and look for evidence in the protocols to explain the changes. They also have brought all their Reading Logs, Speeding-Up Charts, and their Strategy Tracking Chart for more evidence to help them realize and explain their growth or the lack thereof.

to learning from complex academic texts. They can "end the drudgery-filled days of reading without any learning" as a graduate student commented after taking the course. And they may say as did a former student about his chemistry class, "I look forward to the class, readings, and assignments with a vast artillery of skills I can adapt for any reading situation. A subject that I once dreaded is now fascinating to me." Hearing such comments from students fires our enthusiasm for more efforts to improve academic reading.

NOTES

1. A second course, Surviving College Reading, also two credits, was created for students needing more support. It taught a smaller subset of the strategies from the ARS course, those deemed most essential for comprehending and remembering what was read. The course allocated almost twice the class time to each strategy. This method has also been highly successful in helping college students improve as metacognitively aware and strategic academic readers.
2. We improved the attitude survey, giving it stronger psychometric properties and a factor structure that helps interpret the scores (Isakson, Isakson, Plummer, & Chapman, 2015).

REFERENCES

ACT (2014). *The condition of college & career readiness, 2014, national.* Retrieved from http://www.act.org/research/policymakers/cccr14/pdf/CCCR14National-ReadinessRpt.pdf.

Afflerbach, P., Pearson, P. D., & Paris, S. G. (2008). Clarifying differences between reading skills and reading strategies. *The Reading Teacher, 61*(5), 364–73. DOI:10.1598/RT.61.5.1.

Alexander, J. E., & Filler, R. C. (1976). *Attitudes and reading*. Newark, DE: International Reading Association.

Alexander, P. A., & Jetton, T. L. (2000). Learning from text: A multidimensional and developmental perspective. In M. L. Kamil, P. B. Mosenthal, P. D. Pearson, & R. Barr (Eds.), *Handbook of reading research* (Vol. III, pp. 285–310). Mahwah, MJ: Lawrence Erlbaum.

Armbruster, B. B., Echols, C. H., & Brown, A. L. (1983). The role of metacognition in reading to learn: A developmental perspective. Reading Education Report N. 40.

Baier, K., Hendricks, C., Warren-Gorden, K., Hendricks, J. E., & Cochran, L. (2011). College students' textbook reading, or not! *American Reading Forum Annual Yearbook* (Vol. 31). Retrieved from http://americanreadingforum.org/yearbook/11_yearbook/documents/BAIER%20ET%20AL%20PAPER.pdf.

Baker, L., & Brown, A. L. (1984). Metacognitive skills and reading. In P. D. Pearson (Ed.), *Handbook of reading research* (pp. 353–94). New York: Longman.

Boise State University (2013). *Literacy: Undergraduate Catalog*. Boise, ID: Author. http://registrar.boisestate.edu/catalogs/online/programs/coe/literacy/c-ed-ltcy.shtml.

Brigham Young University (2015). *Student Develop Classes*. Provo, UT. https://ccc.byu.edu/helpful-classes.

Brown, J. I., Fishco, V. V., & Hanna, G. (1993). *Nelson-Denny Reading Test: Manual for Scoring and Interpretation, Forms G & H*. Austin, TX: PRO-ED, Houghton Mifflin Harcourt, and Riverside Publishing.

Caverly, D. C., Nicholson, S. A., & Radcliffe, R. (2004). The effectiveness of strategic reading instruction for college developmental readers. *Journal of College Reading and Learning, 35*(1), 25–49.

Clump, M. A., Bauer, H., & Bradley, C. (2004). The extent to which students read textbooks: A multiple class analysis of reading across the psychology curriculum. *Journal of Instructional Psychology*, *31*, 227–29.

Dartmouth College (2105). Miniversity Course. Reading your textbooks effectively and efficiently. Retrieved from http://www.dartmouth.edu/~acskills/success/reading.html.

Dewey, J. (1910). *How we think*. Lexington, MA: D. C. Heath.

Duke, N. K., & Pearson, P. D. (2002). Effective practices for developing reading comprehension. In A. E. Farstrup & S. J. Samuels (Eds.), *What research has to say about reading instruction*, 3rd ed. (pp. 205–42). Newark, DE: International Reading Association.

Dunlosky, J., & Rawson, K. A. (2012). Overconfidence produces underachievement: Inaccurate self evaluations undermine students' learning and retention. *Learning and Instruction, 22,* 271–80.

Ericsson, K. A., & Simon, H. A. (1984). *Protocol analysis: Verbal response data.* Cambridge, MA: MIT Press.

Fenstermacher, G. D. (1994). The knower and the known: The nature of knowledge in research on teaching. In L. Darling-Hammond (Ed.), *Review of Research in Education* (pp. 3–56). Washington, DC: American Educational Research Association.

Flavell, J. H. (1976). Metacognitive aspects of problem solving. In L. B. Resnick (Ed.), *The nature of intelligence* (pp. 231–35). Hillsdale, NJ: Lawrence Erlbaum.

Hacker, D. J. (1998). Self-regulated comprehension during normal reading. In D. J. Hacker, J. Dunlosky, & A. C. Graesser (Eds.), *Metacognition in educational theory and practice* (pp. 165–91). Mahwah, NJ: Lawrence Erlbaum.

Harvard Bureau of Study Counsel (2013). The reading course. Online. http://www.bsc.harvard. edu/icb/icb.do?keyword=k73301&tabgroupid=icb.tabgroup127159.

Holschuh, J. P., & Aultman, L. P. (2009). Comprehension development. In R. F. Flippo & D. C. Caverly (Eds.), *Handbook of college reading and study strategy research*, 2nd ed. (pp. 121–44). New York: Routledge.

Hong-Nam, K., & Leavell, A. G. (2011). Reading strategy instruction, metacognitive awareness, and self-perception of striving college developmental readers. *Journal of College Literacy and Learning*, *37*, 3–17.

Isakson, M. B. (2007). *Line Read Rate Test*. Unpublished informal test. In possession of the author. Provo, UT.

Isakson, M. B., with Isakson, R. L. (2016). *Learn more and read faster: A handbook of advanced reading strategies for college success*, 3rd ed. Provo, UT: BYU Academic Publishing.

Isakson, M. B., & Isakson, R. L. (2013, August). *Student to scholar: Teaching college students to read like their professors.* Poster session presented at the meeting of the American Psychological Association, Honolulu, HI.

Isakson, M. B., & Isakson, R. L. (2013, November). *College students can complete their reading on time and with in-depth learning and engagement—if they know how.* Paper presented at the meeting of the College Reading and Learning Association, Boston, MA.

Isakson, M. B., & Isakson, R. L. (2013, December). Metacognitively aware, purposeful, and strategic: What professors do as readers that college students would benefit from doing. Paper presented at the meeting of the Literacy Research Association, Dallas, TX.

Isakson, M. B., & Plummer, K. J. (2016). *The Reliability and Validity Evidence of a Metacognitive Performance Assessment, The PAMA.* Manuscript in preparation.

Isakson, R. L. (2010). *College Students Attitudes toward Reading.* Unpublished manuscript. Counseling and Career Center, Brigham Young University, Provo, UT.

Isakson, R. L., Isakson, M. B., Plummer, K. J., & Chapman, S. B. (2015). The development and validation of the *Isakson Survey of Academic Reading Attitudes (ISARA).* Manuscript in preparation.

James, W. (1890). *The principles of psychology.* New York: Holt.

Ku, K. Y. L., & Ho, I. T. (2010). Metacognitive strategies that enhance critical thinking. *Metacognition and Learning, 5,* 251–67.

Linderholm, T. (2006). Reading with purpose. *Journal of College Reading and Learning*, *36*(2), 70–80.

Magno, C. (2010). The role of metacognitive skills in developing critical thinking. *Metacognition and Learning*, *5,* 137–56. DOI:10.1007/s11409-010-9054-4.

Maier, J., & Richter, T. (2014). Fostering multiple text comprehension: How metacognitive strategies and motivation moderate the text-belief consistency effect. *Metacognition and Learning*, *9*(1), 51–74.

Maki, R. H. (1998). Test predictions over text material. In D. J. Hacker, J. Dunlosky, & A. C. Fraesser (Eds.), *Metacognition in educational theory and practice* (pp. 117–44). Mahwah, NJ: Lawrence Erlbaum.

Manz, S. L. (2002). A strategy for previewing textbooks: Teaching readers to become THIEVES. *The Reading Teacher*, *55*, 434–35.

Mokhtari, K., & Reichard, C. A., (2002). Assessing students' metacognitive awareness of reading strategies. *Journal of Educational Psychology, 94*(2), 249–59. DOI:10.1037//0022-0663.94.2.249.

Nist, S. L., & Holschuh, J. L. (2000). Comprehension strategies at the college level. In R. F. Flippo & D. C. Caverly (Eds.), *Handbook of college reading and study strategy research* (pp. 75–104). Mahwah, NJ: Erlbaum

Nist, S. L., & Simpson, M. L. (2000). College studying. In M. L. Kamil, P. B. Mosenthal, P. D. Pearson, & R. Barr (Eds.), *Handbook of reading research* (Vol. III, pp. 645–66). Mahwah, NJ: Erlbaum. .

Pacello, J. (2014). Integrating metacognition into a developmental reading and writing course to promote skill transfer: An examination of student perceptions and experiences. *Journal of College Reading and Learning, 44*(2), 119–40.

Pecorari, D., Shaw, P., Irvine, A., Malmström, H., & Mezek, S. (2012). Reading in tertiary education: Undergraduate student practices and attitudes. *Quality in Higher Education, 18*, 235–56.

Pressley, M., & Afflerbach, P. (1995). *Verbal protocols of reading: The nature of constructively responsive reading.* Hillsdale, NJ: Lawrence Erlbaum.

Pressley, M., & Gaskins, I. W. (2006). Metacognitively competent reading comprehension is constructively responsive reading: How can such reading be developed in students? *Metacognition and Learning, 1*(1), 99–113.

Shanahan, C., Shanahan, T., & Misischia, C. (2011). Analysis of expert readers in three disciplines: History, mathematics, and chemistry. *Journal of Literacy Research, 43*(4), 393–429. DOI:10.1177/1086296X11424071. http://jlr.sagepub.com/content/43/4/393.

Sheorey, R., & Mokhtari, K. (2001). Differences in the metacognitive awareness of reading strategies among native and non-native readers. *System*, 29, 431–49.

Simpson, M. L., & Nist, S. L. (2002). *Encouraging active reading at the college level.* In C. C. Block & M. Pressley (Eds.), Comprehension instructions: Research-based best practices (pp. 365–79). New York: Guilford.

Snyder, B. L., & Pressley, M. (1990). *What do adults do when studying for a test with unpredictable questions?* Technical Report, London, Canada: University of Western Ontario, Department of Psychology. As cited in Pressley, M., El-Dinary, P. B., & Brown, R. (1992). Skilled and not-so-skilled reading: Good information processing and not-so-good information processing. In M. Pressley, K. R. Harris, & J. T. Guthrie (Eds.), *Promoting academic competence and literacy in schools* (pp. 91–127). San Diego, CA: Academic Press.

Springer, S. E., Wilson, T. J., & Dole, J. A. (2014). Ready or not: Recognizing and preparing college-ready students. *Journal of Adolescent & Adult Literacy, 58*(4), 299–307.

Thiede, K. W., Anderson, M. C. M., & Therriault, D. (2003). Accuracy of metacognitive monitoring affects learning of texts. *Journal of Educational Psychology*, *95*(1), 66–73.

Thorndike, E. L. (1917). Reading as reasoning: A study of mistakes in paragraph reading. *Journal of Educational Psychology, 8,* 323–32.

Tucker, B. (2012). The flipped classroom. *Education Next, 12* (1), 82–83.

University of California Board of Regents. (2008). *University of California Undergraduate Experience Survey (UCUES).* Berkeley, CA: Author. Retrieved at www.studentresearch.ucsd.edu/sriweb/surveys/ucues/2008/core2008.pdf.

University of Georgia (2015). Course information. http://www.georgiacenter.uga.edu/courses/reading-writing/speed-reading-study.

Van Blerkom, M. L., & Van Blerkom, D. L. (2004). Self-monitoring strategies used by developmental and non-developmental college students. *Journal of College Reading and Learning*, *34*(2), 45–60.

Veenman, M. V. J., Van Hout-Wolters, B. H. A. M., & Afflerbach, P. (2006). Metacognition and learning: Conceptual and methodological considerations. *Metacognition and Learning*, *1*(1), 3–14.

Weinstein, C. E., Acee, T. W., & Jung, J. (2011). Self-regulation and learning strategies. New Directions for Teaching and Learning, No. 126, Summer, Wiley Online Library, 45–53. Retrieved from link from http://onlinelibrary.wiley.com/doi/10.1002/tl.443/abstract.

Zohar, A., & David, A. B. (2009). Paving a clear path in a thick forest: A conceptual analysis of a metacognitive component. *Metacognition and Learning, 4*, 177–95. DOI:10.1007/s11409-009-9044-6.

Chapter 9

Metacognitive Reading Strategies Instruction for Students in Upper Grades

Stephan E. Sargent

ABSTRACT

In the upper grades, educators often presume that students already know and use metacognitive reading strategies while reading. Nonetheless, countless students arrive at school unskilled and unaware of these important strategies. This chapter discusses the relationship between metacognition and reading proficiency among students in upper elementary and middle school grades. It also offers various strategies aimed at enhancing students' awareness and use of metacognitive reading strategies when reading academic texts.

FRAMING THE ISSUE

Many people recall a time when they read a challenging chapter for a demanding course. Some readers recall "reading" the entire selection (pronouncing all of the words), only later to realize that the passage made little or no sense. Take the following paragraph, for example:

Sarah and Mark were having a wonderful Easter. They couldn't stop laughing when their father came hopping across the yard in his white costume with a fuzzy tail. They were enjoying hunting for beautiful colored eggs and placing them in their baskets. Both of them were really surprised when he gave them a beautiful krashanky, which they placed in their baskets with the other eggs (Cooper, 1988, p. 83).

While many are able to decode the words correctly, most readers are not sure about the meaning after reading and struggle to make sense of what they read. However, at this point, a skilled reader typically stops and realizes a challenge exists. This is because "good readers constantly monitor their comprehension as they read" (Richek, Caldwell, Lennings, & Lerner, 2002, p. 227). Likely, the reader is constantly monitoring the status of his/her own thinking and applying "fix-up" strategies as needed (Reutzel & Cooter, 2007). Here, the reader might use context clues to infer that a krashanky is a type of beautifully decorated Easter egg. The reader could also use a dictionary or ask the teacher. Such monitoring enables readers to make sense of what they read and thus restores comprehension.

Conversely, Richek, Caldwell, Lennings, & Lerner contend that "Students with reading problems generally lack metacognition in reading. Because they often do not expect reading to make sense, they let their eyes move over the text and proceed on, unconcerned that they understand almost nothing" (2002, p. 227). Such readers continue calling the words but often do not understanding what is read. Richek, Caldwell, Lennings, & Lerner call the awareness of a person's mental activities while reading and the ability to control them metacognition (2002). Afflerbach noted that students need to learn and use metacognitive skills to continue developing literacy skills, even in the upper grades (Devries, 2015; Afflerbach, Cho, Kim, Crassas, & Doyle, 2013).

Metacognition and reading are closely related. Research supporting this assertion is not new. Even in the 1980s researchers realized the pivotal role metacognition plays in the construction of meaning from text. Today, this finding is widely accepted (Barker & Beall, 2009). The National Reading Panel also discovered that students need to have processes in place to monitor and repair comprehension as needed to read beyond an initial level (The National Reading Panel, 2000).

Studies have found that for both elementary school and middle school students, metacognition may be used as a significant predictor of reading comprehension. Because of the relationship between metacognition and reading comprehension, many teachers include it in the literacy curriculum. Moreover, studies support that metacognitive knowledge can be fostered through effective classroom practice (Barker & Beall, 2009). As metacognition improves, many times comprehension does as well. In turn, metacognitive skills further are enhanced. This recursive process helps a student become a more effective reader. Barker and Beall acknowledge that many factors impact reading comprehension. While metacognition is important, the prudent educator must address multiple other factors impacting comprehension as well (Barker & Beall, 2009).

MAKING THE CASE FOR METACOGNITIVE READING STRATEGIES INSTRUCTION

Literacy professionals often hear that students in the primary grades learn to read, while in grades four and above they read to learn. While there is some truth in this dated adage, reading teachers often realize it is inaccurate. Far too many upper elementary students and beyond assume a passive orientation to reading, often simply reading to quickly finish an assigned text. Unfortunately, a passive stance toward reading is one reason why low-achieving students experience difficulty in reading (Jenkins, Heliotis, Hayes, & Breck, 1986). Fortunately, literacy researchers have found that by helping students develop an awareness of metacognition, struggling readers can increase their learning (van Der Brock & Kremer, 2000; Barker & Beall, 2009). Struggling readers often lack awareness and use of metacognitive reading strategies before, during, and after reading. For instance, unskilled readers may not understand how or why to create a purpose for reading. When reading comprehension fails, they may not be aware of "fix-up" strategies that will help alleviate the problem. Struggling readers of fail to evaluate their understanding after reading. Pressley sheds hope on their situation. He states, "The case is very strong that teaching elementary, middle school, and high school students to use a repertoire of comprehension strategies increases their comprehension of text" (2000, p. 547). When teachers model these strategies and have students practice them independently over long periods of time, reading often improves.

The terms reading strategies and reading skills are commonly encountered and even more commonly confused. Strategies are both deliberate and goal-oriented. Strategies often help the reader decode unfamiliar text, identify the meaning of words, and comprehend text. If a reader comes across a particularly difficult passage and struggles to construct meaning, he/she might reread the passage, stopping after each sentence or paragraph to check for meaning. This is an example of a strategy. The reader is using it on purpose (deliberate) and employing it to meet a goal (understand the text), both hallmarks of a reading strategy.

If the reader above chose to use this reading strategy throughout the year and it worked well, use of this strategy would likely require less effort and awareness. Afflerbach et al. contend that in this case "deliberate reading strategies become fluent reading skills" (2008, p. 368). Reading skills require neither deliberate control of the reader nor a conscious awareness. As a student reads an easy passage, he/she likely relies on the internalized skills. However, as reading becomes challenging, the same reader may revert to using deliberate strategies to construct meaning from the text. Current thinking is "teach children many strategies, teach them early, re-teach them often, and connect assessment with reteaching" (Afflerbach, Pearson, & Paris, 2008, p. 371). While not all strategies work and become internalized skills with every reader, as children find strategies that work for them, the strategies will likely become skills, providing for enhanced performance with very little effort.

Reading strategies have multiple purposes. For example, setting a purpose for reading, making predictions, and previewing texts before reading all serve different purposes yet often bolster reading proficiency. Strategies that help older students enhance metacognition typically have two major characteristics. First, such strategies help the reader think about his/her thinking while reading. Second, these strategies help the student repair failing comprehension during reading (Reutzel & Cooter, 2007). A meta-analysis of programs designed to enhance metacognition revealed that the most effective strategies to use require self-questioning and identification of text consistencies (The National Reading Panel, 2000). The same research also found that strategies designed to bolster metacognition most always include two pedagogical techniques: instruction in background knowledge and providing explicit access to the "ordinarily hidden processes of comprehension" that are often unknown to new or struggling readers (Snow, Burns, & Griffin, 1998, pp. 220–21). The seven practical strategies described in this chapter, while not exhaustive, include these major characteristics and are designed to help students in the older grades enhance metacognitive skills.

While a plethora of reading strategies are available, the following are vital: generating questions, constructing mental images, summarizing, and analyzing stories (Presley, 2000). While these are modeled and taught explicitly, students often use the strategies in tandem while reading. Reciprocal teaching, described later in the chapter, exemplifies this combination of strategies.

Skilled readers often use a group of strategies simultaneously, especially when engaged in deep and complex text. For instance, they set a purpose for reading, preview text, and monitor their text understanding at the same time. Duke found that instead of working with strategies individually, they may be taught in clusters and quickly used as sets instead of alone (Duke, 2008). Not only are students able to use these together, but data gathered when students use strategies in tandem shows particularly strong results for bolstering reading achievement (Reutzel et al., 2005). Having carefully designed instructional activities (e.g., Transactional Strategies Instruction, Concept-Oriented Reading Instruction, Collaborative Strategic Reading) while learning to use a suite of strategies together is crucial for students to effectively understand what they read.

PEDAGOGICAL IMPLICATIONS

Metacognition and reading strategies that promote it often lead to heightened reading ability. A student who thinks about his/her thinking and uses strategies as needed will more likely construct meaning from a passage. Hopefully the strategies he/she utilizes will become so imbedded that they become lifelong reading skills. On the other hand, a student who fails to think about thinking and monitor comprehension is much less likely read a passage and fail to construct meaning. The strategies described in this chapter are especially applicable for older readers from the fourth grade and up. These strategies are best used in the guided-reading portion of a reading lesson, when the teacher (often in small groups) focuses on comprehension with text at the instructional level of reading. Ideally, once a strategy is introduced, modeled, practiced, and used, it should be continued. Pressley recommends using teaching strategies over years. Many schools have adopted four or five reading strategies which are taught across disciplines in all of the upper grade levels. The seven strategies described here are immediately usable in the classroom and will likely enhance metacognition and reading proficiency.

TEACH STUDENTS TO MONITOR OR CHECK FOR MEANING WITH THE "SAY SOMETHING" TECHNIQUE

The "Say Something" strategy helps students respond to a text. While reading, students take turns making a statement at a predetermined stopping point (a sentence, paragraph, etc.) about what has been read. Perhaps most basic, this strategy holds great power to enhance student use of metacognition. Unfortunately, when some students finish reading a selection they have little grasp of what has been "read." Walker describes this strategy, asking students to stop regularly while reading and ask one of four questions of themselves (2012). These include:

- Did what I just read make sense to me?
- Can I retell it in my own words?
- Are there any words that I do not understand?
- Are any sentences confusing to me?

Each question above requires explicit instruction and modeling in the classroom prior to use. These questions make an important yet easy to construct poster in the room or bookmark, reminding students to regularly apply this strategy. If students are unable to answer these four questions in the affirmative, then stop and proceed no further until the selection makes sense. As students are reading any genre (fiction or nonfiction), this strategy safeguards against "word-calling" and reading without meaning. For example, when working with a small group of students, the teacher begins by demonstrating this strategy with a child in the group. The pair first decides if the reading will be oral or silent. The two take turns reading and say something about what they have read each time they switch turns. The teacher might ask,

"Did what I just read make sense to me?" and answer the question. The other partner might ask, "Are there any words that I do not understand?" Now, the teacher discusses with the entire group how the strategy worked. Finally, the teacher asks each member of the group to break into pairs and try the strategy with a text selection. This guided practice sets the stage for individual use of the strategy in the future.

USE PAINT COLOR CARDS TO SUPPORT STUDENTS' THINKING ABOUT READING

Reading teachers have long known that adding a manipulative piece to instruction often helps students better implement and remember to use a specific strategy, even with older children. Tanny Mcgregor (2007) describes an innovative technique using paint color cards (available at all paint stores) to help students as they "think about their thinking" (p. 23). First, the teacher obtains enough paint cards at a local store that sells paint so that all students have one. Usually these are given to teachers at no charge. Then, the teacher models how the "color gradients can clearly represent the levels of a reader's understanding" (Mcgregor, 2007, p. 23). For example, after modeling the reading of a selection, the teacher might say she understood it very well and consequently choose the most intense color on the coloring card to describe his/her understanding of the passage. Later, he/she again reads a passage, but if meaning is not constructed, the teacher might choose the lightest color's name on the card to describe the grasping of the text. Students often name the different shades on the cards to help them "think about their thinking" (p. 23). Teachers and students, individually or collectively, may create guidelines using this technique. For example, if a student's reading is described at or below a certain color or level on the color card, the student might benefit from using a fix-up strategy. Conversely, if the student describes his/her experience reading a passage as the second color from the most intense, perhaps continuing reading is the best option. This strategy, while directly asking students to be metacognitive, is especially effective because of the hands-on component.

SHOW STUDENTS HOW TO USE CLICK OR CLUNK TO FIND OUT IF READING MAKES SENSE

A well-loved strategy called "Click or Clunk" (Carr, 1985; Reutzel & Cooter, 2007) used by many teachers inaccurate and incomplete comprehension of texts. Too often, students read an entire passage and only when they reach the end realize they have not constructed meaning from the text. Using

"Click or Clunk" helps develop metacomprehension and bolster reading proficiency. First, the students divide the text to be read into small, meaningful units (e.g., sentence, paragraph, section, etc.) prior to reading. After reading that amount of text, students stop and ask if that section "clicked" and made sense or if it "clunked" and was confusing. If the text "clicked" the students continue reading. However, if it "clunked," they apply one of five fix-up strategies (Reutzel & Cooter, 2007, p. 304):

i. Read on.
ii. Reread the sentence.
iii. Go back and reread the paragraph.
iv. Seek information from the glossary or reference materials.
v. Ask someone near you who may be able to help, such as one of your peers.

Modeling of each "fix-up" strategy is essential for success. For example, if a student read a passage and it did not make sense, the teacher might model reading on in the text. Often after reading a few more sentences, the text in question will make sense. Conversely, the teacher might also model rereading the sentence. Perhaps a word left out or hearing the sentence again will clarify the question. The teacher should also model reading a part of the text and come across an unknown or confusing word. At this point, the teacher may model use of reference materials to find the definition for the word. Lastly, the teacher will model how to ask someone nearby for help without disturbing others (e.g., a peer, paraprofessional, etc.). Only after the teacher has modeled these fix-up strategies should students begin using the strategy alone. Again, these make an excellent poster or bookmark, which will help student remember to use this technique. Using "Click or Clunk," students not only realize whether or not their reading makes sense, but they also discover what to do when comprehension fails. This strategy works equally well with all genres of text.

USE THOUGHT BUBBLES TO MAKE THINKING VISIBLE

Tanny McGregor describes a fun, yet effective way to "get inside your teacher's head" to share metacognitive strategies (McGregor, 2007, p. 20). This technique is a variation on the time-tested "Think Aloud" strategy. Unlike traditional thought bubbles seen in comics, this thought bubble is two feet wide and made from white poster board. The center is cut out with a space for the "thinkers" face. McGregor describes the importance of modeling this strategy using herself and another teacher in the building. One is the reader and the other the "thinker," holding the thought bubble in front of his/

her face. As the reader shares the text aloud (seated), the "thinker" (standing) will "explicitly demonstrate how proficient readers think while they are reading" (McGregor, 2007, p. 20). The reader stops regularly, affording the "thinker" the opportunity to share the thoughts in his/her mind. For example, if the reader read: "The bear was snoozing," the "thinker" might reply, "I'm not sure of the word snooze. I know bears sleep in the winter, but let's keep reading and the author might make this clearer to me." This continues about half-way through a picture book. Next, the teacher lets volunteers take the place of being the "thinker." Such modeling ensures students understand how the process works before attempting it without teacher direction. Finally, students utilize the strategy in pairs. For students (or classes) who struggle to know what to think, Walker (2012) recommends providing variations of the following stems on a poster in the classroom to get the process started.

I bet . . . *(students predict what will happen next)*

I see in my head . . . *(students visualize what they see in there head while listening)*

This reminds of a time . . . *(students connect the story to their experiential background)*

This word/sentence was confusing to me, so I will . . . *(students identify a problematic piece of the selection and identify a way to solve it)*

As students have the opportunity to practice, taking turns between reader and "thinker," they develop the capacity to think while reading. Again, this focus on metacognition will lead to enhanced comprehension of text.

UTILIZE CLOZE PASSAGES

For many year, the "Cloze" strategy has not only been highly effective in bolstering students' comprehension, but also has been useful in enhancing metacognitive awareness. Cloze is a strategy where every third, fifth, seventh, or tenth word is deleted. Most teachers omit approximately ten words out of a 250-word passage. Students are asked to fill in the missing words. The teacher may retype the passage or simply use a marker to remove the words that are deleted. Recently, technology has enabled the teacher to make cloze passages online. The following URL creates free cloze passages when the teacher types the text or cuts/pastes text into the website: http://l.georges.online.fr/tools/cloze.html.

Typically, the first and last sentences are left intact. Proper nouns are generally not deleted. Students are encouraged not to guess randomly. Instead, they think about the words around the deletion (context clues), the passage itself, as well as their own background knowledge. Cloze passages are easily created for any genre of reading, fiction or nonfiction. Successfully completing such exercises helps focus students' attention to comprehension and ultimately enhance metacognitive awareness.

A teacher using cloze passages might first look at a sentence from the passage, such as the one below (Walker, 2012, p. 143):

> "Sam started to explain, but sobs choked her. She cried so hard __________ it was a long __________ before her father understood __________."

The teacher models how to look at the words and meaning of the sentence to decide what word(s) would best fit in the blank. After practicing together, the teacher has students utilize the same process. Afterward, the teacher asks students to review his/her choices and tell what strategies he/she used to decide on the word selected. Subsequently, students may use this strategy alone.

UTILIZE THE REQUEST PROCEDURE TO SUPPORT STUDENTS' COMPREHENSION MONITORING

The ReQuest procedure (Walker, 2012) is designed to help students monitor their reading comprehension processes while reading. Ultimately, this strategy helps students to begin asking themselves questions as they read. By so doing, the likelihood of monitoring their reading and thinking is enhanced. First, the teacher selects a text that the students will be encountering, which has multiple new words and concepts. This may be a fiction or expository text. The teacher begins by modeling. He/she reads the first paragraph aloud and then asks and answers a question that he/she poses. The teachers model asking appropriate questions that promote critical thinking (as opposed to questions that may be answered with yes/no). After sufficient demonstrating, the teacher asks the students again to read a paragraph. This time the students take turn asking the teacher questions. For example, the student might ask, "What was the main point of the paragraph?" The teacher models answering the questions appropriately, using corroboration from the text. This provides students the opportunity to create questions with input from the teacher and also see and hear the teacher respond appropriately. Ultimately, the students will ask themselves questions as they read. According to Lenski, Johns, and Wham, so doing will "help them monitor and understand what they are reading" (2003, p. 167).

USE RECIPROCAL TEACHING TO PROMOTE MULTIPLE STRATEGY USE

Though a bit more complicated than the other strategies described, Reciprocal Teaching allows the students and teacher to exchange roles, using four key techniques: prediction, question generation, summarizing, and clarifying (Palinscar & Brown, 1984; Richek, Caldwell, Jennings, & Lerner, 2002; Snow, pp. 221–23; Reutzel & Cooter, 2007). Each of these requires extensive instruction and modeling prior to students using them alone. To model, the teacher first selects an appropriate book and prepares a poster showing the four associated strategies. First, the teacher helps the class predict the content of the book from the title and pictures. Next, the teacher reads the text (or has the students read the text). After this, the teacher assists the class to generate appropriate questions from the text. Often the teacher asks the students to think of questions that might be on a test or that they would like to discuss with peers. The teachers then discuss these questions with the class, emphasizing that the answer to the question should be likely to be found in the text. Afterward, the teacher summarizes (briefly) the selection previously read. Creating a brief summary is often a challenge for students. Often the students are asked to summarize the selection in one sentence, preventing the summary from being as long or longer as the selection read. The teacher may provide one sentence that summarizes the passage, later asking students to do the same. Finally, the teacher helps the students clarify confusing vocabulary, passages, content, and the like. When students are reluctant to find confusing content, some teachers have asked them to think of something in the text that would be confusing to a child who is younger. Usually, students then readily share what they in fact do not understand.

Once students are comfortable with predictions, forming questions, clarifying, and summarizing, the teacher divides the class into small groups. One person in each group is assigned to be the "teacher." He/She will organize the group to read, first making predictions. The leader will then ask students to read the text. Finally, the "teacher" asks someone in the group to generate questions, summarize, and clarify. When the passage is completed, the student acting as "teacher" chooses someone else to assume that role (Reutzel & Cooter, 2007, pp. 309–10).

CONCLUDING THOUGHTS

Most teachers encounter regularly encounter students who read a passage of text yet struggle to construct meaning. Research has shown that students with reading problems generally lack metacognition in reading. Fortunately, many strategies are available for students to apply that will bolster metacognition and reading proficiency. Vacca and Gove (2012) remind teachers that students rely on "metacognitive strategies to engage their mind in the dialogue so that they can understand, respond to, question, and even challenge the author's ideas" (p. 232). Speaking to the importance of metacognitive strategies, this quote reiterates the importance of students using strategies such as those mentioned above. As these strategies are deliberately used to meet a goal with a text, they hopefully will become so internalized that they become skills, used without deliberate thinking. Click or Clunk, Cloze, Thought Bubbles, Paint Color Cards, ReQuest, and Reciprocal Teaching are but a few of the many metacognitive strategies available for older readers. Devries claims, "Eventually, students will use metacognitive strategies independently to monitor their reading processes and comprehension" (Devries, 2015, p. 28). However, enhancing reading for school purposes is but one benefit of teaching and having students apply metacognitive strategies. As Laura Robb states, "When you teach self-monitoring, you provide students with tools that enable them to solve problems throughout their life" (2003, p. 125). What better gift could a reading teacher give a student?

REFERENCES

Afflerbach, P., Pearson, D. P., & Paris, S. G. (2008). Clarifying differences between reading skills and reading strategies. *The Reading Teacher, 61*(5), 364–73.

Afflerbach, P., Cho, B-Y, Kim, J-Y, Crassas, M. E., & Doyle, B. (2013). Reading: What else matters besides strategies and sills? *The Reading Teacher, 66*(60), 440–48.

Carr, E. (1985). The vocabulary overview guide: A metacognitive strategy to improve vocabulary comprehension and retention. *Journal of Reading, 28*(8), 684–89.

Cooper, J. D. (1988). *The what and how of reading instruction.* Columbus, OH: Glencoe.

Devries, B. A. (2015). *Literacy assessment and intervention for classroom teachers.* Scottsdale, AZ: Holcomb Hathaway Publishers.

Dewitz, P., & Carr, E. M. (1987, December). Teaching comprehension as a student directed process. In P. Dewitz (Chair), Teaching reading comprehension, summarizing and writing in content area. Symposium conducted at the National Reading Conference, Florida.

Duke, N. K. (2008, July). Building comprehension through strategy instruction. Presented at the National Reading First Conference, Nashville, TN.

Jenkins, J. R., Heliotis, J., Haynes, M., & Bweck, K. (1986). Does passive learning account for readers' comprehension deficits in ordinary reading situations? *Learning Disability Quarterly, 9*, 60–76.

Lenski, S. D., Wham, M. A., & Johns, J. L. (2003). *Reading and learning strategies: Middle grades through high school.* Dubuque, IA: Kendall-Hunt.

McGregor, T. (2007). *Comprehension connections: Bridges to strategic reading.* Portsmouth, NH: Heinemann.

National Institute of Child Health and Human Development. (2000). *Report of the National Reading Panel. Teaching children to read: An evidence-based assessment of the scientific research literature on reading and its implications for reading instruction* (NIH Publication No. 00-4769). Washington, DC: U.S. Government Printing Office.

Pressley, M. (2000). What should comprehension instruction be the instruction of? In M. L. Kamil, P. B. Mosenthal, & P. D. Pearson (Eds.), *Handbook of reading research* (pp. 545–61). Mahwah: Erlbaum.

Reutzel, D. R., & Cooter, R. B. (1999). *Balanced reading strategies and practices.* Upper Saddle River, NJ: Merrill.

Reutzel, D. R., & Cooter, R. B. (2005). *Teaching children to read: The teacher makes the difference*, 5th Ed. Upper Saddle River, NJ: Merrill.

Reutzel, D. R., & Cooter, R. B. (2007). *Strategies for reading assessment and instruction*, 3rd ed. Upper Saddle River, NJ: Pearson.

Richek, M. A., Caldwell, J. S., Jennings, J. H., & Lerner, J. W. (2002). *Reading problems: Assessment and teaching strategies*, 4th ed. Boston: Allyn and Bacon.

Robb, L. (2003). *Teaching reading in social studies, science, and math.* New York: Scholastic.

Snow, C. E., Burns, M. S., & Griffin, P. (Eds.) (1998). *Preventing reading difficulties in young children.* Washington, DC: National Academy Press.

Vacca, J. L., Vacca, R. T., & Gove, M. K. (2012). *Reading and Learning to Read*, 8th ed. New York: Longman.

Van Der Brock, P., & Kremer, K. E. (2000). The mind in action: What it means to comprehend during reading. In B. M. Taylor, M. F. Graves, & P. Van Der Brock (Eds.), *Reading for meaning: Fostering comprehension in the middle grades* (pp. 1–31). Newark, DE: International Reading Association, and New York: Teachers College Press.

Walker, B. J. (2012). *The diagnostic teaching of reading*, 7th ed. Upper Saddle River, NJ: Pearson.

Chapter 10

Improving Reading Comprehension Through Metacognitive Reading Strategies Instruction for Students in Primary and Elementary Grades

Melinda Smith

ABSTRACT

Reading instruction in the early grades tends to emphasize decoding and word recognition strategies during the *Learning to Read* stage. Complex metacognitive strategy instruction is usually considered more appropriate in the mid to upper elementary stage of *Reading to Learn.* However, research indicates that complex comprehension strategies can be effectively taught at all grade levels with all learners. Providing extensive, appropriate comprehension-strategy instruction beginning in the primary grades can and should be the strong foundation to build upon for early readers. This chapter provides a set of strategies aimed at improving students' reading comprehension performance by encouraging metacognitive awareness and self-regulation among primary and elementary grade students.

As every primary grade reading teacher can attest, some children learn to read easily. They acquire critical concepts about reading and writing even before they enter formal instruction. They often begin school with a wealth of early literacy experiences. Once instruction begins, they progress to develop fast and accurate word recognition skills, leaving more time and the mental resources to devote to deriving meaning from the text (Samuels, 1987). Successful readers note the structure and organization of text, monitor their understanding while reading, create mental notes and summaries, anticipate what will happen next, revise and evaluate their thinking as they navigate through the text. These readers are active processors of text (Baker & Brown, 1984).

For other children, learning to read can be extremely difficult and frustrating. Many children begin school having significantly fewer opportunities to engage in meaningful literacy-related experiences than their peers. They typically read slower and less accurately, understand the meaning of fewer words, rarely monitor their understanding and use few of the effective strategies of good readers (Pressley & Afflerbach, 1995). These students struggle with comprehension because of slow and inadequate decoding skills, low interest, minimal preparation and inadequate background knowledge and vocabulary to aid in interpreting text.

There is no question the need and importance of fostering reading comprehension and monitoring strategies for all readers beginning in the primary grades. The challenge for the primary grade teachers is that they are serving students who vary widely in their command of English, their decoding proficiency, and their experiential backgrounds. It comes as no surprise that many primary grade teachers have not emphasized comprehension-strategy instruction in their curriculum. Delaying comprehension monitoring instruction until children have reached the intermediate grades is denying them the experiences that help them develop this most important of reading dispositions (Kragler, Walker, & Martin, 2005; Pearson & Duke, 2002; Reutzel, Smith, & Fawson, 2005). The good news is research demonstrates the comprehension processing abilities of all young children can be increased significantly when students are taught complex comprehension strategies, specifically metacognitive strategy instruction (Block, Rogers, & Johnson, 2004). In fact, teachers can and need to begin teaching metacognitive comprehension strategies as early as kindergarten. Emerging readers are capable of using these higher thinking skills to bring meaning to the text. Comprehension can occur when any reader is able to act on, and respond to a text in a way that demonstrates deep understanding. (Brassell & Rasinski, 2008).

Reading comprehension is a complex process. It involves a series of cognitive actions that work together to construct meaning (Baker & Brown 1984; Block & Pressley 2002; Farstrup & Samuels, 2002; Pearson, 2002). A reader's comprehension is influenced by a variety of internal factors including: cognitive processing abilities, perceptions, beliefs, motivation and problem-solving strategies. There is a fine line between perception and metacognition (Lyons, 2003). Both types of processing form the foundation of comprehension. Research shows that we perceive what our brain tells us to notice. However, if we do not have the background experiences to relate to the reading event, the message or related understanding is lost (Dorn & Saffos, 2005).

Metacognition can be defined as a reader's awareness of what he or she is thinking about while reading and the ability to monitor one's own thinking (Brown, 2002). Metacognition and comprehension results from the mind's ability to make connections and ask questions related to the reading event. If the reader cannot determine questions about the reading then true thinking about their thinking and comprehension cannot occur. Metacognition is characterized by (a) choosing thinking and problem-solving strategies to fit specific learning situations, (b) clarifying purposes for learning, (c) monitoring personal comprehension though self-questioning, and (d) taking corrective action when comprehension fails (Echevarria, Vogt, & Short, 2000). This understanding creates the challenge for all teachers, particularly for primary teachers, who are also dealing with the skills of learning to read. First we must fully understand metacognition and the comprehension process and then we must be able to apply this understanding to our work with students.

Metacognitive reading strategy instruction is increasing in grades K–3. Research has proven that as early as age five, children can initiate metacognitive processes. Young children can describe and monitor their own comprehension effectively when they talk about what they think when they read. They can select specific thinking processes to make meaning before, during and after reading (Brown, 2002). Young students can be taught how to correct misunderstanding in the process of comprehending text (Block et. al, 2004). Young children even have the ability to evaluate their own comprehension; however, most students will not engage such metacognitions without being taught how to apply these strategies (Baker, 2002; Block et al., 2004). Studies have shown that teaching metacognitive strategies to improve comprehension to primary grade students has positive effects both on standardized measures and formative measures (Shanahan, Callison, Carriere, Duke, Pearson Schatschneider, & Torgenson, 2010; Stahl, 2004, 2014). While there is no evidence to show students who were taught how to use metacognitive strategies while reading actually used the specific strategies when reading on their own (National Reading Panel, 2000). Instead, researchers propose that when students are taught how to use strategies flexibly while reading, their interactions with and their thinking about the text are heightened, leading to deep or close, reading that in turn improves their reading comprehension (Taylor, Pearson, Garcia, Stahl, & Bauer, 2006). Another important benefit of metacognitive strategy instruction is that students' motivation to read is enhanced, which frequently results in their reading more text than they did prior to instruction (National Reading Panel, 2000).

Many of our youngest students have had limited adult modeling and mentoring experiences in which a "mentor" explains the thinking processes they use when they encounter reading difficulties (Baker, 2002; Block et al., 2004). Metacognitive reading strategy instruction is proven to be valuable because it can provide early and struggling readers the opportunities to observe and participate in activities and experiences designed to explain, model and scaffold the thinking processes that they use when they encounter reading difficulties (Baker, 2002; Block & Pressley, 2002; Block & Rodgers, 2004). This research is supported by the theoretical work of Lev Vygotsky's (1978). The Vygotskian zone of proximal development is defined as the distance between what a learner can do alone and what the learner can do with assistance. Vygotsky's work demonstrated that students learn best when their learning is scaffolded. Wood, Bruner, and Ross (1976) used the term scaffolding to describe instruction that provides a temporary support system during the child's construction of knowledge. In the beginning, while learning new information, high levels of support are provided by a more knowledgeable mentor (teacher) and over time the learner assumes more responsibility for the task as he or she internalizes the language and behaviors related to that task. Scaffolding must be employed over time as a teacher gradually releases responsibility to the child (Pearson & Gallagher, 1983). There is evidence that this gradual release of responsibility works well for comprehension instruction due to the complexity and multidimensional nature of the comprehension processes. Young readers, through experiencing modeling and scaffolding, can see that planning before they read is necessary, and they should be monitoring their understanding during reading (Block, Gambrell, & Presseley, 2002; Block & Pressley, 2002). What a learner can do today with support he or she will be able to accomplish independently in the future.

Students must also be taught how to self-regulate their reading in order for metacognitive comprehension-strategy instruction to be effective. Self-regulation occurs when students know how to transfer what they learned in the classroom about monitoring their understanding to their own independent reading, internalize and apply the appropriate strategies to repair, facilitate, or enhance their comprehension, and set goals for their reading (Stahl & Garcia, 2015). Self-regulated learners choose from several strategies to accomplish a reading goal. If the chosen strategy is unsuccessful, they will opt for a different strategy. As a result, students need to be adept with a variety of metacognitive reading strategies to ensure they have options if a particular strategy proves ineffective. Good readers have also demonstrated that they do not use comprehension strategies one at a time, but instead they activate a set of strategies to comprehend text. (Reutzell et al., 2005). As a result, recent research promotes multiple strategy instruction where students are taught how to use and coordinate multiple strategies as they read (Gersten, Fuchs, Williams, & Baker, 2001; Neufeld, 2005; Pearson & Duke, 2002; Reutzel et al., 2005). To help student internalize their use of strategies, Almasi (2003) recommends that you make sure your students (1) know the purpose and usefulness of comprehension strategies, (2) have a variety of comprehension strategies at their disposal, (3) have heightened metacognitive knowledge so that they know when they are not comprehending, (4) be able to analyze the reading task or activity, and (5) be motivated to use the appropriate strategies (p. 13). Heightened metacognitive knowledge occurs when readers interrupt their reading or that of the teacher to say, "That doesn't make sense." Or "I don't understand what that means." Young readers can demonstrate the flexible use of strategies when they can (on their own without prompting) say "I need to go back are read that again, I'm confused." As students become older, more strategic readers, they should be able to select strategies according to what they know about themselves as readers, the text they are reading, the task or activity for which they are reading and the context in which the reading act takes place (National Reading Panel, 2000; Stahl & Garcia, 2015).

Research indicates that six metacognitive processes that can be taught effectively to students in grade K–3 (Block, Rodgers, & Johnson, 2004, p. 148) are described as follows:

1. *Semantic processes*: checking the meaning of individual words.
2. *Syntactic processes*: attending to the grammatical structure of sentences and phrases.
3. *Evaluating informational completeness*: verifying that all parts of a text that have been read are understood.
4. *Evaluating textual cohesiveness*: evaluating the understanding of ideas throughout the text.
5. *Noting the direction of a character's thoughts*: identifying the clues in a character's personality and interaction with other characters revealing the reason the author depicted the character in that way.
6. *Comparing what is read to similar events in readers' lives*: applying text to the students' lives by reflecting and thinking as they read.

The ultimate goal of teaching these metacognitive processes is to equip K–3 students to pause, reflect and then effectively apply metacognitive strategies in order to connect what is happening in the text to their own lives (Trimble, 1994). When researchers taught young students to use these metacognitive processes they found that both strong and weak comprehenders benefited equally from the instruction. Metacognition could be developed, even if literal comprehension and decoding proficiencies were below grade level (Baker, 2002, Block & Rodgers, 2004).

To reinforce the six metacognitive processes, specific metacognitive reading strategies should be taught. The key to helping young readers focus their thinking on key ideas while reading is to model or think-aloud what you do to overcome comprehension problems and then scaffold support as they navigate the text and monitor their own understanding. By practicing and applying metacognitive reading strategies, students will become good readers, capable of handling any text across a curriculum. With that in mind, consider the following three main reasons to teach metacognitive reading strategies to K–3 readers and struggling readers including EL students (Block & Mangierri, 2003).

1. **To enable students to develop a deeper understanding of text**
   Good readers know how to use cognitive and metacognitive reading strategies together to develop a deeper understanding of a book's theme or topic. They learn or construct knowledge (using cognitive strategies) through a variety of methods, and then recognize (using metacognitive strategies) when they lack understanding and, consequently, choose the right tools to correct the problem.
2. **To take students' thinking to a higher level**
   For many students, explaining their thought process is a challenging. They may think, "How do I explain what I think? I don't know what to say. My teacher usually helps me out." These students need opportunities to take their thinking to a higher level and express themselves clearly. Small-group activities, especially those with a teacher's guidance, provide them with the right opportunities.
3. **To guide students into becoming strong readers**
   Active readers develop a plan for reading and set a specific purpose. They decide which strategies they may need to comprehend and if their comprehension breaks down, what adjustments they will need to make. Once the metacognitive reading strategies are grasped, students will transfer their use from their school lives to their personal lives and will continue to apply them as they mature.

Ways to help readers become successful thinkers about their thinking (Pressley & Afflerbach, 1995):

1. Develop a plan *before* reading.
2. Monitor their understanding of text; use "fix-up" strategies when meaning breaks down *during* reading.
3. Reflect and evaluate their thinking *after* reading.

PLAN (BEFORE READING)

- Successful readers plan before reading, and K–3 students, struggling readers and EL students must learn the steps needed to accomplish this task. With teacher-directed extensive modeling using kid-friendly language and examples and opportunities to practice on their own, all readers should be able to
- Think about the text's topic.
- Think about how text is organized and how these features can help in understanding the topic.
- Read the title and author, front and back cover blurbs, and table of contents.

- Study illustrations, photos, and graphics, including labels and captions.
- Skim for boldfaced words, headings and subheadings, and summaries.
- Think about what they know about the topic, what connections they can make, and what questions they want answered.

MONITOR (DURING READING)

Successful readers take charge of their reading by monitoring their own comprehension, and K–3 students, struggling readers and EL students need direct instruction on how and why to do this. The first step is recognizing whether or not confusion exists by asking, "Do I understand what I just read?" or "What does the author really want me to know about this text?" Readers who take responsibility for their own comprehension constantly question the text and their reactions to it.

Pressley and Afflerbach (1995) identified other ways that readers monitor comprehension during reading are to:

- make connections
- make predictions
- make inferences
- use context clues
- use text features
- identify text structures
- use graphic organizers to pinpoint particular types of text information
- write comments or questions on self-stick notes or in the margins

Readers can become confused during reading for a variety of reasons (Tovani, 2000):

- The voice inside the reader's head is not talking to him any longer about the text. It may simply be reciting the text.
- The reader's mind begins to wander; he is no longer reminding himself to "pay attention."
- The reader can't remember what has been read.
- The reader can't answer his own questions.
- The reader re-encounters a character but does not remember how or when the character was introduced in the story.

Teaching students how to actively monitor their understanding of the text during reading and how to apply fix-up strategies when it breaks down will ensure all readers a deeper grasp of the text.

EVALUATE (AFTER READING)

When successful readers finish reading, they can reflect on the strategies they used to determine whether their strategies worked or whether they should try something different next time. Because this evaluative, reflective component of the metacognitive process is so valuable, model and practice it with your K–3 students, those that struggle and EL students at every opportunity (whole group, shared reading, guided reading, and teacher read-aloud).

HELPING STUDENTS THINK ABOUT THEIR THINKING: CLASSROOM METACOGNITIVE STRATEGIES THAT BENEFIT ALL READERS

In the remaining portion of this chapter, specific metacognitive strategies are provided that will enable teachers to promote and support students' metacognitive awareness with the goal of enhancing reading comprehension performance for all readers. These activities provide opportunities for children to engage in metacognitive and meaning-making comprehension strategy use. In addition, these activities will enable students to adopt different notions of the purposes and value of reading for deep meaning. This strategy instruction can be applied to all readers: primary, struggling elementary readers, as well as first- and second-language learners.

The format provided here is for basic introduction and beginning activities to practice the strategies. For mastery, continued practice will need to occur daily. Teaching students how to use the metacognitive reading strategies will be most successful with a gradual release of responsibility model. The explicit nature of this instruction is to show students HOW we think when we read.

Step 1: Teacher Modeling (I do, you watch)
(There needs to be LOTS of modeling as strategies are introduced and practiced.)
Step 2: Guided Practice (I do, you help)
Step 3: Independent Practice (You do, I help)
Step 4: Application of Strategy (You do, I watch)

GETTING STARTED

Introducing metacognitive reading comprehension strategies to students feels like a daunting task and one of the most challenging things is to know how to get started. The good news is, introducing these comprehension strategies can be quick, easy, and fun if approached that way. Keep explanations simple, in language that all students can understand and offer students a reasonable amount of new information tied to concrete activities that can inform, but not overwhelm them.

First, introduce the term metacognition. Discuss what this big word means and brainstorm with students what they think it means to think about our thinking. Teachers should use more concrete vocabulary whenever possible when working with younger students, but make an exception in the case of this word because there is no other word that means "thinking about our thinking." Explain to the students that they are going to learn some strategies that will help them think while they are reading. Boyles (2004), identified kid-friendly names for abstract metacognitive reading strategies. Breaking these strategies into familiar, concrete concepts helps students grasp the meaning in a manageable way. The strategies discussed here will be: Connecting, Picturing (Visualization), Wondering (Questioning), Guessing (Predicting), Noticing and Figuring Out (simplified version of Synthesis and Inference) (Boyles, 2004).

As readers, we don't only use one strategy per text. Teachers, must stress that message as strategies are introduced. The strategies we use while reading a text depend on the readability of the text, our background knowledge of the topic, and our interest while reading. The goal is for students to be able to use these comprehension strategies flexibly. However, for introduction sake it is usually best to define and provide examples of one strategy at a time. This will enable the students to get a clear understanding of what each term means and how each strategy contributes to their understanding of any text that they read (Boyles, 2004).

For primary readers, struggling readers and readers whose first language is not English, a gradual introduction to these strategies is best. For these readers an introduction of just two strategies, Connecting and Picturing, which are the most concrete, is a good place to begin instruction. Even the most challenged readers need to be exposed to more than just one strategy right from the start so that they have options in applying the strategies. Even if they can't connect to a particular text from their own experiences, maybe the text will allow the student to make a strong picture in their mind. Provide opportunities to actively practice these two strategies for a couple of weeks before moving on to introduce two more (Boyles, 2004). This plan of introducing these six metacognitive comprehension strategies, two at a time requires approximately six weeks and might unfold in the classroom like this.

WEEKS 1 AND 2

On the first day, introduce and explain the Connecting and Picturing strategy pair in language that is clear and simple enough for all readers to understand.

After the first day, be sure to review the basic definition at the beginning of every lesson. Subsequently model connecting and picturing for the students, Model the integrated use of these comprehension strategies a few times each week in whole-class Read-Aloud/Think-Aloud sessions using appropriate books.

EXPLAINING CONNECTING

Good readers make a lot of different mental connections as they read. They connect the reading to their background knowledge, to their own life, to another text and to the larger world. Students need to understand how and why good readers make these connections as they read. The simple truth is making connections with any text will help us to want to keep reading it.

MAKING CONNECTIONS: TEXT-TO-SELF, TEXT-TO-TEXT, TEXT-TO-WORLD STRATEGY

Schema theory explains how our previous experiences, knowledge, emotions, and understandings affect what and how we learn (Anderson and Pearson, 1984). Schema is the background knowledge and experience readers bring to the text. Good readers draw on prior knowledge and experience to help them understand what they are reading and are thus able to use that knowledge to make connections. Struggling readers often move directly through a text without stopping to consider whether the text makes sense based on their own background knowledge, or whether their knowledge can be used to help them understand confusing or challenging materials. By teaching students how to connect to text,_they are able to better understand what they are reading (Harvey & Goudvis, 2000). Accessing prior knowledge and experiences is a good starting place when teaching strategies because every student has experiences, knowledge, opinions, and emotions that they can draw upon.

Keene and Zimmerman (1997) concluded that students comprehend better when they make different kinds of connections: Text-to-self, Text-to-text, and Text-to-world.

Text-to-self connections are highly personal connections that a reader makes between a piece of reading material and their own experiences. An example of a text-to-self connection might be, "This part of the story reminds me of riding horses on my aunt's farm when I was a little girl."

Sometimes when reading, readers are reminded of other things that they have read, other books by the same author, stories from a similar genre, or perhaps on the same topic. These types of connections are text-to-text connections. Readers gain insight during reading by thinking about how the information they are reading connects to other familiar text. "This character has the same problem that I read about in a story last year," would be an example of a text-to-text connection.

Text-to-world connections are the larger connections that a reader brings to a reading situation. We all have ideas about how the world works that goes far beyond our own personal experiences. We learn about things through the internet, television, movies, magazines, and newspapers. Often it is the text-to-world connections that teachers are trying to enhance when they teach lessons in science, social studies, and literature. An example of a text-to-world connection would be when a reader says, "I saw a TV show that talked about things described in this article."

To effectively use this strategy, teachers should spend time modeling for students how to make meaningful connections. The easiest connection to teach is text-to-self. Teachers should model text-to-self connections initially with selections that are relatively close to the student's personal experiences. A key phrase that prompts text-to-self connections is, "this reminds me of . . ." Next, teachers should model how to make text-to-text connections. Sometimes when we read, we are reminded of other texts we have read. Encourage students to consider the variety of texts they have experienced which will help them understand the new selection. Finally, teachers should model how to make text-to-world connections. When teachers suspect that students may lack the ability to make meaningful connections, classroom instruction will be necessary to bridge the gap between reading experiences and author assumptions. Building the necessary background knowledge is a crucial means for providing text-to-world support and may be used to preempt reading failure. Harvey and Goudvis (2000) caution that merely making connections is not sufficient. Students may make some connections that can distract them from the text. Throughout instruction, students need to be challenged to analyze how their connections are contributing to their understanding of the text. Text connections should lead to text comprehension.

Below are examples of questions that can be used to help students connect. These connection questions can be made into an anchor chart (table 10.1).

Connecting statements can be made into anchor charts for students to use as a reference or teachers can use as prompts for classroom discussions.

Connecting Statements

- This part reminds me of . . .
- I felt like . . . (Character) when I . . .
- If that happened to me I would . . .
- This book reminds me of . . . (Another text) because. . . .
- I can relate to . . . (Part of text) because one time . . .
- Something similar happened to me when . . .

Table 10.1 Making Connections.

Text-to-self	*Text-to-text*	*Text-to-world*
What does this remind me of in my life?	What does this remind me of in another book I've read?	What does this remind me of in the real world?
What is this similar to in my life?	How is this text similar to other things I've read?	How is this text similar to things that happen in the real world?
How is this different from my life?	How is this different from other books I've read?	How is this different from things that happen in the real world?
Has something like this ever happened to me?	Have I read about something like this before?	How did that part relate to the world around me?
How does this relate to my life?		
What were my feelings when I read this?		

EXPLAINING PICTURING (VISUALIZATION)

Picturing the story or visualizing, strengthens reading comprehension skills as students gain a more thorough understanding of the text they are reading by consciously using the words to create mental images. As students gain more deliberate practice with this skill, the act of visualizing text becomes automatic. Students who visualize as they read not only have a richer reading experience but they can recall what they have read for longer periods of time. (Harvey & Goudvis, 2000). When a reader can picture the words on the page as if they were watching a movie or if they can picture themselves actually in the story, they will create personal links that will help them remember and relate to what they have read or listened to at a much deeper level. This makes for a more meaningful reading experience and promotes continued reading.

PRACTICING THE PICTURING (VISUALIZATION) STRATEGY

Ask students to close their eyes. Read a text or example that uses descriptive language. Read a portion and stop. Then ask the students to open their eyes and share with a shoulder partner or with the class what their "movie" looked like as the story was read. Continue this activity through several portions of the story. This is a great way to introduce the strategy, but it is also a useful way to monitor how well the students visualize in their everyday reading.

Picture This (Visualizing)

Good readers use their senses to make pictures in their head.

- I can see . . .
- I can smell . . .
- I can hear . . .
- I can feel . . .
- I can taste . . .
- I can imagine . . .

Provide the students with opportunities in whole group, small group and independent work times to practice making pictures in their minds.

WEEKS 3 AND 4

Continue the same format as above, focusing on the next strategies: Wondering and Guessing. These strategies will enable students to see how questions can lead to predictions. Practice incorporating these two strategies for a couple of weeks. Students should be given opportunities to practice all four of these strategies in whole-class modeling sessions and small-group practice sessions (Boyles, 2004).

EXPLAINING WONDERING/QUESTIONING

Questions help students deepen their understanding of the text they are reading. Zimmerman and Hutchins (2003) state "Questions send readers on quests. They cause readers to seek, pursue, and search for answers for deeper understanding." The teacher should briefly discuss with students what good readers might wonder about before, during and after they read. Before reading students can ask themselves: what is this story/text going to be about? What do I know about this story/topic? Have I read anything like this before? What do the pictures tell me? During reading they should ask themselves questions such as, what will happen next in the story? Why did that happen? How is this story going to end? Wondering is what makes readers want to read (Boyles, 2004).

HOW TO USE THE GENERATING QUESTIONS STRATEGY

Create an anchor chart. Discuss how asking questions while reading keeps us engaged in the story and betters our comprehension. Model this strategy with "think-alouds" as a story is read. After modeling the types of questions that could be asked while reading (and how this helped your comprehension), introduced the game "Guess my Question." This game will get the more competitive students attention! Read a book aloud, then stopped at certain points and say, "Guess my question." Call on students until they come up with a question that would make sense for that part in the story. This game gets the students to really think about potential questions to ask while reading.

Another activity to practice questioning is to take a quick picture walk through a picture book, give each child a large sticky note and tell them to write a question they had about the story based on the pictures. Encourage students to start with the phrase, "I wonder if . . ." Discuss all the questions once your students have finished writing. You could provide a border at the bottom of the chart (below) to place the sticky notes. This activity could be modified to cover other questions on the Anchor Chart. These activities can be done in whole group and small guided-reading group settings.

Wondering (Questioning)	
Ask questions before, during, and after reading. You Should Ask Questions: • When you are curious about something. • When you want to clarify something. • When you want to think deeper about the topic.	
Thin Questions—Right There in the Book: • When? • Where? • Who? • What? • Why?	

Thick Questions—Think and Search to Find • I wonder if . . . ? • How did . . . ? • Why did . . . ? • What might . . . ? • What do you think . . .? • What would happen . . . ? • How would you feel if . . . ?	

EXPLAINING GUESSING (PREDICTING)

Introducing the Guessing (Predicting) strategy is the perfect follow-up to the Wondering (Questioning) strategy. Ask students to think about what they do when they have wondered about something they were reading or listened to in a read-aloud. Discuss their responses and then model this using a read-aloud. Stop at a given point and ask what are they wondering about? They probably will ponder it for a while and then venture a guess about what is happening. Once we make a guess, we usually want to read carefully to find out if our guess was right or wrong and if our thinking was on target.

Explain to students that making predictions is like being a detective. They can find clues in the book title, the illustration on the front cover, as well as pictures inside the book to predict what the story is about. Students may be inclined to take the easy way out and say the book is about a princess or a dog but that's not good enough. Have them also predict what a character will do or an important event that may take place.

This Guessing (Predicting) strategy is not always thought of as a stand-alone metacognitive strategy. It is usually considered a component of inferring. However, for young children it is a critical strategy to introduce as a precursor to inferring. Guessing (Predicting) sets the stage for students to monitor their own understanding of text, formulate reasonable guesses and then check to see if the guesses are correct. This process helps a reader to notice when their thinking about the text is on track and when it is off track (Boyles, 2004).

Students can now integrate use of the four comprehension strategies that have been introduced: Connecting, Picturing, Wondering, and Guessing.

WEEKS 5 AND 6

The last strategies introduced are Noticing and Figuring Out. These two comprehension strategies are logically paired together because in order for a reader to figure out (infer and synthesize), he must notice the details the author has provided. To draw a conclusion or integrate the text elements into a connected whole, the reader must notice the details the author has chosen to write about (Boyles, 2004).

EXPLAINING NOTICING

To introduce the Noticing strategy, hold up a children's picture book and ask the question "What are some of the things good readers notice as they read?" The student's immediate response is typically, "They notice the pictures!" That is a great start, but we want readers to notice important verbal clues: words, sentences and paragraphs that offers evidence of the text's meaning. Some of the best clues in stories might be the details about the characters, clues to identifying the problem, or sentences that specify important events. Helpful clues for a reader to notice in informational, nonfiction could be the words in bold print or the words that lead us to the main ideas. Now that we have noticed them, what should we do with these clues? They need to recognize that when we find clues in text, we should file them away carefully in our mind so we can pull them out later to see how they all fit together—as main ideas and themes (Boyles, 2004).

Good readers also notice when they stop understanding what they are reading, when none of the clues they've gathered while reading makes sense. This process helps a reader to notice when his thinking about the text is on track and when it is off track. The goal is for students to notice the role of their reading comprehension strategies in addition to their rereading and using word-level strategies to untangle text. Any and all of these strategies can help a struggling reader to get their comprehension back on track (Boyles, 2004).

EXPLAINING FIGURING OUT

Figuring it out is a simplified version of the two metacognitive strategies: synthesis and inference. These are extremely abstract ideas for younger elementary, struggling, and EL students to understand. However, these concepts can be grasped if we make the language we use to explain these reading strategies meaningful for all readers. Figuring Out moves the reader beyond the construction of basic knowledge to a deeper understanding of text. Explaining to students the way to Figuring Out is like being a detective. Using the clues the author leaves you, combined with the things you already know, helps you to figure out what the author is really trying to convey. When you can really figure out (synthesize) the meaning of a text, you have used all of your reading comprehension strategies very well. You have made the appropriate connections, created some great pictures in your mind, wondered, guessed and noticed a lot of clues all along while you were reading. And all of this information has helped to figure out the author's meaning (Boyles, 2004).

Following working on these last two strategies for a short time, perhaps another two weeks, these final strategies can be added to the rest of the strategy repertoire. The students can now draw upon all six thinking strategies: Connecting, Picturing, Wondering, Guessing, Noticing, and Figuring Out as they read, whether in teacher-guided whole groups, small groups, or independently.

After the students have watched and listened to the modeling of all the metacognitive strategies, encourage them to think along (with you) about their use of these strategies and to verbalize examples of their use of these strategies. Conclude each modeling session with a discussion of how comprehension strategies help us to become good readers (Boyles, 2004).

If the students *are not* yet reading, their practice using these strategies in small groups must begin with hearing a text read to them. The students can use strategy picture cue cards (that you make) to identify and talk about their comprehension-strategy choice after hearing each chunk of text read out loudly. Even students who can't read like to use these cards to demonstrate and discuss the strategies they use to understand text that is read to them (Boyles, 2004).

If the students *are* ready for reading in these small-group practice sessions, be careful to choose texts that match their reading abilities. Many of the early guided-reading books won't have much content to demonstrate use of reading comprehension strategies. But, nonfiction selections offer some potential for demonstrating these strategies (Boyles, 2004).

The goal of the initial strategy explanations and beginning practice is not mastery, the goal is simply to set a foundation that readers can build upon. When all strategies have been introduced, make an anchor chart of the Metacognitive Thinking Stems (McGregor, 2007) as a reminder of all metacognitive strategies to use when reading (see below).

Students can and will learn much more about these metacognitive strategies as they get familiar with and more comfortable using them as they read. Primary grade students and struggling elementary readers (both native and nonnative speakers of English) can be taught how to effectively select and use appropriate comprehension strategies based on what they know about themselves as readers through self-regulation and the ability to transfer their

Metacognition: Thinking Stems

- I'm thinking . . .
- I'm noticing . . .
- I'm wondering . . .
- I'm picturing . . .
- I'm feeling . . .
- It reminds me of . . .
- I'm figuring out . . .

use of strategies. Comprehension-strategy instruction can teach these students how to use metacognitive strategies flexibly to resolve comprehension problems and enhance their comprehension of both narrative and informational texts. Appropriate, specific instruction will enable these learners to determine whether they understand what has been read and how to take appropriate steps to correct the comprehension problems that emerge.

REFERENCES

Almasi, J. F. (2003). *Teaching strategic processes in reading.* New York: Guilford Press.

Anderson R. C., & Pearson, P. D. (1984). A schema-theoretic view of basic processes in reading comprehension. In P. D. Pearson (Ed.), *Handbook of reading research* (pp. 255–91). New York: Longman.

Baker, L. (2002). Metacognition in comprehension instruction. In C. C. Block & M. Pressley (Eds.), *Comprehension instruction: Research-based best practices* (pp. 77–95). New York: Guilford Press.

Baker, L., & Brown, A. L. (1984). Metacognitive skills and reading. In R. Barr, M. L. Kamil, P. Mosenthal, & P. D. Pearson (Eds.), *Handbook of reading research* (Vol. 2, pp. 353–94). White Plains, NY: Longman.

Block, C. C., Gambrell, L., & Pressley, M. (Eds.). (2002). *Rethinking comprehension.* San Francisco: Jossey-Bass.

Block, C. C. & Mangieri, J. N. (2003). *Exemplary literacy teachers: Literacy success in grades K–5.* New York: Guilford Press.

Block, C. C., & Pressley, M. (Eds.). (2002). *Comprehension instruction: Research-based best practices.* New York: Guilford Press.

Block, C. C., Rodgers, L. L., & Johnson, R. B. (2004). *Comprehension Process Instruction: Creating Reading Success in Grades K–3.* New York: Guilford Press.

Boyles, N. N. (2004). *Constructing Meaning through Kid-Friendly Comprehension Strategy Instruction.* Gainesville: Maupin House.

Brassell, D., & Rasinski, T. (2008). *Comprehension that works: Taking students beyond ordinary understanding to deep comprehension.* Huntington Beach, CA: Shell.

Brown, R. (2002). Straddling two worlds: Self-directed comprehension instruction for middle schoolers. In C. C. Block & M. Pressley (Eds.), *Comprehension Instruction: Research-based best practices* (pp. 337–50). New York: Guilford Press.

Dorn, L. & Soffos, C. (2005). *Teaching for deep comprehension: A reading workshop approach.* Portland, MN: Stenhouse.

Echevarria, J., Vogt, M., & Short, D. (2000). *Making content comprehensible for English language learners.* Needham Heights, MA: Allyn & Bacon.

Farstrup, A. & Samuels, S. J. (Eds.). (2002). *What research has to say about reading instruction,* 3rd ed. Newark, DE. IRA.

Gersten, R., Fuchs, L. S., Williams, J. P., & Baker, S. (2001). Teaching reading comprehension strategies to students with learning disabilities: A review of research. Review of Educational Research, 71(2), 279–320.

Harvey, S., & Goudvis, A. (2000). *Strategies that work: Teaching comprehension to enhance understanding.* Portland, ME: Stenhouse.

Keene, E., & Zimmerman, S. (1997). *Mosaic of Thought.* Portsmouth, NH: Heinemann.

Kragler, S., Walker, C. A., & Martin, L. E. (2005). Strategy instruction in primary content textbooks. *The Reading Teacher,* 59(3), 254–61.

Lyons, C. (2003). *Teaching struggling readers how to use brain based research to maximize learning.* Portsmouth, NH: Heinemann.

McGregor, T. (2007). Comprehension connections: *Bridges to Strategic Reading.* Portsmouth, NH: Heinemann.

National Institute of Child Health and Human Development. (2000). *Report of the National Reading Panel. Teaching children to read: An evidence-based assessment of the scientific research literature on reading and its implications for reading instruction (NIH Publication No. 00-4769).* Washington, DC: U.S Government Printing Office.

Neufeld, P. (2005). Comprehension instruction in content area classes. *The Reading Teacher,* 59(4), 302–12.

Pearson, D. P. (Ed.). (2002). *Handbook of Reading Research.* Mahwah, NJ: Lawrence Erlbaum.

Pearson, D. P., & Duke, N. K. (2002). Comprehension instruction in the early grades. In C. C. Block & M. Pressley (Eds.), *Comprehension instruction: Research-based best practices* (pp. 247–58). New York: Guilford.

Pearson, D. P. & Fielding, L. (1991).Comprehension instruction. In R. Barr, M. L. Kamil, P. B. Rosenthal, & P. D. Pearson (Eds.), *Handbook of reading research: Volume II* (pp. 815–60). White Plains, NY: Longman.

Pearson, P. D., & Gallagher M. C. (1983). The instruction of reading comprehension. *Contemporary Educational Psychology, 8,* 317–44.

Pressley, M., & Afflerbach, P. (1995). *Verbal protocols of reading: The nature of constructively responsive reading. Hillsdale,* NJ: Lawrence Erlbaum Associates.

Pressley, M. (2004). The need for research in secondary literacy education. In T. L. Jetton and J. A. Dole (Eds.), *Adolescent literacy research and practice* (pp. 415–32). New York: Guilford.

Reutzel. D. R., Smith, J. A., & Fawson, P. C. (2005). An evaluation for two approaches for teaching reading comprehension strategies in the primary years using science information texts. *Early Childhood Research Quarterly*, 20(3), 276–305.

Samuels, S. J. (1987). Information processing abilities and reading. *Journal of Reading Disabilities, 20*, 18–22.

Shanahan, T., Callison, K., Carriere, C., Duke, N. K., Pearson, P. D., Schatschneider, C., & Torgenson, J. (2010). *Improving reading comprehension in kindergarten through third grade: A practical guide (NCEE 2010-4038).* Washington, DC: National Center for Education Evaluation and Regional Assistance, Institute of Education Sciences, U.S. Department of Education. Retrieved from *whatworks.ed.gov/publications/practiceguides.*

Stahl, K. A. D., & Garcia, G. E. (2015). *Developing reading comprehension: Effective Instruction for All Students in PreK–2.* New York: Guilford Press.

Stahl, K. A. D. (2014). Fostering inference generation with emergent and novice readers. *The Reading Teacher, 67*(5), 384–88.

Stahl, K. A. D. (2004). Proof, practice and promise: Comprehension strategy instruction in the primary grades. *The Reading Teacher, 57*, 598–609.

Stebick, D. M., & Dain, J. M. (2007). *Comprehension Strategies For Your K–6 Literacy Classroom: Thinking Before, During and After Reading.* Thousand Oaks, CA, Corwin Press.

Taylor, B. B., Pearson, P. D., Garcia, G. E., Stahl, K. A. D., & Bauer, E. B. (2006). Improving students' reading comprehension. In K. A. D. Stahl & M. C. McKenna (Eds.), *Reading research at work: Foundations of effective practice* (pp. 303–15). New York: Guilford Press.

Trimble, S. (1994). The scripture of maps, the names of trees: A child's landscape. In G. P. Nathan and S. Trimble (Eds.), *The geography of childhood: Why children need wild places* (pp. 15–32). Boston: Beacon Press.

Vygotsky, L. S. (1978). *Mind in society: The development of higher psychological Processes.* Cambridge, MA: Harvard University Press.

Wilhelm, J. D. (2001). *Improving Comprehension with Think-Aloud Strategies.* New York: Scholastic Inc.

Wood, D. J., Bruner, J. S., & Ross, G. (1976). The role of tutoring in problem solving. *Journal of Child Psychology and Psychiatry, 17*, 89–100.

Zimmerman, S., & Hutchins, C. (2003), *7 Keys to Comprehension.* New York: Three Rivers Press.

Chapter 11

Exploring the Potential of Internet Reciprocal Teaching to Improve Online Reading

Jill Castek

ABSTRACT

This chapter explores an adaptation of Reciprocal Teaching (RT), a well-known instructional intervention for increasing reading comprehension, to address the skills and strategies required when reading online text. When students read online, additional literacy skills are required to navigate and make sense of the vast number of websites and information resources they will encounter. An adapted instructional approach, Internet Reciprocal Teaching (IRT), is a promising practice that promotes group discussion to address searching for information, synthesizing information, critically evaluating information, and communicating ideas online. Instruction in online reading may have beneficial implications for the future success of both thriving and striving readers. A background and rationale is followed by pedagogical implications section that showcases ways to implement this instructional approach.

FRAMING THE ISSUE

New literacies theory suggests that the nature of literacy is rapidly changing and transforming as new information and communication technologies emerge. Supporting students' online reading comprehension in this information-rich online environment, presents unique challenges to reading comprehension instruction. Reciprocal teaching (RT), a discussion routine in which groups of students discuss texts and share understandings together, can be adapted to address the comprehension skills and strategies required for reading on the Internet such as those needed to comprehend search engine results and to synthesize information gathered from multiple websites. When reading and interpreting search engine results, students must learn to select the best resource from among thousands available online and to critically evaluate these information resources to make informed reading choices. Researchers have worked to modify RT to address online reading. The adapted approach has been explored as a promising instructional practice (see Castek, Coiro, Henry, Leu, & Hartman, 2015).

Internet Reciprocal Teaching (IRT) builds on work by Palincsar & Brown's (1984) well-known approach, RT. RT is a widely used and extensively researched approach to teaching strategic reading comprehension strategies during which a group reads a shared text and discusses it dynamically in order to make sense of the ideas and clarify understanding (e.g., Brown & Palincsar, 1989; Hacker & Tenent, 2002; Palincsar & Brown, 1984; Rosenshine & Meister, 1992). The RT instructional model begins with teacher modeling of reading strategies. While working in small groups, teachers and students take turns leading discussions of the text and demonstrating reading strategies: questioning, predicting, clarifying, and summarizing. Eventually, the teacher relinquishes control and students enact the reading strategies and lead the discussion in a collaborative group setting. Over time, these strategies appear to become self-regulated and transfer to new reading contexts.

This approach promotes the interrelationship between strategies while reading in different contexts. The strategies when taught together are more powerful than when implemented in isolation (Hacker & Tenent, 2002; Palincsar & Brown, 1984; Rosenshine & Meister, 1994). Key elements of the RT model include:

- the use of traditional, printed texts, which are often narratives;
- the reading of a common text;
- the teaching of a small group of students, often struggling readers;
- teacher modeling of comprehension strategies;
- a focus on predicting, questioning, clarifying, and summarizing strategies;
- a gradual release of responsibility away from the teacher as students take on use of comprehension strategies;
- collaboration and discussion among all participants in the RT group

A meta-analytic review of sixteen studies (Rosenshine & Meister, 1994) showed that RT had a consistent, large, and positive effect on comprehension outcomes. Median effect sizes across the studies were between 0.34 and 0.60 on teacher-designed tests. Since reading performance in the United States has remained flat for decades, it is important that educators capitalize on instructional models that can be flexibly implemented in different contexts and have shown some success, such as RT.

Promising work in online reading instruction (see Castek, Zawilinski, McVerry, O'Byrne, & Leu, 2011) involved adaptation and extension of a number of the elements of RT. Some changes stemmed from the differences between reading offline and reading online. Others have resulted from moving a small-group instructional model, initially developed for teaching lower performing readers, to meet the needs of self-contained classroom teachers who teach larger numbers of students with a wider range of reading proficiency. Additional changes have resulted from the decision to adapt RT within classrooms where students each have their own computer or digital device. The resulting instructional model, IRT, includes the following key elements:

- the use of online informational texts
- the reading of unique texts students find online (not a common text provided by a teacher)
- the instruction in a classroom made up of students with different experiences with digital tools and online texts
- the integration of both teacher and student modeling of online comprehension strategies
- a focus on questioning, locating, critically evaluating, synthesizing, and communicating strategies as important elements of online reading (see Leu, Coiro, Kinzer, Castek, & Henry, 2013)
- collaboration and discussion among all participants in IRT.

In the sections that follow, additional background about the IRT model is included, followed by a detailed example of an instructional sequence.

Making the Case

Online reading is a process of problem-based inquiry made up of four interdependent areas: (1) locating information; (2) critically evaluating information for relevancy, accuracy, and bias; (3) synthesizing information across multiple text formats; and (4) communicating information to others using multiple modes (Leu et al., 2013).

A promising instructional model, IRT draws on collaborative models of instruction and the use of digital texts combined with the proven intervention, RT, to teach the literacies required for online reading, writing, and communicating. Adaptations made to RT, are categorized into three general areas: the texts used, the strategies taught, and the phases of instruction.

Reader-constructed text. In IRT, as students read on the Internet, they construct their own texts as they search for information and click on links that lead them to different web pages (Coiro & Dobler, 2007). Therefore, the texts used while teaching through IRT vary from student to student based on where they navigate online when searching for topical information. In contrast, when working in RT groups, the students all read from a common text. Additionally, the texts in IRT are most often informational-based texts.

Online literacy strategies. Making sense of digital information requires skills and strategies that are complex, and in some cases unique, to online reading and writing contexts (Afflerbach & Cho, 2009). Online texts and their associated literacy practices are diverse, multiple, and evolve based on the variety of ways learners read, write, view, listen, compose, and communicate information as they access information on the Internet. A sampling of strategies taught through IRT include, but are not limited to: (a) strategies for reading and interpreting search results pages by attending to URLs and the descriptions under the link titles; (b) strategies for making inferences about where different links might lead, and whether clicking on a link might provide relevant information or detract from meeting a specified goal; (c) strategies for critically evaluating information based on relevancy, accuracy, and reliability; and (d) strategies for using a blog, wiki, or other socially networked technology to spark an exchange of ideas. Additional skills and strategies are listed in the IRT Phase I and Phase II checklists (see Castek et al., 2015, pp. 340–44).

Phases of instruction. An emerging model of IRT suggests there are three phases of instruction that differ in degrees of strategy complexity, level of student responsibility for teaching or modeling for others, and degree of independent inquiry and use. Phase I is largely teacher directed and focuses on basic computer and Internet use skills such as file saving, browser basics, and features of email interfaces. During Phase II, the teacher and students share responsibility for modeling while students are engaged in problem-solving activities using the Internet. Lessons focus on locating and critically evaluating information, synthesizing, and communicating on the Internet. Phase III integrates independent inquiry where students use the Internet to investigate self-selected questions and share information within and beyond the classroom via Internet communication tools. These three phases employ variations in scaffolding to support students as they take greater responsibility for their own learning over time.

Pedagogical Implications

IRT instruction can encompasses several distinct Internet reading contexts. Ideally, lessons in each area would be planned and delivered in a series that would move progressively from easier to more complex reading contexts. The following list provides a suggested sequence.

A. **Reading between two web pages (a homepage and one linked webpage).** This series of lessons introduces website structures. Lessons demonstrate how the reading context changes as various navigational paths are taken. Through demonstration, discussion and guided navigation, students learn to follow only those hyperlinks that would best suit their purpose for reading.
B. **Reading within multiple web pages bound to one website**. This series of lessons introduces the process of navigation within multiple layers of hypertext. Hypertext is text that includes links to additional websites that provide more background or information. For novice online readers, navigating multiple links introduces many choices that can make wayfinding through a text challenging. Through demonstration, discussion and guided navigation students learn how to read linked information. Students are taught how to infer the kinds of information that may be linked to various sites and how to use a set of criteria for evaluating what constitutes a quality website and relevant information.
C. **Reading within a search engine**. This series of lessons introduces the use of a search engine and includes how to query search engines, guidelines for reading search results, and ways to search within a site to locate specific information. Students learn to make informed choices about what to read and how to navigate to the sites that contain the information suited to their intended reading purpose.
D. **Reading the entire Web**. This series of lessons teaches students to how to choose a topic of interest, query electronic sources, locate information relevant to their interests, and synthesize the information from multiple sources to come to new understandings. It provides students with the broadest possible reading tasks and contexts where they are able to use all of the strategies they have learned in earlier stages.
E. **Reading (and writing) online messages**. This series of lessons explores the many different comprehension strategies required to infer information presented in a variety of communication contexts: Email, blogs, social networking posts, or other networked communication application. Each of these communication contexts requires unique inferential reasoning skills as compared to offline texts since the recipient(s) of the message are often outside the immediate context. Discussion focuses on how to construct clear messages appropriate for each context.

In all of these contexts, particular emphasis is placed on elements that have been found to play an important role in online reading comprehension (Coiro & Dobler, 2007). Inferential reasoning skills become more complex and multidimensional within Internet reading contexts (Coiro & Dobler, 2007). Readers are continually required to make predictions about where each link they follow may lead. And readers must become skilled in evaluating whether its utility suits their purpose. In addition, recognizing that reading and writing are interrelated processes is an essential part of online reading comprehension. When engaging in online communication, one must take into consideration mode, audience, and purpose to be efficient and effective in sharing ideas.

TEACHING SEQUENCE FOR GUIDED MODELING OF IRT

1. In the modeling phase, leadership rotates. The teacher begins by demonstrating her reading processes, then different students guide the group through the four target strategies for a section of text.
2. The teacher directs students to look at the homepage's title bar, labels, navigational links, any annotations following these links, icons, animations, and the main text on the homepage.
3. Students *predict* what types of information will be found on this page and where links (selected by the teacher) may lead. Discussions focus on how predicting the main structure of a website leads to a more successful and efficient process of reading for information. Through discussion and modeling, students come to better understand the types of informational resources that are linked between web pages.
4. The IRT group reads the textual information revealed upon selecting a particular hyperlink. Students are encouraged to consider the meaning communicated in animations, images, video, or audio clips on the webpage. The leader points out words or concepts that cause confusion. This information will be discussed and *clarified* by the group. Group members consult resources or use context clues. The teacher provides support as needed or asks others in the classroom to assist.
5. The strategy leader within the IRT group generates a *question* relating to the information on the website. Students within the group answer these questions referring back to what they have read. The teacher models questioning strategies while thinking aloud to scaffold students' questioning processes.
6. The leader in each IRT group *summarizes* the section they read. Students describe how their choice of navigational path and selection of links to related information helped to build the summary they constructed. After sufficient time has passed for the IRT groups to summarize, the teacher provides additional models so that summaries remain focused on important points.
7. The process detailed above repeats as group leadership rotates. Groups will *predict* where the embedded links from a homepage lead. Guided navigation in a group context and setting a clear purpose for reading will

help students determine which links are purposeful and which may lead them astray. The same procedure is followed for each new series of links on a target website. Instruction focuses on predicting the path of several links deeper down the website's structure (away from the homepage). The teacher will model how to return to the site's homepage to select alternative navigational paths, following different links to repeat the process. After five links or so have been followed, students share their summaries, generate an overall strategy for the entire text, and clarify any lingering misunderstandings.

Students may find it helpful to have a series of prompts to support the collaborative discussion within an Internet reading context. The prompts help frame the discussion and keep students focused on equity in participation.

INTERNET RECIPROCAL TEACHING PROMPTS

Predict

- Explain what kinds of information will be contained on this webpage.
- Use cues from the website (illustrations, icons, graphics, or subtitles) to support your prediction.
- Identify which links will help you navigate through the text to gather information.
- Describe the types of information you predict will be linked to the website or to buttons on the menu.

Clarify

- Look for words, phrases, links, or features that are unfamilar.
- Discuss the words, images, animations, or concepts that are new, interesting, or confusing.
- Examine the context, substitute a synonym, locate the root word, prefix or suffix and use these pieces as support, ask others, mark the word to look up later; if it is a linked word, examine the link to identify supports that may help you (glossary or other online source).

Question

- Ask questions that begin with who, what, when, where, why, or how.
- Ask main idea questions that aid in identifying key ideas.
- Ask questions that have under the surface answers.
- Ask questions about the navigational path as it relates to summarizing.

Summarize

- Include the main ideas, not all the details.
- Keep the summary concise and focused.
- Stick to the point.

Internet Reciprocal Teaching Practical "How Tos"

1. *Explain* how using a strategy will improve learning. Students need know not only how to *use* a strategy, but also *why* it is useful. If given a purpose, they will put effort into learning it.
2. *Demonstrate* how and when to use a strategy. Demonstrate by "thinking out loud" while showing the how strategy can be used.
3. *Practice* using the strategy. Simply explaining does not mean students will learn *how* to do it. They need to actively practice using the strategy in meaningful ways.
4. *Support* students while they learn the strategy. Students need scaffolding, while learning to use strategies. Scaffolding may include hints, questions, reminders, explanations, or other supports.
5. *Explain* what was learned while reading and using a strategy. This shows that the strategy was valuable to learn because it helped build understanding.
6. *Feedback* can help students know whether they understand how to use the strategy effectively. Feedback should be very specific.
7. *Debrief* with students about how useful the strategy was to them. This can help students make the connection between using the strategy and better comprehension.

Getting Started

1. Choose an area of online reading you'd like to explore with students.
   a. *Examples*: using a search engine, critically evaluating information, synthesizing ideas from multiple sites.
2. Introduce the strategy focus.
3. Assign a purposeful task using the tool you've introduced. Students can work individually or in pairs.
4. Provide time for students to complete the task (observe as students are working).
5. Make note of instances where students are using unique strategies that go beyond the information you taught in the introduction.
6. When a unique strategy is observed, bring it to that students' attention, and ask if they'd be prepared to share and demonstrate their strategy to the class.

Internet Reciprocal Teaching Observation Record
Questioning
Clarifying
Summarizing
Predicting

7. Plan time for students to share/demonstrate to the class what their unique strategy was (and how it was useful to them in completing the task).
8. List these unique strategies as a class on chart paper to use as a reference.

ASSESSMENT TOOLS

In addition to exploring new ways of thinking about IRT instruction, a number of different methodologies and instruments have been developed to formatively assess online reading comprehension. Two instruments can be used to organize these observations

1. *The Internet Reciprocal Teaching Observation Record* is a formative assessment for note taking. It is used to record an individual's reading processes and strategy application. Observation notes are collected to provide guidance and feedback to students to promote growth and improvement.
2. *The Internet Reciprocal Teaching Dialogue Rubric* is used in several ways. In the introductory phase of the group modeling process, it communicates expectations for the application of strategy use in the context of the group dialogue. The rubric is also used as a discussion tool to prompt reflection. Students are invited to suggest revisions to the rubric based on what they have understood to be important about implementing each strategy in an Internet context. The rubric documents students' progress over time during the course of a school year (see figure 11.1).

SUMMARY

This chapter explores the potential of an instructional model called IRT to support students' online reading and comprehension. The approach, suggested instructional sequences, and assessment tools offered here have been developed in conjunction with several classroom teachers using an iterative and formative design process. The resulting tools and techniques have yielded promising results with diverse classrooms. As students gain experience with

Strategy	Beginning 1	Developing 2	Accomplished 3	Exemplary 4
Questioning	Generates simple recall questions that can be answered directly from facts or information found within the website's home page.	Generates main idea questions that can be answered based on information gathered by accessing one or more links to the website's content.	Generates questions requiring inference. Facts and information must be synthesized from one or more links to the website's content and combined with prior knowledge.	Generates questions flexibly that vary in type, based on the content read and dialogue.
Clarifying	Identifies clarification as a tool to enhance understanding and initiates clarification dialogue when appropriate.	Identifies appropriate words for clarification with the dialogue's context.	Assists group in clarifying identified words based on context clues.	Uses strategies for word clarification that can be applied generally across reading contexts.
Summarizing	Summary consists of loosely related ideas.	Summary consists of several main ideas but also many details.	Summary synthesizes main ideas, is complete, accurate and concise.	Summary is accurate, complete, and concise incorporating content vocabulary contained in the text.
Predicting	Demonstrates knowledge of predictions as an active reading strategy.	Directs group predictions to set a clear purpose for reading.	Articulates predictions that build logically from context.	Provides justification for prediction and initiates confirmation or redirection based on information located in the text.

Group Facilitation	Beginning 1	Developing 2	Accomplished 3	Exemplary 4
Group Leadership	Initiates one to two of the strategies in a loosely organized manner.	Provides some leadership in initiating three to four strategies	Leads effectively incorporating all four strategies into a dialogue.	Keeps group on task and skillfully and demonstrates strategies while balancing group participation.
Group Participation	Stays on task mostly listening but contributes little to the dialogue	Stays on task and actively participates in the dialogue.	Actively listens and builds responses around what others have contributed to the dialogue.	Participates in dialogue and actively responds to other students in a strategic manner.

Figure 11.1 Designed for Assessment of Internet Reciprocal Teaching by Jill Castek

the IRT model, they develop not only the skills required for online reading comprehension, but also empowerment in their ability to lead their classmates in acquiring important skills and strategies for reading online. As technologies and digital tools continue to evolve, so too will these instructional strategies. Such is the nature of teaching and learning in a rapidly changing, technologically rich world.

REFERENCES

Afflerbach, P., & Cho, B. (2009). Identifying and describing constructively responsive comprehension strategies in new and traditional forms of reading. In S. Israel and G. Duffy (Eds.), *Handbook of reading comprehension research* (pp. 69–90). Mahwah, NJ: Erlbaum Associates.

Castek, J., Coiro, J., Henry, L., Leu, D., & Hartman, D. (2015). Research on instruction and assessment in the new literacies of online research and comprehension. In S. Parris and K. Headley (Eds.), *Comprehension Instruction: Research-Based Best Practices*, 3rd ed. (pp. 324–44). New York, NY: Guilford Press.

Castek, J., Zawilinski, L., McVerry, G., O'Byrne, I., & Leu, D. J. (2011). The new literacies of online reading comprehension: New opportunities and challenges for students with learning difficulties. In C. Wyatt-Smith, J. Elkins, & S. Gunn (Eds.), *Multiple perspectives on difficulties in learning literacy and numeracy* (pp. 91–110). New York, NY: Springer.

Coiro, J., & Dobler, B. (2007). Exploring the online comprehension strategies used by sixth-grade skilled readers to search for and locate information on the Internet. *Reading Research Quarterly, 42*, 214–57.

Hacker, D. J., & Tenent, A. (2002). Implementing reciprocal teaching in the classroom: Overcoming obstacles and making modifications. *Journal of Educational Psychology, 94*(4), 699–718.

Leu, D. J., Coiro, J., Kinzer, C., Castek, J., & Henry, L. A. (2013). A dual level theory of the changing nature of literacy, instruction, and assessment. In N. Unrau and D. Alvermann (Eds.), *Theoretical models and processes of reading*, 6th ed. (pp. 1150–81). Newark, DE: International Reading Association.

Palinscar, A. S., & Brown, A. L. (1984). Reciprocal teaching of comprehension-fostering and comprehension-monitoring activities. *Cognition and Instruction, 1*, 117–75.

Rosenshine, B., & Meister, C. (1994). Reciprocal teaching: A review of the research. *Review of Educational Research, 64*(4), 479–530.

FURTHER READINGS

Castek, J., Henry, L., Coiro, J., Leu, D., & Hartman, D. (2015). Research on instruction and assessment in the new literacies of online research and comprehension. In S. Parris and K. Headley (Eds.), *Comprehension Instruction: Research-Based Best Practices*, 3rd Ed. (pp. 324–44). New York, NY: Guilford Press.

Henry, L. A., Castek, J., Zawilinski, L., & O'Byrne, I. (2012). Using peer collaboration to support online reading, writing, and communication: An empowerment model for struggling readers. *Reading and Writing Quarterly: Overcoming Learning Difficulties, 28*, 279–306.

Chapter 12

Development of Word Identification in a Second Language

Keiko Koda

ABSTRACT

Efficient word identification is vital to successful reading comprehension. Word form analysis and word meaning retrieval are the main components of word identification. The primary function of the two components is to connect sequences of graphic symbols in a written text with stored knowledge of word forms, word meanings, and real-life experiences. As such, as a mechanism of extracting and integrating information from diverse sources, word identification is linked with every other operation involved in reading comprehension. The primary goals of this chapter include clarifying reader-text interactions in word form analysis and word meaning retrieval, describing cross-linguistic variations in word form analysis, and discussing their implications for the development of word identification skills in a second language.

DEVELOPMENT OF WORD IDENTIFICATION IN A SECOND LANGUAGE

Reading is a process of constructing text meanings based on graphically encoded linguistic information. As such, it entails several interlinked operations, including (a) extracting formal (phonological and morphological) information from a printed word (word form analysis), (b) retrieving the context-appropriate meaning of the word (word meaning retrieval), (c) incorporating the word's meaning into the emerging local text meaning, (d) integrating local text meanings into a coherent whole, and (e) assimilating the consolidated text information into relevant knowledge bases. Of these, word identification encompasses the first two operations (Adams, 1990; Perfetti & Stafura, 2014; Roberts, Christo, & Shefelbine, 2011). Given the evidence supporting the reader's continual engagement in word form analysis and heavy reliance on a word's formal information during text comprehension, word identification should be regarded as a vital process that enables the reader to bring personal knowledge and experiences, both direct and vicarious, into text meaning construction.

Building on current models of reading, this chapter describes (a) what are the roles of the reader's knowledge in word form analysis and word meaning retrieval, (b) how word identification skills vary across languages, and (c) how such cross-linguistic variations affect the development of word identification skills in a second language.

COMPONENT OPERATIONS IN WORD IDENTIFICATION

Word identification entails a number of component operations, including formal information extraction, speedy lexical access, word meaning retrieval, and context-appropriate meaning/sense selection. When these operations are executed successfully in tandem, graphically encoded formal information is connected with various sources of stored knowledge—for example, phonological and morphological forms, lexical entries, word meanings, real-life experiences, and prior knowledge—that are internally available to the reader. The sections below describe what processes word form analysis and word meaning retrieval entail, and how reader-text interactions transpire in those processes.

WORD FORM ANALYSIS

The function of word form analysis is to find out to which word a sequence of graphic symbols corresponds based on the phonological and morphological information extracted from the symbol string. The analysis is necessary because writing systems encode only formal information of words, but not their meanings (Coulmus, 1989). As such, this operation requires the knowledge of the language in which reading is learned and its relationships to the graphic symbols in the writing system.

READER-TEXT INTERACTIONS DURING WORD FORM ANALYSIS

Orthographic processing. Fluent reading requires rapid and effortless access to context-appropriate word meanings. It may seem that good readers recognize words instantly and access their meanings without word form analysis. However, word recognition studies have repeatedly shown that skilled readers are, through automaticity, capable of segmenting and assembling sub-lexical information effortlessly (Ehri, 1998; Shankweiler & Liberman, 1972), and that competent readers are adept at pronouncing both individual letters and nonsense letter strings (Hogaboam & Perfetti, 1978; Siegel and Ryan, 1988; Wagner, Torgesen, & Rashotte, 1994). These findings suggest that what seems like instant holistic performance is not attributable to whole-word retrieval, but rather, children's accumulated knowledge of the orthography in their writing system (Adams, 1990; Ehri, 1994, 1998, 2014). Seidenberg and McClelland (1989) define English orthographic knowledge as "an elaborate matrix of correlations among letter patterns, phonemes, syllables, and morphemes" (1989, p. 525). Similarly, Ehri (2014) contends that orthographic processing entails "the formation of letter-sound connections to bond the spellings, pronunciations, and meanings of specific words in memory" (2014, p. 5). Once acquired, therefore, word-specific orthographic representations are responsible for sight word reading, spelling, and vocabulary learning.

Phonological processing. Phonological processing refers to the processes involved in accessing, storing, and manipulating a word's phonological information (Torgesen & Burgess, 1998). Studies consistently document that weak readers are poor at phonological processing and that their deficiencies tend to be "domain-specific, longitudinally predictive, and relatively unaffected by non-phonological factors—such as general intelligence, semantic, or visual processing" (Share & Stanovich, 1995, p. 9). It is widely acknowledged that the ability to extract the phonological information from the written form of a word is causally related to reading achievement. The primary function of phonological processing is to afford quick access to stored meanings of familiar spoken words (Frost, 1998). Word (both real and pseudo-word) naming performance is known to be a powerful predictor of reading success among children in the initial grades (Bowers, Golden, Kennedy, & Young, 1994; Share & Stanovich, 1995; Torgesen & Burgess, 1998).

Morphological processing. Morphemes are the smallest functioning unit in the composition of words. In learning to read, children rely on their emerging understanding of morpheme forms, functions, and concatenation rules. This knowledge plays an important role in learning to read English and other languages whose writing systems directly represent morphological information (Frost, 2002; Ehri, 2014; Ku & Anderson, 2003; Nunes & Bryant, 2006).

As an illustration, the English orthography is alphabetic, in nature, and generally bound by phonemic constraints. However, its strong tendency to preserve morphological information in the grapheme disallows phonemic constituents to fully account for its orthographic conventions. For example, distinct orthographic patterns are used to differentiate two unrelated morphemes sharing the same pronunciation, such as "sale" and "sail." Conversely, shared morphemes are spelled identically despite their distinct pronunciations, as in "anxious/anxiety" and "electric/electricity," or the past tense marker "-ed" (e.g., /-d/ in moved, /-t/ in talked, /-ɪd/ in visited).

Morphological processing in word form analysis becomes more central to reading comprehension, word meaning retrieval, and word meaning inference, as children move through the grades in school. According to Nagy and Anderson (1984), roughly 60 percent of the new words children encounter in printed school materials are structurally transparent multi-morphemic words, such as "fire-fight-er" and "un-lady-like." This implies that the meaning of at least half the new words children encounter could be inferred by segmenting a word into its morphological constituents. The ability to analyze the printed form of a word through morphological segmentation enables children to identify familiar functional elements in the word, and in so doing, allows them to extract partial information from the word they have never seen before (Ku & Anderson, 2003). Without such competence, children would be unable to fill semantic gaps created by unfamiliar words during reading, which would hamper their text comprehension.

Word meaning retrieval

Based on widely acknowledged definitions of vocabulary knowledge (Nation, 2001; Schmitt, 2014; Anderson & Nagy, 1991), this section discusses what it means to know a word's meaning and how this knowledge bridges the core semantic information of the word and the reader's real-life experiences. Anderson & Nagy (1991) contend that conventional models of word meanings equate word meanings with abstract core semantic information that defines the set of entities or events to which a word refers, and that this knowledge must include the representations of the situations in which the word appears. By adding the situation-specific dimension to word meaning knowledge, Anderson and Nagy explain how this knowledge allows the graphic form of a word to evoke the reader's real-life experiences associated with the word. They argue that a viable model of word meanings, particularly in the context of reading research, must include (a) context-free abstract meanings for the commitment to parsimony of representation and (b) context-bound meanings for the preservation of their connections to real-life knowledge.

As a complex construct, word meaning knowledge emerges gradually through repeated encounters with a word referring to a particular object, event, or property in particular situations. In this regard, the vast majority of words have multiple references. For example, the word "house" evokes different images of houses the reader has previously encountered in real-life situations—ranging from a large mansion to a decrepit shack with a leaking roof. To assimilate the word into the emerging local text meaning, word meaning retrieval must include the process of selecting the right meaning, or reference, that is semantically congruent both with the local text meaning and the reader's real-life experience. Thus, the selection of the context-appropriate meaning is constrained by the word form, local text meaning, and prior knowledge.

These multiple constraints seem to imply that word meaning retrieval entails two distinct sets of mappings—one between word forms and abstract meanings and the other between situation-specific word meanings and real-life experiences. Such a postulation is plausible because the knowledge of word forms (phonological and morphological information) has an arbitrary relation to experience-based representations. As a mediator, the context-sensitive dimension of word meaning knowledge in a way serves as a pass-code to stored prior knowledge as it includes "information about the things to which words refer—be they related to the external world or to internal states of the mind" (Schreuder & Flores d'Arcais, 1992, p. 422).

Reader-text interactions during word meaning inference. When encountering an unknown word during reading, the reader needs to "infer" its meaning based on its printed form, the local text meaning, and prior knowledge. Færch, Haastrup, and Phillipson (1984) defines word meaning inference as the process in which the reader makes informal guesses about the meaning of a word based on all cues that are visually available in a text and his prior knowledge. Based on this definition, word meaning inference is included in this section as a special case of word meaning retrieval.

Word meaning inference is achieved through systematic integrations of information stored in multiple knowledge sources. In describing a sequence of the operations required for word meaning inference, Sternberg (1987) likens it to a process of knowledge acquisition: (a) selective encoding (selecting cues in a text that are relevant for the purpose of inferring the meaning of the focal word), (b) selective combination (integrating relevant cues to form a hypothesis about a possible meaning of the word), and (c) selective comparison (relating the hypothesized meaning to stored knowledge for the purpose of validating the hypothesis). When the semantic and functional information of these contextual cues are accessed in stored knowledge, they jointly create semantic and syntactic constraints, and in so doing, reduce the number of plausible candidates for the meaning of the word to be inferred. Successful inference occurs when the hypothesized meaning of the word is semantically consistent with the local text meaning, as well as conceptually plausible and fitting in with the reader's real-life experience and prior knowledge.

From a meaning construction perspective, Nagy and Anderson (1984) underscore the importance of word form analysis—morphological segmentation, in particular—in word meaning inference. Although the combined contribution of the local text meaning and the reader's prior knowledge is limited to the formulation of a specific scenario that is described in the text (Nagy & Gentner, 1990; Nagy & Scott, 2000), such top-down scenarios are too broad to provide sufficient semantic constraints and are likely to generate too many candidates for the meaning of the word to be inferred. L2 inference studies have in fact shown that morphological analysis is one of the most frequently used strategies by adult learners during word meaning inference (Nassaji, 2003); and that the ability to analyze a word's morphological structure is a strong predictor of word meaning inference (Zhang & Koda, 2012).

To summarize, word identification entails two major operations—word form analysis and word meaning retrieval. Word form analysis is a process of connecting the graphically encoded formal information of a word with stored knowledge of the orthography, phonology, and morphology of the word. Word meaning retrieval, on the other hand, involves systematic integrations of the word's formal information, its abstract meaning, context-sensitive meaning, the local context meaning, and real-life experiences associated with the word. Through these operations, word identification, a central joint, integrates information extracted from reader-external input sources and information retrieved from reader-internal resources for the purpose of constructing text meaning meanings.

CROSS-LINGUISTIC VARIATION IN WORD IDENTIFICATION

Word form analysis requires a set of language-specific skills that is optimal for mapping a word's phonology and morphology onto the graphic symbols that encode the formal information. For example, Chinese has a large number of homophones. In speech, many of them are distinguished by lexical tone. In writing, however, tonal information is not graphically encoded. Instead, morphological distinction is signaled by a character's graphic component that indicates the semantic category of the word the character stands for, as shown in [功 ("strength") and 貢("tribute")]. The characters share one component 工 which specifies their pronunciation. Their morphological identity is distinguished by the other component in each character (力 "power" in 功 and 貝 "money" in 貢) (Taylor & Taylor, 1995). Explicit morphological distinction in the grapheme makes Chinese characters a powerful tool for communication among speakers of mutually unintelligible languages and dialects in China. The prominence of the grapheme-morpheme relationship in Chinese characters has two implications for word form analysis in Chinese: (1) graphically complex and structurally similar characters must be visually distinguished; and (2) the graphic components within a character must be isolated. Chinese word form analysis thus relies heavily on visual analysis and segmentation of graphically complex characters.

In contrast, word form analysis in the Korean writing system, hungul, involves grapheme-phonology mappings at two, syllable and phoneme, levels. Like English, the hungul is an alphabetic system, in which each symbol represents a distinct phoneme. Unlike English, individual symbols must be packaged into blocks to form syllables. Reflecting the dual-unit representations, Korean children develop sensitivity to both syllables and phonemes, and the skills to manipulate phonological information at the phoneme and syllable levels are both strong predictors of their word reading ability (McBride-Chan, Wagner, Muse, Chow, & Shu, 2005).

Hebrew reading acquisition serves another example. It is a root-derived language and a word's base is a root morpheme. Root morphemes generally consist of three consonants (e.g., *gdl*) that convey abstract semantic information (e.g., "largeness"). Hebrew word formation entails intertwining root morphemes with word-pattern morphemes. Each word-pattern morpheme comprises built-in slots for the root's consonants to fit into. The Hebrew orthography encodes consonantal root morphemes, certain vowels (represented by letters that can also stand for consonants), as well as consonants that appear in patterns, prefixes, and suffixes. Reflecting the visible grapheme-consonant linkage, children learning to read Hebrew are known to develop stronger sensitivity to consonants than vowels (Tolchinsky & Teberosky, 1998; Geva, 2008). Studies involving adult readers, however, present a more complex picture, by demonstrating that word identification efficiency is affected by lexical factors, such as word frequency (Frost, Katz, & Bentin, 1987), letter sequence (Frost, 2012), and morphological structural transparency (Feldman et al., 1995). These findings would seem to suggest that Hebrew readers rely on solid lexical representations to supply the unspecified information in graphemes in identifying the lexical entry of printed words.

Collectively, these findings suggest that word form analysis entails a command of the cognitive mechanisms that allow children to detect recurring patterns of graphic symbols that systematically correspond to specific language elements, and then, to adapt their grapheme-to-language mappings to the emerging patterns of correspondences among graphemes, phonemes/syllables, and morphemes. In short, word analysis skills are closely attuned to the grapheme-language relationships is a particular writing system, and therefore, vary systematically across languages. Such cross-linguistic variations have implications for reading acquisition in another language because the language-specific mapping skills, once mastered at the level of automaticity in one language, have lasting impacts on word form analysis in later acquired languages.

DEVELOPMENT OF L2 WORD IDENTIFICATION

Dual-language involvement is a major characteristic that distinguishes L2 reading from L1 reading. From a language-specific perspective, much of L2 research has addressed individual and developmental variations in L2 word identification attributable to transferred L1 reading skills. Cumulative evidence suggests that (1) corresponding subskills are systematically related between two language, (2) that transferred skills alter the way L2 print information is processed among linguistically diverse L2 readers, (3) that structural similarities between two languages are directly related to L2 processing efficiency, and (4) that the knowledge of the target language affects the way transferred L1 skills contribute to L2 word identification.

Impacts of L1 Word Form Analysis Skills

Transfer has long been a major theoretical concept in L2 learning research. In early days, transfer was conceived of as the reliance on L1 knowledge to compensate for an insufficient grasp of L2 knowledge. In recent years, transfer is seen as the ability to learn new skills by drawing on previously acquired resources (August & Shanahan, 2006; Genesee, Geva, Dressler, & Kamil, 2006), and those resources are described as a reservoir of knowledge, skills and abilities that is available to learners when learning to read in a new language (Riches & Genesee, 2006). Under these newer views of transfer, L2 reading studies have investigated to what extent and how L1 reading ability affects L2 reading development. A large number of biliteracy studies, for example, have demonstrated systematic cross-linguistic relationships in a variety of subskills, including phonological awareness (Bialystok & McBride-Chang, 2005; Branum-Martin, Fletcher, Carlson, Ortiz, Carlo, & Francis, 2006; Durgunoglu, Nagy, & Hancin, 1993; Wade-Woolley & Geva, 2000; Wang, Perfetti, & Liu, 2005), decoding (Abu-Rabia, 1997; Da Fontoura & Siegel, 1995; Durgunoglu, Nagy, & Hancin, 1993; Geva & Siegel, 1999; Gholamain & Geva, 1999; Wade-Woolley & Geva, 2000), syntactic awareness (Abu-Rabia, 1995; Da Fontoura & Siegel, 1995), and working memory (Abu-Rabia, 1995; Da Fontoura & Siegel, 1995; Geva & Siegel, 1999; Gholamain & Geva, 1999). These results clearly indicate that L1 reading subskills indeed are a potential resource that could provide substantial facilitation in learning a new set of subskills in another language.

Within the transfer framework, another line of studies has examined how transferred L1 skills—word form analysis skills, in specific—affect processing behaviors during L2 word identification. Typically, in these studies, the magnitude of a particular experimental manipulation is compared among L2 learners with contrasting L1 backgrounds. For example, ESL learners with alphabetic (e.g., Spanish) and morphosyllabic (e.g., Chinese) L1 backgrounds can be contrasted in their reliance on phoneme-level analysis during phonological processing. Because alphabetic systems require segmenting and manipulating phonemic information, alphabetic readers have learned to rely on phoneme-level analysis. In contrast, phonological processing in morphosyllabic systems does not entail phonemic analysis because the phonological unit encoded in morphosyllabic systems is a syllable. It can be hypothesized then that blocking phonemic information will induce different reactions among ESL learners with alphabetic and morphosyllabic L1 backgrounds. While efficiency in phonological processing among alphabetic ESL learners would be seriously impaired when phonemic information is made unavailable, that among morphosyllabic learners would be far less affected by this manipulation.

The studies testing this and other similar hypotheses generally confirm that L2 learners with contrasting L1 backgrounds respond differently to a variety of experimental manipulations (e.g., Akamatsu, 2003; Brown & Haynes, 1985; Green & Meara, 1987; Koda, 1998, 1999); and that the observed differences are identifiable with the processing demands imposed by the language-specific structural properties of the participants' respective first languages (e.g., Koda, 1989, 1990, 1993; Ryan & Meara, 1990). Viewed collectively, the results make it plain that L1 word form analysis skills not only impose lasting impacts on L2 reading development, but also systematically alter processing behaviors during L2 word identification.

L1 and L2 Joint Impacts

In recent years, increased attention has been given to the joint impacts stemming from the language-specific demands imposed by L1 and L2 structural properties. The primary hypothesis tested in this research is to what extent the degree of structural similarity between two languages affects the magnitude of the facilitation stemming from transferred L1 skills in L2 word identification. Muljani, Koda and Moates (1998) shed light on the issue by testing the effect of orthographic distance on L2 word identification efficiency. Comparing lexical-decision performance among proficiency-matched adult ESL learners with similar (Indonesian employing a Roman-alphabetic system) and dissimilar (Chinese using a morphosyllabic system) L1 backgrounds, the researchers found that only Indonesian participants benefited from intra-word structural congruity (i.e., spelling patterns that are consistent between English and Indonesian). However, the Indonesian superiority essentially disappeared when they processed incongruent items whose spelling patterns were unique to English. These results are illuminating because they not only demonstrated that structural similarity between two languages has general facilitative impacts, but also that accelerated efficiency occurs only when L1 and L2 word forms share similar structural properties. The clear implication is that enhanced efficiency attributable to orthographic distance is far more restricted and localized than has been assumed.

Similar findings have been reported in studies comparing the impacts of L1 skills on L2 morphological processing in structurally congruent and incongruent L2 words among ESL learners with related (Korean: alphabetic, concatenative) and unrelated (Chinese: morphosyllabic, non-concatenative) L1 backgrounds (Koda, 2000). Not surprisingly, Korean learners were more efficient in morphological segmentation than their proficiency-matched Chinese counterparts, but their efficiency gap was substantially reduced when they were confronted with structurally incongruent L2 words whose structural properties are unique to English. Segmentation efficiency in structurally incongruent words was far less affected by orthographic distance presumably because word form analysis in those words requires structural insights that had not yet been available to either Korean or Chinese ESL learners at the point of data collection. Here again, the findings suggest that the effect of structural similarity between two languages is systematic and specific, and thus, predictable from variations in the language-specific demands imposed by the structural properties of the two languages involved.

More recent studies have explored cross-linguistic interactions that transpire between transferred L1 skills and L2 structural properties during L2 word identification, using a variety of experimental tasks, including semantic category judgment (Wang, Koda, & Perfetti, 2003), associative word learning (Hamada & Koda, 2008), and word meaning retrieval (Wang & Koda, 2007). To isolate the impact stemming from L1 skills from the impact of L2 language-specific demands, L2 stimulus words were manipulated in one way or another, and the magnitude of the effect of such manipulations was compared between two learner groups each representing a distinct first language. In such a design, the extent to which a particular manipulation affects both groups is used as the basis for gauging the impact of the L2, and the extent to which the effect of the manipulation varies between the two learner groups serves as an index of the L1 impact.

For example, Hamada and Koda (2008) compared impact of L1 word form analysis skills on L2 phonological processing and on L2 word meaning retrieval between two groups of proficiency-matched adult ESL learners with alphabetic (Korean; congruent) and morphosyllabic (Chinese; incongruent) L1 backgrounds. It was hypothesized that congruity in the internal structure of printed words between two languages would facilitate L2 phonological processing, which, in turn, would enhance semantic information encoding and retention of novel L2 words. As predicted, structural similarity between two languages was found to have a facilitative impact on L2 word identification performance. The study revealed that Korean ESL learners performed significantly better than Chinese learners in both phonological processing and word meaning retrieval. Their data also showed that both groups performed better with regularly spelled words than their irregularly spelled words. Although the Korean superiority was significant (L1 impact), the group difference was neutralized by the spelling regularity effect (L2 impact), resulting in a nonsignificant Group (Korean vs. Chinese) × Spelling regularity (regular vs. irregular) interaction effect. Taken as a whole, these findings suggest that L1 skills and L2 structural properties both have significant impacts on L2 word identification, and that, of the two, the L2 effect is a more powerful predictor of both L2 phonological processing and word meaning retrieval.

In sum, L2 word identification studies have shown that the language-specific demands stemming from the properties of two languages jointly shape L2 word identification subskills. Studies that directly compared the effect of L1 skills and that of L2 structural properties consistently suggest that L2 demands have a stronger impact than L1 skills on L2 word identification development.

L2 Linguistic Constraints on L1 Skills Transfer

Given that L2 word identification is affected by both transferred L1 skills and L2-soecific processing demands, a logical question to pursue is how the two variables relate to each other as major factors influencing the formation of L2 word identification subskills. Since the inception of L2 reading research in the 1970s, the significance of L2 linguistic knowledge has been recognized. Yorio (1971), for example, maintained that conceptual processing, such as guessing and predicting, is hindered by "the imperfect knowledge of the language" (p. 108). Clarke (1980) also argued that "limited control over the language 'short circuits' the good reader's system causing him/her to revert to poor reader strategies when confronted with a difficult or confusing task in the second language" (p. 120). Based on these early contentions. Alderson (1984) posed a cerebrated question: "Is second language reading a language problem or a reading problem?" In the subsequent decades, the question has prompted a number of empirical studies, in which the relative contributions of L1 reading ability and L2 linguistic knowledge to L2 reading ability. Their findings consistently suggest that L2 linguistic knowledge accounts for much greater proportions of variances (30–38 percent) in L2 reading comprehension than does L1 reading ability (10–16 percent) (e.g., Bernhardt & Kamil, 1995; Bossers, 1991; Carrell, 1991; Yamashita, 2002).

The relative proportions of the two variables corroborate the results from the cross-linguistic experiments described above. The convergence of evidence suggests that the knowledge of the target language is the stronger force driving L2 reading development. It should be noted, however, that the two lines of studies critically differ in their conceptualizations of the relationship between L1 reading ability and L2 linguistic knowledge. While Alderson's formulation and subsequent related studies assume that the contributions of the two variables to L2 reading ability are mutually exclusive and independent, the experimental studies conceptualize L1 and L2 effects as an index of relative sensitivity to the structural properties of two languages in the representations of L2 word forms, assuming that their effects coalesce in the process of jointly shaping L2 reading subskills. If the latter is the case, two implications arise: (1) the two variables are functionally interdependent; and (2) their reciprocity changes over time as learner-internal resources—L2 proficiency, in particular—changes. To date, however, little is known about how the knowledge of the target language affects the utility and utilization of L1 reading ability during L2 word identification. Empirical explorations of possible linguistic constraints on the contribution of L1 skills to L2 reading are currently under way.

Zhang and Koda (2012) compared the facilitation from two facets of L1 morphological awareness (sensitivity to the structural properties of compound and derivational morphemes) to the formation of corresponding L2 awareness facets. They also examined the relative contributions of L1 and L2 morphological awareness to L2 word meaning inference. Their participants were Grade 6 Mandarin speaking children learning English as a foreign language in China. The study yielded a series of complex and illuminating findings. First, the cross-linguistic relationships varied between compound (used both in L1 and L2) and derivational awareness facets (dominant in English). Compound facet was more strongly related than derivational facets between the two languages. Intralingually, the two L2 morphological awareness facets significantly contributed to word meaning inference in Chinese and English. Interlingually, however, neither of the L1 morphological awareness facets made direct contributions to L2 word meaning inference. A subsequent analysis revealed that the contribution of L1 compound awareness to L2 word meaning inference was significant when it was mediated by L2 compound awareness, as well as by L1 word meaning inference. However, such mediated facilitation was not found in L1 derivational awareness. These findings seem to suggest that for transferred L1 skills to be functional in L2 reading, they must be linguistically conditioned in the target language to be adjusted to the language-specific demands of L2 processing tasks. The complex intralingual and interlingual relationships indicate that there is a possibility that the mutually exclusive contributions of L1 reading ability and L2 linguistic knowledge assumed by Alderson's formulation and related studies might have underestimated the involvement and contributions of L1 reading ability to L2 reading development.

In his dissertation study, Miller (2013) more directly addressed linguistic constraints on the contribution of L1 reading skills to L2 word meaning inference. His participants were college learners of English as a foreign language in Japan. As did Zhang and Koda (2013), Miller found that the contribution of L1 reading ability to L2 word meaning inference was recognized when it was mediated by a requisite subskill (L2 sentence comprehension) for L2 word meaning inference. His data further demonstrated that the mediated L1 effect was considerably stronger in high proficiency EFL learners than in their lower proficiency counterparts. These findings corroborate those from the Zhang & Koda study described above, suggesting that the knowledge of the target language strongly affects the extent to which transferred L1 skills are assimilated into L2 word identification. In brief, the emerging evidence provides empirical support for the hypothesized constraints imposed by the language-specific properties and the knowledge of those properties on both the utility and utilization of transferred L1 reading skills.

SUMMARY AND FUTURE RESEARCH DIRECTIONS

The importance of word identification is widely acknowledged in reading research. Four conclusions can be drawn from a significant body of L1 reading research: (1) reading comprehension results from continual interactions between text information and stored knowledge of the reader; (2) accurate and speedy word form analysis has a direct impact on word meaning retrieval; (3) the skills required for word form analysis evolved gradually through cumulative experiences of decoding and encoding printed words; and (4) those skills are closely attuned to the structural properties of printed words in the language in which reading is learned. These research insights have significant implications for L2 reading development.

In conceptualizing word identification development in a second language, the chapter has considered three additional issues uniquely associated with dual-language involvement: (a) L1 impacts, (b) L1-L2 joint impacts, and (c) linguistic constraints on the utilization of L1 skills. Collectively, findings from L2 reading studies suggest that (1) corresponding L1 and L2 subskills are systematically related; (2) that L2 word identification is achieved through diverse procedures among learners with diverse L1 backgrounds; (3) that

L2 learners are sensitized to the structural properties of two languages; and (4) that L2 linguistic knowledge affects the way L1 subskills contribute to L2 word identification. Taken as a whole, the emerging evidence has yielded some significant clue that could guide us in shaping agendas for further explorations to enhance our understanding of complex cross-linguistic interactions during L2 reading and their relations to individual differences in word identification efficiency and its development.

REFERENCES

Abu Rabia, S. (1995) Learning to read in Arabic: Reading, syntactic, orthographic and working memory skills in normally achieving and poor Arabic readers. *Reading Psychology, 16*, 351–94.

Adams, M. J. (1990). *Beginning to read.* Cambridge, MA: MIT Press.

Akamatsu, N. (2003). The effects of first language orthographic features on second language reading in text. *Language Learning, 53*(2), 207–31.

Alderson, J. C. (1984). Reading in a foreign language: A reading problem or a language problem? In J. C. Alderson & A. H. Urquhart (Eds.), *Reading in a Foreign Language* (pp. 1–24). London: Longman.

Anderson, R. C., & Nagy, W. E. (1991). Word meaning. In R. Barr, M. L. Kamil, P. Mosenthal, & P. D. Pearson (Eds.), *Handbook of reading research* (Vol. II, pp. 512–38). New York: Longman.

August, D., & Shanahan, T. (Eds.). (2006). *Developing literacy in second-language learners: Report of the National Literacy Panel on Language-Minority Children and Youth.* Mahwah, NJ: Lawrence Erlbaum.

Bernhardt, E. B., & Kamil, M. L. (1995). Interpreting relationships between L1 and L2 reading: Consolidating the linguistic threshold and the linguistic interdependence hypotheses. *Applied Linguistics, 16*, 15–34.

Bialystok, E., McBride-Chang, C., & Luk, G. (2005). Bilingualism, language proficiency, and learning to read in two writing systems. *Journal of Educational Psychology*, *97*, 580–90.

Bossers, B. (1991). On thresholds, ceilings and short-circuits: The relation between L1 reading, L2 reading and L2 knowledge. *AILA Review, 8*, 45–60.

Bowers, P., Golden, J., Kennedy, A., & Young, A. (1994). Limits upon orthographic knowledge due to processes indexed by naming speed. In V. W. Berninger (Ed.), *The varieties of orthographic knowledge I: Theoretical and developmental issues* (pp. 173–218). Dordrecht, The Netherlands: Kluwer.

Branum-Martin, L., Fletcher, J. M., Carlson, C. D., Ortiz, A., Carlo, M., & Francis, D. J. (2006). Bilingual phonological awareness: Multilevel construct validation among Spanish-speaking kindergarteners in transitional bilingual education classrooms. *Journal of Educational Psychology, 98,* 170–81.

Brown, T. & Haynes, M. (1985). Literacy background and reading development in a second language. In T. H. Carr (Ed.), The development of reading skills (pp. 19–34). San Francisco, CA: Jossey-Bass.

Carrell, P. L. (1991). Second language reading: Reading ability or language proficiency? *Applied Linguistics, 12*, 159–79.

Clarke, M. A. (1980). The short circuit hypothesis of ESL reading—or when language competence interferes with reading performance. *The Modern Language Journal, 64*, 203–09.

Coulmas, F. (1989). *The writing systems of the world*. Cambridge, MA: Blackwell.

Cummins, J. (1979). Linguistic interdependence and the educational development of bilingual children. *Review of Educational Research, 49*, 222–51.

Cummins, J. (1984). *Bilingualism and special education: Issues in assessment and pedagogy*. San Diego, CA: College-Hill Press.

Cummins, J. (2000). *Language, power, and pedagogy: Bilingual children in the crossfire*. Clevedon: Multilingual Matters.

Cummins, J., Swain, M., Nakajima, K., Handscombe, J., & Green, D. (1981). *Linguistic interdependence in Japanese and Vietnamese students*. Report prepared for the Inter-America Research Associates, June. Toronto: Ontario Institute for Studies in Education.

Da Fontoura, H. A., & Siegel, L. S. (1995). Reading syntactic and memory skills of Portuguese-English Canadian children. *Reading and Writing: An International Journal, 7,* 139–53.

Durgunoglu, A. Y., Nagy, W. E., & Hancin, B. J. (1993). Cross-language transfer of phonemic awareness. *Journal of Educational Psychology, 85,* 453–65.

Ehri, L. C. (1994). Development of the ability to read words: Update. In R. Ruddell, M. Ruddell, & H. Singer (Eds.), *Theoretical models and processes of reading*, 4th ed. (pp. 323–58). Hillsdale, NJ: Erlbaum.

Ehri, L. C. (1998). Grapheme-phoneme knowledge is essential to learning to read words in English. In J. L. Metsala & L. C. Ehri (Eds.), *Word recognition in beginning literacy* (pp. 3–40). Mahwah, NJ: Erlbaum.

Ehri, L. C. (2014). Orthographic mapping in the acquisition of sight word reading, spelling memory, and vocabulary learning. *Scientific Studies of Reading, 18*, 5–21.

Færch, C., & Kasper, G. (1987). Procedural knowledge as a component of foreign language learners' communicative competence. In T. Slama-Cazacu (Ed.), *Psycholinguistics: AILA Review 1986* (Vol. 3, pp. 7–23). New York: Cambridge University Press.

Feldman, L. B., Frost, R., & Pnini, T. (1995). Decomposition words into their constituent morphemes: Evidence from English and Hebrew. *Journal of Experimental Psychology: Learning, Memory and Cognition, 21*, 1–14.

Fowler, A. E., & Liberman, I. Y. (1995). The role of phonology and orthography in morphological awareness. In L. B. Feldman (Ed.), *Morphological Aspects of Language Processing* (pp. 157–88). Hillsdale, NJ: Erlbaum.

Frost, R. (1998). Towards a strong phonological theory of visual word recognition: True issues and false trails. *Psychological Bulletin, 123*, 71–99.

Frost, R. (2012). Towards a universal model of reading. *Behavioral and Brain Sciences, 35*, 263–329.

Frost, R., Katz, L., & Bentin, S. (1987). Strategies for visual word recognition and orthographic depth: A multilingual comparison. *Journal of Experimental Psychology: Human Perception and Performance, 13*, 104–15.

Genesee, F., Geva, E., Dressler, C., Kamil, M. L. (2006). Synthesis: Cross-Linguistic relationships. In D. August & T. Shanahan (Eds.), *Developing literacy in second-language learners: Report of the National Literacy Panel on Language-Minority Children and Youth* (pp. 153–83). Mahwah, NJ: Lawrence Erlbaum

Geva, E. (2008). Facets of metalinguistic awareness related to reading development in Hebrew: Evidence from monolingual and bilingual and bilingual children. In K. Koda & A. M. Zehler (Eds.), *Learning to read across languages: Cross-linguistic relationships in first and second language literacy development* (pp. 154–87). Mahwah, NJ: Lawrence Erlbaum.

Geva, E., & Siegel, L. S. (2000). Orthographic and cognitive factors in the concurrent development of basic reading skills in two languages. *Reading and Writing, 12*, 1–30.

Gholamain, M. & Geva, E. (1999). Orthographic and cognitive factors in the concurrent development of basic reading skills in English and Persian. *Language Learning, 49,* 183–217.

Goodman, K. S. (1973). Psycholinguistic universals of the reading process. In F. Smith (Ed.), *Psycholinguistics and reading* (pp. 21–29). New York: Holt, Rinehart and Winston.

Green, D. W., & Meara, P. (1987). The effects of script on visual search. *Second Language Research, 3,* 102–17.

Hamada, M., & Koda, K. (2008). Influence of first language orthographic experience on second language decoding and word learning. *Language Learning, 58*, 1–31.

Hogaboam, T. W., & Perfetti, C. A. (1978). Reading skill and the role of verbal experience in decoding. *Journal of Educational Psychology, 70,* 717–29.

Koda, K. (1988). Cognitive process in second language reading: Transfer of L1 reading skills and strategies. *Second Language Research, 4,* 133–56.

Koda, K. (1989). The effects of transferred vocabulary knowledge on the development of L2 reading proficiency. *Foreign Language Annals, 22*, 529–42.

Koda, K. (1990). The use of L1 reading strategies in L2 reading. *Studies in Second Language Acquisition, 12,* 393–410.

Koda, K. (1993). Transferred L1 strategies and L2 syntactic structure during L2 sentence comprehension. *Modern Language Journal, 77,* 490–500.

Koda, K. (1998). The role of phonemic awareness in L2 reading. *Second Language Research, 14,* 194–215.

Koda, K. (1999). Development of L2 intraword structural sensitivity and decoding skills. *Modern Language Journal, 83,* 51–64.

Koda, K. (2000). Cross-linguistic variations in L2 morphological awareness. *Applied Psycholinguistics, 21,* 297–320.

Ku, Y-M., & Anderson, R. C. (2003). Development of morphological awareness in Chinese and English. *Reading and Writing: An Interdisciplinary Journal, 16,* 399–422.

Legarretta, D. (1979). The effects of program models on language acquisition of Spanish speaking children. *TESOL Quarterly, 13*, 521–34.

Miller, R. T. (2013). Cross-linguistic influences on L2 semantic gap filling and its component sub-skills (Doctoral dissertation). Carnegie Mellon University, Pittsburgh, PA.

Muljani, M., Koda, K., & Moates, D. (1998). Development of L2 word recognition: A Connectionist approach. *Applied Psycholinguistics, 19,* 99–114.

Nagy, W., & Anderson, R. C. (1984). How many words are there in printed school English? *Reading Research Quarterly, 19,* 304–30.

Nagy, W., & Gentner, D. (1990). Semantic constraints on lexical categories. *Language & Cognitive Processes, 5,* 169–201.

Nagy, W. E., & Scott, J. A. (2000). Vocabulary processes. In M. L. Kamil, P. B. Mothenthal, P. D. Pearson, & R. Barr (Eds.), *Handbook of reading research* (Vol. III, pp. 269–84). Mahwah, NJ: Erlbaum.

Nassaji, H. (2003). Higher-level and lower-level text processing skills in advanced ESL reading comprehension. *The Modern Language Journal, 87*, 261–76.

Nation, I. S. P. (2001). *Learning vocabulary in another language.* Cambridge: Cambridge University Press.

Nunes, T., & Bryant, P. (2006). *Improving literacy by teaching morphemes.* London: Routledge.

Perfetti, C. A. (1985). *Reading ability.* New York: Oxford University Press.

Perfetti, C. A., & Stafura, J. (2014). Word knowledge in a theory of reading comprehension. *Scientific Studies of Reading, 18*, 22–37.

Riches, C., & Genesee, F. (2006). Crosslanguage and crossmodal influences. In F. Genesee, K. Lindholm-Leary, W. Saunders, & D. Christian (Eds.), *Educating English language larners: A synthesis of research evidence* (pp. 64–108). New York: Cambridge University Press.

Roberts, T. A., Christo, C., & Shefelbine, J. A. (2011). Word recognition. In M. L. Kamil, P. D. Pearson, E. Birr Moje, & P. Mosenthal (Eds.), *Handbook of reading research* (Vol. IV, pp. 229–58). New York: Longman.

Ryan, A., & Meara, P. (1991). The case of invisible vowels: Arabic speakers reading English words. *Reading in a Foreign Language, 7,* 531–40.

Schmitt, N. (2014). Size and depth of vocabulary knowledge: What the research shows. *Language Learning, 64*, 913–51.

Schreuder, R., & Flores d'Arcais, G. B. (1992). Psycholinguistic issues in the lexical representation of meaning. In W. Marslen-Wilson (Ed.), *Lexical representation and process* (pp. 409–36). Cambridge, MA: MIT Press.

Seidenberg, M. S., & McClelland, J. L. (1989). A distributed, developmental model of word recognition and naming. *Psychological Review, 96,* 523–68.

Shankweiler, D., & Liberman, I. Y. (1972). Misreading: A search for causes. In J. F. Kavanaugh & I. G. Mattingly (Eds.), *Language by eye and by ear* (pp. 293–317). Cambridge, MA: MIT Press.

Share, D., & Stanovich, K. E. (1995). Cognitive processes in early reading development: Accommodating individual differences into a model of acquisition. In J. S. Carlson (Ed.), *Issues in education: Contributions from psychology* (Vol. 1, pp. 1–57). Greenwich, CT: JAI.

Siegel, L. S., & Ryan, E. B. (1988). Development of grammatical sensitivity, phonological, and short-term memory in normally achieving and learning disabled children. *Developmental Psychology, 24,* 28–37.

Skutnabb-Kangass, T., & Toukomaa, P. (1976). *Teaching migrant children's mother tongue and learning the language of the host country in the context of socio*

cultural situation of the migrant family. Helsinki: the Finnish National Commission for UNESCO.
Sternberg, R. J. (1987). Most vocabulary is learned from context. In M. G. McKeown & M. E. Curtis (Eds.), *The Nature of Vocabulary Acquisition* (pp. 89–105). Hillsdale, NJ: Erlbaum.
Taylor, I., & Taylor M. M. (1995). *Writing and literacy in Chinese, Korean, and Japanese*. Philadelphia: John Benjamins.
Tolchinsky L., & Teberosky, A. (1998). The development of word segmentation and writing in two scripts. *Cognitive Development, 13,* 1–25.
Torgesen, J. K., & Burgess, S. R. (1998). Consistency of reading-related phonological processes throughout early childhood: Evidence from longitudinal-correlational and instructional studies. In J. L. Metsala & L. C. Ehri (Eds.), *Word recognition in beginning literacy* (pp. 161–88). Mahwah, NJ: Erlbaum.
Troike, R. C. (1978). Research evidence for the effectiveness of bilingual education. *NABE Journal, 3,* 13–24.
Wade-Woolley, L., & Geva, E. (2000) Processing novel phonemic contrasts in the acquisition of L2 word reading. *Scientific Studies of Reading, 4*, 295–311.
Wagner, R. K., Torgesen, J. K., & Rashotte, C. A. (1994). The development of reading-related phonological processing abilities: New evidence of bi-directional causality from a latent variable longitudinal study. *Developmental Psychology, 30,* 73–87.
Wang, M., & Koda, K. (2005). Commonalities and differences in word identification skills among learners of English as a second language, *Language Learning, 55,* 71–98.
Wang, M., Koda, K., & Perfetti, C. A. (2003). Alphabetic and non-alphabetic L1 effects in English semantic processing: A comparison of Korean and Chinese English L2 learners. *Cognition, 87,* 129–49.
Wang, M., Perfetti, C. A., & Liu, Y. (2005). Chinese-English biliteracy acquisition: Cross-language and writing system transfer. *Cognition, 97*, 67–88.
Yamashita, J. (2002). Mutual compensation between L1 reading ability and L2 language proficiency in L2 reading comprehension. *Journal of Research in Reading, 25*, 81–95.
Yorio, C. A. (1971). Some sources of reading problems in foreign language learners. *Language Learning, 21,* 107–15.
Zhang, D., & Koda, K. (2012). Morphological awareness, lexical inferencing vocabulary knowledge and L2 reading comprehension: Testing direct and indirect effects. *Reading and Writing, 25*, 1195–1216.

Index

About the Editor

Kouider Mokhtari (Interdisciplinary PhD, Ohio University) currently serves as the Anderson-Vukelja-Wright Endowed Professor of Education within the School of Education at The University of Texas at Tyler, where he engages in research, teaching, and service initiatives aimed at enhancing teacher practice and increasing student literacy achievement outcomes.

Mokhtari's research focuses on the acquisition of language and literacy by first- and second- language learners, with particular emphasis on children, adolescents, and adults who can read but have difficulties understanding what they read. One of his coauthored books, *Preparing Every Teacher to Reach English Learners: A Practical Guide for Teacher Educators* (2012), received the 2013 American Association of Colleges for Teacher Education (AACTE) Outstanding Book Award. The award recognizes exemplary books that make a significant contribution to the knowledge base of educator preparation or of teaching and learning with implications for educator preparation.

Mokhtari's work in literacy earned him the 2014 John C. Manning Public School Service Award from the International Reading Association (IRA). This prestigious award recognizes a professor of reading education who has demonstrated his or her commitment to public education and has spent significant time working with public school teachers and their students in classrooms, demonstrating approaches and techniques that have been shown to improve reading instruction.

About the Contributors

Peter Afflerbach is professor of education at the University of Maryland. Dr. Afflerbach's research interests include individual differences in reading and reading development, reading assessment, reading comprehension and the verbal reporting methodology. Afflerbach is a standing member of the Reading Committee of the National Assessment of Educational Progress (NAEP) and a member of the Literacy Research Panel of the International Reading Association. Afflerbach has served as chair of the Literacy Assessment Committee of the International Reading Association and on the Common Core State Standards Review and Feedback Panels.

Janice F. Almasi is the Carol Lee Robertson Endowed Professor of Literacy Education at the University of Kentucky. Her research focuses on comprehension and the strategic processing that occurs while children read and discuss text with peers.

Linda Baker is a professor of psychology at the University of Maryland, Baltimore County. Research interests include metacognition and comprehension monitoring, literacy development, motivation for reading, parents' educational beliefs and practices, and instructional interventions. She is a fellow of the American Psychological Association and the American Educational Research Association.

Jill Castek is an associate professor in the Department of Teaching, Learning, and Sociocultural Studies in the College of Education at the University of Arizona. She works collaboratively with multidisciplinary colleagues from across the university on Technology Enhanced Language Learning (TELL). Her research explores digital literacy and STEM learning.

Susan Chambers Cantrell is an associate professor of literacy education in the Department of Curriculum and Instruction at the University of Kentucky. Her research focuses on teachers' efficacy beliefs and the ways in which classroom instruction influences reading.

Annamary L. Consalvo is an assistant professor of literacy at The University of Texas at Tyler where she teaches undergraduate and graduate courses. Research interests include the study of writing conferences in secondary contexts; disciplinary and adolescent literacy; and ways in which multiliteracies and new literacies inform teaching and learning in the twenty-first century.

Thomas D. Griffin is a research professor in the Department of Psychology, University of Illinois at Chicago. His research interests include individual differences that affect learning in science, and the impact of beliefs on the comprehension process and acceptance of scientific theories.

Keiko Koda is a professor in the Department of Modern Languages at Carnegie Mellon University. Her research interests include second-language reading, biliteracy development, foreign language instruction and assessment.

Richard L. Isakson, PhD, is an emeritus professor, Counseling and Career Center, Brigham Young University. He is currently an academic reading consultant with Isakson Literacy, LLC. His research interests are improvement of college reading and measurement of attitudes toward academic reading.

Marné B. Isakson, PhD, is a retired secondary reading teacher and retired adjunct professor, Brigham Young University. She developed, coordinated, and taught academic reading courses at BYU. Currently, she is an academic reading consultant with Isakson Literacy, LLC. Her interests include improving instruction and assessments for academic reading.

P. David Pearson is a professor in the programs in Language and Literacy and Human Development at the Graduate School of Education at the University of California, Berkeley, where he served as dean from 2001 to 2010. Pearson's current research projects include Seeds of Science/Roots of Reading—a Research and Development effort with colleagues at Lawrence Hall of Science in which reading, writing, and language as are employed as tools to foster the development of knowledge and inquiry in science. Pearson is the founding editor of the *Handbook of Reading Research,* now in its fourth volume; he edited *Reading Research Quarterly* and the *Review of Research in Education*; and he has served on the Editorial Review Board for some twenty educational journals. Pearson's awards include the 1989 Oscar Causey Award (NRC) for contributions to reading research, and the 1990 William S. Gray Citation of Merit (IRA) for contributions to reading research and practice.

D. Ray Reutzel is dean of the College of Education, University of Wyoming. For fourteen years, Reutzel was Emma Eccles Jones Endowed Professor at Utah State University. He has authored 230+ publications and received $16+ million in research funding. He is currently executive editor of the *Journal of Educational Research* and President-Elect of the *Reading Hall of Fame.*

Margaret Rintamaa is an assistant professor of middle level education in the Department of Curriculum and Instruction at the University of Kentucky. Her research interests include the preparation of middle-level teachers, and the motivation and engagement of struggling adolescent readers.

Stephan E. Sargent is a professor of reading in the College of Education at Northeastern State University in Broken Arrow, Oklahoma. His research interests focus on how to best support struggling readers through the use of traditional and alternative texts.

Diane L. Schallert is a professor of educational psychology at The University of Texas at Austin with teaching duties that include undergraduate teacher preparation and graduate courses in learning, psycholinguistics, and discourse processes. Her research interests are focused on the interface between discourse, motivation/emotion, and learning, situated in social and cultural contexts.

Melinda L Smith, is a professor of reading education at Northeastern State University. Her more than thirty years in education include public school teaching and extensive experience working with primary grade struggling readers in clinical settings. Her research interests included reading acquisition, struggling readers, and comprehension.

Keith W. Thiede is associate dean for research and advanced programs in the College of Education at Boise State University. His research has focused on finding ways to improve the accuracy of metacognitive monitoring. He has also examined the role of monitoring in learning.

Marcel V. J. Veenman is director of the Institute for Metacognition Research, which aims at facilitating metacognition in education. He published over 100 scientific articles and book chapters on metacognition and self-regulation.

Until 2012, he was founding editor of the international journal *Metacognition and Learning*.

Jennifer Wiley is a professor in the Department of Psychology, University of Illinois at Chicago. Her research interests include contexts that support comprehension and metacomprehension when learning from informational texts.

Made in the USA
Middletown, DE
02 September 2024

60216177R00161